Chapter 1: The Chosen City

The road from Nazareth to Capernaum wound through the hills like a serpent of dust and broken promises. Jesus walked it alone, his sandals raising small clouds with each step, his shadow stretching long in the afternoon sun. Behind him, invisible but felt, lay the smouldering ruins of every relationship he'd ever known.

They had tried to kill him. His neighbours. His childhood friends. The men he'd worked beside in the carpenter shop. The women who had brought their broken furniture to Joseph's door. The rabbi who had taught him his letters. All of them transformed in an instant from familiar faces to a murderous mob, intent on throwing him from the cliff at the edge of town. His crime? Reading Isaiah in the synagogue. Claiming the ancient promises were fulfilled. Speaking truth to people who preferred their Messiahs theoretical and distant, not standing before them with sawdust under his fingernails and a local accent on his tongue.

"No prophet is accepted in his hometown," he murmured to the empty road. The words tasted bitter and true, like medicine that heals while it burns.

A merchant's cart rumbled past, the driver eyeing him with the casual suspicion reserved for solitary travellers. Jesus stepped aside, letting it pass. The man would reach Capernaum by nightfall, spreading news as merchants do. By tomorrow, the fishing town would know that the young rabbi from Nazareth was coming. They would wonder why. They would gossip and speculate and prepare their hearts for scandal or salvation, depending on their inclination.

Jesus paused at a rise in the road, looking back one last time at the hills that cradled Nazareth. Somewhere among those whitewashed houses, his mother was explaining his absence to neighbours who alternated between sympathy and suspicion. His brothers were probably relieved—James especially, always so concerned with respectability, with not making waves in a world that punished those who disturbed its surface.

"I'm sorry, Mama," he whispered to the wind. But he wasn't, not really. Sorry for her pain, yes. Sorry for the whispers she would endure, the looks, and the careful distances people would keep. But not sorry for speaking truth. Not sorry for beginning what he'd come to begin.

The road descended toward the valley, and with each step, Nazareth faded further into memory. Ahead, the Sea of Galilee waited like a promise of new beginnings. Its waters had called to him in dreams, sometimes silver with moonlight, sometimes dark with storms. Always alive. Always changing. Nothing like the staid predictability of a carpenter's shop, where wood remained wood and nails remained nails and nothing ever transformed into more than it appeared.

As the sun began its descent toward the western hills, Jesus reached the crossroads where the path to Capernaum branched from the main trade route. Here, the Via Maris—the Way of the Sea—carried the commerce of empires from Damascus to Egypt. Spices from the East, purple dye from Tyre, slaves from everywhere—all of it flowed along this ancient artery while Galilee's lifeblood leaked slowly away in taxes and tributes.

He sat on a milestone, Roman numerals proclaiming the distance to nowhere that mattered to him. His feet ached from the journey, and his stomach reminded him that he'd eaten nothing since the bread his mother had pressed into his hands that morning, tears streaming down her face.

"You have to go, don't you?" she'd said. Not a question. An acknowledgement. She'd known this day would come since the angel's visit thirty years ago. Known it when the shepherds had burst into the stable, babbling about heavenly choirs. She knew it when Simeon had prophesied over her infant, speaking of swords and sorrow. She'd known it every time she'd watched him pause in his work, staring at something beyond the walls of their home.

"Yes," he'd answered simply. "It's time."

She'd nodded, aged beyond her years by the weight of carrying heaven's secret. "Then go with God, my son. But remember—you will always have a home with me."

Home. The word sat strangely in his mind now. The foxes had holes, the birds had nests, but where would the Son of Man lay his head? Not in Nazareth, certainly. Perhaps not anywhere anymore. Perhaps home was no longer a place but a purpose, no longer walls and a roof but the invisible kingdom he'd come to proclaim.

A group of fishermen passed, nets slung over shoulders, heading toward the lake for the night's work. They glanced at him curiously—a rabbi, by his dress, but walking alone without disciples or servants. One of them, a weather-beaten man with arms like tree trunks, paused.

"Are you heading to Capernaum, Rabbi?"

Jesus nodded.

"Best hurry then. Gates close at sunset, and you don't want to spend the night outside the walls. There have been bandits on the roads lately. Desperate men doing desperate things." He spat to the side. "Times are hard since Herod started his building projects. Taxes bleed us dry while he plays at being Caesar."

"Thank you for the warning," Jesus said. "May your nets be full tonight."

The fisherman laughed, but not unkindly. "From your mouth to God's ears, Rabbi. Though lately, it seems like God's gone fishing somewhere else, if you know what I mean."

They moved on, their rough voices fading into the distance, leaving Jesus alone with the implications of that casual blasphemy. God has gone fishing somewhere else. Is that what they thought? That the Almighty had abandoned his people to Rome's grip and Herod's greed? That heaven had closed its ears to the cries of the poor and oppressed?

He stood, brushing dust from his robe. No more delay. Capernaum waited, and with it, the beginning of everything. The choosing of the twelve. The healings would draw crowds like honey draws flies. The teachings that would shake foundations and topple carefully constructed hierarchies. The kingdom of God breaking in like a thief in the night, stealing away everything people thought they knew about power and glory and the nature of divine love.

The last mile passed quickly, urgency lending speed to his tired feet. As the fisherman had predicted, the sun touched the horizon just as Capernaum's walls came into view. Unlike Jerusalem's mighty fortifications, these were modest—more suggestion than statement, designed to keep out wild animals and casual thieves rather than armies. The town sprawled beyond them, houses and shops spilling down to the water's edge where boats bobbed like sleeping birds.

The gate guard barely glanced at him, more interested in closing up for the night than questioning late travellers. Jesus passed through into streets already growing quiet as shopkeepers shuttered their stalls and families gathered for evening meals. The smell of cooking fish and baking bread made his stomach clench with hunger.

He knew no one here. Had no relatives to claim hospitality from, no letters of introduction to smooth his way. By choice, he'd come empty-handed to this city by the sea, carrying nothing but the words that burnt in his bones like fire.

But he knew where he was going. Dreams and prayer had shown him the house—modest but sturdy, built near the shore where the fishermen beached their boats. A house that would become more than a house. A centre. A refuge. A place where the kingdom of God would first take visible form in shared meals and heated discussions, in the laughter of unlikely friends and the transformation of ordinary men into fishers of humanity.

The streets grew narrower as he approached the lake, the grand houses of merchants and tax collectors giving way to the humbler dwellings of those who wrestled their living from the water. Here, nets hung drying on walls. Here, the smell of fish permeated everything. Here, men with permanently bent backs and women with hands raw from mending nets lived out their days in the shadow of empire, dreaming small dreams and dying small deaths.

Until now.

He found the house exactly where he'd known it would be. Lamplight spilt from the windows, and voices carried on the evening air—a woman scolding, children laughing, and a man's deeper tones beneath it all. Jesus stood at the gate, suddenly uncertain. In dreams and visions, this had seemed so clear. But now, faced with the reality of interrupting a family's evening meal, of inserting himself into lives that had rhythm and routine without him...

The door opened before he could knock. A woman stood silhouetted against the light, wiping her hands on her apron. She was perhaps forty, with the kind of face that had been pretty before work and worry etched their lines. Her eyes, though, remained young—quick and intelligent, taking in his appearance with one comprehensive glance.

"You'll be the rabbi from Nazareth," she said. Not a question. Jesus blinked. "How did you—"

"My fool of a husband has been talking about nothing else for three days. Ever since he heard you speak at the shore last week. "The kingdom of heaven is at hand," he keeps saying, like that explains why the nets need mending or the roof needs patching. She stepped aside. "You'd better come in before the neighbours see and the gossip starts. Though knowing this town, it's probably too late for that."

The house's interior was exactly as he'd seen it—low-ceilinged but clean, with that particular order that comes from making do with little. Children peered at him from behind a curtain that divided the sleeping area. The smell of fish stew made his mouth water.

"Miriam!" A man's voice boomed from the back room. "Who is it?"

"Your rabbi," she called back, her tone suggesting complex feelings about that possessive pronoun. "The one you've been mooning over like a lovesick boy."

Heavy footsteps, and then he was there—Simon, called Peter, though Jesus knew that without being told. Big as a house, with hands that could crush stone and eyes that held surprising depths. He stopped dead when he saw Jesus, his mouth opening and closing like one of his fish.

"Master," he breathed. "You came. You actually came."

"Did you doubt I would?"

Peter's laugh was shaky. "I... yes. No. I don't know. When you spoke at the shore, when you looked at me and said the kingdom was coming... I felt something. Here." He thumped his chest with one massive fist. "Like lightning. Like drowning. Like being born. But then you walked away, and I thought maybe I'd imagined it. Maybe the sun had been too hot, or the wine too strong the night before.

"Simon." Miriam's voice held fond exasperation. "Let the man sit before you talk his ears off. He's been walking all day by the look of him."

She was already moving, efficient as a general directing troops. A bowl of water appeared for his feet. A cup of wine—watered, but welcome. A place at their table as natural as if he'd always belonged there.

The children crept closer, emboldened by their mother's acceptance of this stranger. A girl of perhaps twelve, all knees and elbows and curious eyes. A younger boy, maybe eight, with his father's broad features in miniature. They stared at Jesus with the frank assessment of the young.

"Are you really a rabbi?" the boy asked. "You don't look like the ones at synagogue."

"Matthias!" His mother's voice was sharp. "Mind your manners."

But Jesus smiled. "What does a rabbi look like, in your opinion?"

The boy considered this seriously. "Old. And fat. And they smell like dusty scrolls and disapproval."

Peter choked on his wine. Miriam looked mortified. But Jesus laughed—really laughed, for the first time since leaving Nazareth. "Then I suppose I'm not a proper rabbi at all. I'm not old, certainly not fat, and I hope I smell more like road dust than disapproval."

8

"You smell like outside," the girl offered shyly. "Like wind and walking and far places."

"Anna has a poet's heart," Miriam said, serving the stew with practiced movements. "Gets it from her grandmother, God rest her soul. Always seeing more than what's there."

"Or perhaps," Jesus said gently, meeting the girl's eyes, "seeing exactly what's there, just more clearly than most."

Anna blushed and ducked her head, but he caught her small smile.

The meal passed in a strange mixture of ordinary and extraordinary. The food was simple—fish stew with barley bread, olives from their own tree, and watered wine that tasted of home. The conversation started carefully, circling around the obvious questions. But gradually, as the wine loosened tongues and the children grew comfortable with his presence, deeper currents emerged.

"They say you claim Isaiah's prophecies for yourself," Peter said finally, pushing aside his empty bowl. "They say the synagogue in Nazareth tried to stone you for blasphemy."

"They say many things," Jesus replied. "What do you say?"

Peter's struggle was visible on his face—a man used to simple truths grappling with mystery. "I say... I say when you spoke at the shore, my heart burnt. I say I've been fishing these waters for twenty years, and I've never felt what I felt when you looked at me. I say either you're the greatest deceiver who ever lived, or..." He swallowed hard. "Or you're what my heart tells me you are."

"And what does your heart tell you?"

The big fisherman looked around his humble home—at his wife, his children, the nets in the corner, and the patched roof above. Everything he was, everything he'd built, everything safe and known. Then he met Jesus's eyes.

"That following you will cost me everything," he said quietly. "And that not following you will cost me more."

Miriam's hand found her husband's, squeezing tight. Jesus saw her fear and her faith warring in that simple gesture. She knew what this meant. Knew her life was about to be upended by this stranger at her table. But she also knew her husband, knew he'd been dying slowly in nets and routine, and knew something in him needed what Jesus offered more than it needed safety.

"Where will you stay tonight, Master?" she asked, practical even in the face of transformation.

"I hadn't—"

"Here," Peter said firmly. "You'll stay here. We have room. Not much, but enough. This house is yours for as long as you need it."

Jesus looked around the cramped space, calculating. A family of four in a two-room house, now adding a fifth. They would be sleeping on top of each other, privacy a forgotten luxury. And yet the offer was genuine, given from hearts that understood hospitality as a sacred duty.

"For tonight," he agreed. "Tomorrow, we'll see what God provides."

Later, after the children had been put to bed and Miriam had retreated to give the men privacy, Jesus and Peter sat on the flat roof, looking out over the lake. The moon had risen, turning the water to molten silver. Fishing boats dotted the surface, their lamps like fallen stars.

"I wasn't always a fisherman," Peter said suddenly. "My father wanted me to study, to become a scribe. Said I had the mind for it, even if I didn't have the patience. But then he died, and someone had to feed the family. So I took up his nets." He flexed his hands, scarred and callused from years of rope work. "Sometimes I wonder what words feel like instead of water. What it's like to wrestle with ideas instead of storms."

"You'll find out," Jesus said softly.

Peter turned to look at him. "Will I? When you call me to follow—and you will call, won't you?—what becomes of all this?" He gestured at the house below, the town around them, and the life he'd built. "Miriam deserves better than a husband who abandons her for dreams. The children need their father. This isn't just about me."

"No," Jesus agreed. "It never is. The kingdom of God doesn't come in isolation. It comes in community, in the messy intersections of daily life. Your family, Peter—they're not obstacles to following me. They're part of it. Watch and see."

They sat in comfortable silence, each lost in thought. Below them, Capernaum settled into sleep. Dogs barked. A baby cried and was hushed. The eternal rhythms of human life, playing out while heaven prepared to break in.

"Why here?" Peter asked eventually. "Why Capernaum? It's not Jerusalem. It's not even a particularly important town. Just fishermen and tax collectors, merchants and soldiers. Nothing special."

Jesus smiled in the darkness. "Do you know what Capernaum means? Village of Comfort. But also the Village of Nahum—the prophet who spoke comfort to those who thought God had forgotten them. This town sits at the crossroads of nations, where Jew and Gentile mix, where the religious authorities have less grip, and where people are desperate enough to hope for something new."

He stood, looking out over the sleeping town. "Jerusalem has its temple, its priests, and its careful interpretations of law. But the kingdom of God doesn't come through committees and hierarchies. It comes like seeds scattered on the ground—some rocky, some thorny, some good. It comes where people fish for survival and hunger for more than bread. It comes here, Peter. Among the ordinary. Among the overlooked. Among those who have ears to hear."

Peter stood too, moved by something in Jesus's voice. "When do we start?"

"We've already begun," Jesus said. "Tomorrow, I teach in your synagogue. Some will hear. Some will rage. Some will see signs and wonders and still not believe. But you, Peter—you've already heard. Your heart has already said yes, even if your mind needs time to catch up."

"My mind may never catch up," Peter admitted. "I'm a simple man, Master. I know fish and weather, nets and markets. This kingdom you speak of... I don't understand it."

"But you feel it," Jesus said. "That's enough for now. Understanding will come with walking. Faith grows by exercise, not explanation."

A cool wind rose off the lake, carrying the smell of water and distance. Both men shivered slightly, drawing their cloaks closer.

"We should sleep," Peter said. "Dawn comes early for fishermen."

"One more thing," Jesus said as they moved toward the stairs. "Your brother Andrew—he works the boats with you?"

"When he's not off listening to that wild man in the wilderness. John the Baptiser has his ear these days. Andrew's always been the spiritual one in the family."

"Invite him to synagogue tomorrow. Tell him..." Jesus paused, choosing his words carefully. "Tell him the one John promised is here."

Peter's eyes widened. "You? You're the one John speaks of? The one whose sandals he's not worthy to untie?"

"I am who I am," Jesus said simply. "Tomorrow, Andrew can decide for himself what that means."

They descended into the house, Peter's mind clearly racing. Jesus bedded down in the main room, insisting he needed no special accommodation. But sleep was slow in coming. Through the thin walls, he could hear Peter and Miriam whispering—her fears, his certainties, their shared wonder at this disruption of their ordinary lives.

Outside, Capernaum slept on, unaware that its destiny had shifted. Tomorrow, the synagogue would echo with words that would ripple across the world. Tomorrow, demons would shriek and flee. Tomorrow, the sick would be healed, the dead raised, and the poor would hear good news that actually sounded good.

But tonight, there was only this—a stranger welcomed, a family's hospitality, and the kingdom of God as quiet as breathing in a fisherman's house.

Jesus closed his eyes, feeling the road's exhaustion in his bones. But beneath the tiredness, something else stirred. Anticipation. Joy. The deep satisfaction of puzzle pieces clicking into place. Nazareth had rejected him, as he'd known they would. But Capernaum… Capernaum would become the centre from which the kingdom radiated outward like ripples on water.

In the darkness, he smiled. Tomorrow, Peter would begin to understand what those ripples might become—waves that would eventually swamp the boat of everything familiar and safe. But tonight, let him sleep in ignorance. Let him hold his wife and dream his fisherman's dreams one last time before everything changed.

The moon traced its path across the sky. The lake whispered its ancient secrets to the shore. And in a modest house in an unremarkable town, the Word made flesh prepared to speak new worlds into existence.

The kingdom of heaven was at hand. Closer than breath. Nearer than a heartbeat. As present as the love that had opened a door to a stranger and as powerful as the God who chose the weak to shame the strong.

Capernaum slept. But it would not sleep much longer.

Dawn came with the cries of gulls and the creak of boats launching. Jesus woke to find the house already stirring, Miriam moving efficiently in the pre-dawn darkness to prepare breakfast. Peter was gone—down to the boats, she explained, to help Andrew bring in the night's catch before synagogue. "He didn't sleep much," she said, not quite meeting Jesus's eyes. "I haven't seen him this worked up since our wedding night." She blushed at her own words. "I mean... that is..."

"I understand," Jesus said gently. "New beginnings are always terrifying and wonderful in equal measure."

She nodded, grateful for his easy acceptance. "Will you... what will you do to him? To us? I need to know. The children need stability. I can't have their father running off to—" She stopped, unable to articulate fears that had no shape yet.

Jesus accepted the bread she offered, thinking carefully before answering. "I will ask him to fish for people instead of fish. I will show him a kingdom not built with hands. I will teach him to walk on water and calm storms and speak with the authority of heaven. But I will not take him from you, Miriam. The kingdom of God is not built on broken families but on healed ones. Trust me in this."

She wanted to. He could see it in her eyes—the desperate desire to believe that this disruption might lead to something better, not worse. But she'd lived too long in a world where prophets demanded everything and delivered ashes.

"My mother named me for Moses's sister," she said suddenly. "The one who watched over him in the river, who danced when Pharaoh drowned, who challenged him when he forgot the people's needs. She said I'd need Miriam's courage to be a fisherman's wife." She met his eyes directly. "Will I need it more to be a disciple's wife?"

"Yes," Jesus said honestly. "But you'll also find joy Miriam never knew. Your husband will become who he was always meant to be. And you—you'll be part of a story that mothers will tell their daughters for generations."

She busied herself with unnecessary tasks, processing this. "The children will go with neighbours during synagogue. But I'll be there. In the women's section, where they think we can't cause trouble." A smile ghosted across her face. "They don't know fishermen's wives very well."

The sun was fully risen by the time Peter and Andrew returned, hauling baskets of fish that would go to market after worship. Andrew was smaller than his brother, with the intense eyes of a seeker and the calloused hands of a worker—an interesting combination that spoke of a man caught between worlds.

He studied Jesus with frank curiosity as they washed for synagogue. "Peter says you're the one John speaks of."

"What does John say?" Jesus asked.

"That the kingdom is coming like fire. That the axe is at the root of the trees. That one comes whose sandals he's unworthy to untie, who will baptise with the Holy Spirit and with fire." Andrew's eyes searched Jesus's face. "You don't look like fire."

"Not yet," Jesus agreed. "But the day is young."

The synagogue of Capernaum was modest compared to Jerusalem's glories, but it had a dignity born of community pride. Built of local black basalt, it squatted near the centre of town like a hen gathering chicks. Already, people were streaming in for Sabbath worship—fishermen scrubbed clean of scales, merchants in their finest robes, mothers herding children, and old men who'd claimed the same seats for decades.

Jesus entered with Peter's family, noting how people noticed. The stranger in town. The rabbi from Nazareth. Already, whispers were starting.

The service began as services always began—with the Shema, that ancient declaration of God's oneness that bound Israel together across distance and difference. "Hear, O Israel, the Lord our God, the Lord is one..." Jesus spoke the words with the congregation, feeling their power fresh. One God. Not the fractured pantheon of Rome with its competing deities and conflicting demands. One. Whole. Complete. Holy.

The reading was from Isaiah—fitting, given what had happened in Nazareth. But this was a different passage, one that spoke of light dawning in Galilee, of people walking in darkness seeing great illumination. The reader, an elderly man with trembling hands, gave each word careful weight.

When he finished, the synagogue ruler—a fussy man named Jairus whom Jesus would come to know well—stood to ask if any visiting rabbi wished to teach. His eyes found Jesus immediately, curiosity and caution warring in his expression.

Jesus stood slowly, feeling the weight of the moment. In Nazareth, he'd claimed Isaiah's promises for himself and nearly died for it. Here, in this village of comfort by the sea, what word would he bring?

He made his way to the front, accepting the scroll with steady hands. But instead of reading further, he rolled it carefully and set it aside. The congregation stirred, uncertain. Visiting rabbis usually expounded on the text, parsing words and phrases with scholarly precision. This departure from protocol was... unsettling.

"The kingdom of heaven," Jesus began, his voice carrying easily through the packed room, "is like a fisherman casting his net into the sea."

In the men's section, Peter straightened. Andrew leaned forward. Even the children, supposedly too young to understand, grew still.

"The net goes deep, where human eyes can't see. It gathers fish of every kind—clean and unclean, large and small, those that swim in schools and those that hunt alone. And when it's full, the fisherman draws it to shore."

He paused, letting them sit with the image. Every person in Capernaum understood nets and fish and the daily gamble of casting into depths that might yield feast or famine.

"You think you know what comes next," he continued. "The sorting. The clean fish were kept, and the unclean were thrown back. The law observed, the boundaries maintained. But what if I told you the kingdom's net doesn't work that way? What if I told you that in God's kingdom, the very nature of clean and unclean is transformed?"

Murmurs now, some interested, some disturbed. The Pharisees in the front row were frowning, already composing objections.

18

"You've heard it said, 'Love your neighbour and hate your enemy.' But I say to you, love your enemies. Pray for those who persecute you. When a Roman soldier compels you to carry his pack one mile, carry it two. When a tax collector—" He paused, his eyes finding a well-dressed man trying to shrink into his seat. "—when a tax collector takes your cloak, offer your tunic as well."

The murmurs grew louder. This was dangerous talk. Seditious, even. Romans and tax collectors were the enemy. Everyone knew that. To suggest otherwise...

"The kingdom of heaven," Jesus pressed on, his voice rising over the noise, "is not coming with signs to be observed. People won't say, 'Look, here it is!' or 'There it is!' Because the kingdom of God is within you. Among you. As present as breath and as hidden as yeast in dough."

"By what authority do you speak these things?" One of the Pharisees had stood, his face flushed with indignation. "You twist the scriptures to suit yourself. You speak of enemies as friends and render the Law meaningless with your pretty parables."

Jesus turned to face him fully, and something in his gaze made the man step back. "I speak of a kingdom where the last are first and the first are last. Where prostitutes and tax collectors enter before priests and scholars. Where a Samaritan's compassion shames a Levite's purity. Does this threaten you?"

"It threatens the very foundations of our faith!" the Pharisee sputtered. "Without the Law, without distinctions between clean and unclean, we're no different from the pagans who surround us!"

"And if I told you," Jesus said softly, but every ear strained to hear, "that God loves those pagans as much as He loves you? That the rain falls on the just and unjust alike? That the kingdom's invitation extends to every tribe and tongue and nation?"

The synagogue erupted. Some shouted in anger, some in wonder. The synagogue ruler was calling for order, his voice lost in the chaos. And then—
"Be silent!"

The voice that came from Jesus was unlike anything they'd heard. It carried authority that bypassed argument and struck directly at the soul. The room fell quiet as if slapped.

But the silence lasted only a moment before it was broken by something worse than shouting. A scream—inhuman, tortured, and full of rage and terror. From the back of the room, a man lurched forward, his movements jerky and wrong, like a marionette with tangled strings.

Everyone knew him. Levi the madman, they called him. He lived in the tombs outside town, cutting himself with stones, howling at the moon. Sometimes he wandered into town, and parents would hurry their children inside. The synagogue attendants were already moving to restrain him, to drag him out before he disrupted worship further.

But Jesus raised a hand, and they froze.

Levi—or the thing wearing Levi's body—crawled closer, its movements becoming more distorted with each foot of progress. When it spoke, the voice was layered, as if multiple throats were trying to use the same mouth.

"What have you to do with us, Jesus of Nazareth?" The words were garbled, full of hatred and fear. "Have you come to destroy us? I know who you are—the Holy One of God!"

The congregation gasped. Even those who'd been shouting moments before fell silent. This was beyond theological debate. This was the collision of kingdoms made visible—darkness recognising light and shrieking at the recognition.

Jesus stepped down from the platform, approaching the writhing man with measured steps. No fear in his movements. No hesitation. Just terrible, tender purpose.

"Be silent," he said again, but gently this time. Then, with authority that shook dust from the rafters: "Come out of him!"

What happened next would be debated in Capernaum for years. Some said Levi convulsed so violently he seemed to levitate. Others swore they saw shadows flee from him like bats from a cave. A few claimed the temperature dropped so suddenly their breath misted in the air.

But everyone agreed on this: one moment Levi was a tangle of limbs and inhuman sounds, and the next he was lying still on the synagogue floor, breathing normally, his eyes clear for the first time in years.

"Levi?" someone whispered. "Is that... is that you?"

The man sat up slowly, looking around in wonder. "I... where am I? How did I..." His eyes found Jesus, and his face crumpled. "Master. Oh, Master. I was lost in the dark for so long. So long. But you called me back. You called me home."

He crawled forward—not with the jerky movements of possession but with the desperate gratitude of the rescued—and grasped Jesus's feet. "Thank you. Thank you. Thank you."

Jesus helped him stand, steadying him with gentle hands. "Go home, Levi. Rest. Eat. Live. The kingdom of God has come near to you today."

The synagogue remained frozen, watching this impossible transformation. The madman made whole. The possessed set free. And it had been done with words. Just words. No elaborate rituals, no calling on higher authorities, no negotiations with the darkness. Just an authoritative command, and evil had fled like smoke before wind.

"By what authority..." the Pharisee from before began, but his voice trailed off. The answer was obvious to anyone with eyes to see. This wasn't the authority of scribes who quoted other scribes who quoted still other scribes. This was original authority. Source authority. The kind of authority that spoke worlds into being and could speak demons out of them.

"Who is this man?" someone whispered. And then louder, spreading through the crowd: "Who is this? What is this teaching? With authority he commands even the unclean spirits, and they obey him!"

Jesus looked around the synagogue—at faces shocked, frightened, hopeful, and hostile. All the reactions he'd known would come. All the seeds that would grow into either faith or rejection.

"The kingdom of heaven is at hand," he said simply. "Today, you've seen its power. Darkness cannot stand before it. Sickness must yield to it. Even death itself will prove powerless against it. But the question isn't whether the kingdom is real. The question is whether you'll enter it."

He moved toward the door, the crowd parting before him like water. At the threshold, he turned back. "I'll be teaching by the shore this evening. Anyone who has ears to hear, let them come and listen."

Then he was gone, leaving behind a synagogue in chaos and a man made whole and a hundred questions hanging in the incense-heavy air.

Peter found him an hour later, sitting on a large rock by the water's edge. The big fisherman's face was a study in conflicting emotions—awe, fear, excitement, and confusion all warring for dominance.

"The whole town's talking," he said without preamble. "Some say you're a prophet. Some say you're dangerous. The Pharisees are meeting with the Herodians—and those two groups agreeing on anything is a miracle in itself." He paused. "Levi's at home with his family. First time in five years. His mother can't stop crying."

"And what do you say, Simon?" Jesus asked.

Peter sat heavily beside him, staring out at the lake he knew so well. "I say my life just got a lot more complicated." He picked up a stone and skipped it across the water. "But also... also more alive than it's ever been. When you spoke in there, when you faced down that demon... I felt it again. That lightning in my chest. That drowning sensation. Like the whole world shifted, and suddenly I could see colours I never knew existed."

"That's the kingdom breaking in," Jesus said. "Your eyes are adjusting to new light."

"Will it always be like this? Demons screaming and Pharisees plotting, and everything I thought I knew turned upside down?"

"Often, yes. The kingdom comes with power, but power disrupts. It heals, but healing hurts those who profit from sickness. It frees, but freedom terrifies those who've made peace with their chains." Jesus turned to look at him. "I told you following me would cost everything."

"I know." Peter's voice was quiet but firm. "I've been thinking about it all through service. What you said about fishing for people. I don't understand it, not really. But I understand this—when you walked into my house last night, something in me woke up. Something I didn't even know was sleeping. And now..." He spread his hands helplessly. "Now I can't go back to sleep. Can't pretend the kingdom isn't knocking at my door."

"And Andrew?"

Peter grinned, the expression transforming his weathered face. "Are you kidding? He's ready to leave everything and follow you right now. Always was the impulsive one. I had to tell him to wait, to let you actually call him first. But he's vibrating like a plucked string. Says you're everything John promised and more."

"And Miriam?"

The grin faded. "She's scared. But also... proud? It's hard to explain. She keeps touching my face like she's seeing me for the first time. She told me whatever I decide, she'll support. But I could see the fear in her eyes. Fear of losing me. Fear of what following you might mean for the children."

"Bring her to the shore this evening," Jesus said. "Let her hear for herself. The kingdom isn't just for men who fish. It's for women who mend nets and children who play in the sand and anyone whose heart hungers for more than bread."

They sat in companionable silence as the afternoon wore on. Other people began to gather, drawn by curiosity or desperation or that indefinable pull of the Spirit moving human hearts. Some Jesus recognised from the synagogue. Others were clearly hearing about the morning's events second- or thirdhand.

By the time the sun began its descent toward the western hills, a considerable crowd had formed. They spread along the shore like a human amphitheatre, some sitting on rocks, others standing in family groups, and children running between the adults playing impromptu games.

Jesus stood, and conversations gradually died. In the synagogue, he'd had to compete with tradition and expectation and the weight of religious authority. Here, with the lake as a backdrop and the sky as a ceiling, he could speak unencumbered.

"A sower went out to sow," he began, his voice carrying easily across the water. "And as he sowed, some seeds fell along the path, and birds came and devoured them..."

The parable unfolded like a flower, simple on the surface but revealing depths to those who looked closer. Peter, sitting with his family near the front, watched Miriam's face soften as she listened. Whatever she'd expected—perhaps thunder and demands and the harsh rhetoric of revolution—this wasn't it. This was a teacher who understood soil and seed, who spoke of farming to fishermen, and who somehow made it make sense.

When he finished the parable, hands shot up like wheat stalks. Questions, so many questions. "What does the seed represent?" "Who are the birds?" "Are we the soil or the sower?"

Jesus answered some directly, others with more stories. The kingdom is like a mustard seed. The kingdom as a pearl. The kingdom is like treasure hidden in a field. Each image building on the last, creating a mosaic of meaning that couldn't be captured in simple definitions.

A woman pushed forward, dragging a boy of perhaps ten. His arm hung useless at his side, withered and twisted. "Teacher," she called out, desperation giving her courage. "My son. Born this way. The priests say it's punishment for sin—mine or his father's; they can't agree. But you cast out a demon this morning. Can you... would you..."

The crowd grew quiet, leaning in. This was what many had come for. Not just words but power. Not just teaching but transformation.

Jesus beckoned them closer. The boy was trying to hide his arm, shame written across his young face. Years of stares and whispers and being excluded from games had taught him his place in the world's hierarchy.

"What's your name?" Jesus asked gently.

"David," the boy whispered. "Like the king. My mother hoped... but I'm not much of a warrior with one arm."

"David killed Goliath with one stone," Jesus said. "Not two. And he played the harp so beautifully that demons fled from the music. Tell me, David, do you want to be healed?"

It seemed an obvious question, but the boy hesitated. "The priests say suffering makes us holy. That God gives us burdens to bear for His glory."

"And what does your heart say?"

David looked up then, meeting Jesus's eyes. "My heart says I want to throw stones with the other boys. I want to help my father with the nets. I want to dance at my sister's wedding without everyone staring."

Jesus smiled. "Then stretch out your hand."

For a moment, nothing happened. The boy looked at his withered arm, then back at Jesus, confusion clear on his face. The crowd held its breath.

"Stretch out your hand," Jesus repeated, and this time there was something more in the words. Not just invitation but enablement. Not just command but capacity.

David's eyes widened. Slowly, impossibly, the withered arm began to move. Muscles that had never worked started to flex. Fingers that had been frozen curled and uncurled. The arm straightened, lengthened, and filled out until it matched its twin perfectly.

The boy stared at his restored limb in wonder, then let out a whoop of pure joy. "Mama! Mama, look! I can move it! I can—" He scooped up a stone and hurled it far out into the lake, laughing and crying simultaneously.

His mother fell to her knees, sobbing prayers of gratitude. The crowd erupted in amazement, pressing closer, everyone suddenly remembering an ailment that needed attention.

"Please!" "My daughter!" "My father!" "Just a touch!" "Have mercy!"

Jesus raised his hands for quiet. "The sun is setting. Sabbath is ending. Bring those who are sick to Peter's house. I'll see them there."

It was a masterful move, Peter realised. The Sabbath restrictions would prevent the Pharisees from organising immediate opposition. By the time the sun fully set and work was permitted, Jesus would be dealing with people in a private home, not the public square.

As the crowd began to disperse, many heading to fetch sick relatives, Jesus turned to Peter. "Your house is about to become very crowded."

Peter looked at Miriam, who nodded slowly. "Let them come," she said. "If this is the kingdom breaking in, let it break in through our door."

The next hours were a blur of bodies and needs and miracles that became almost routine in their frequency. The house overflowed. The courtyard filled. The street beyond became an impromptu waiting room for the desperate and hopeful.

Fevers broke at a touch. Blind eyes opened. Lame legs strengthened. Demons fled shrieking into the night. And through it all, Jesus moved with calm purpose, never hurried, never overwhelmed, treating each person as if they were the only one who mattered.

Peter tried to manage the crowd, directing traffic and keeping order. But his eyes kept returning to Jesus, trying to understand what he was seeing. This wasn't the distant God of the Temple, accessible only through priests and sacrifices. This was divinity with dirt under its fingernails, touching lepers without flinching, speaking tenderly to those whose minds had broken under life's weight.

"Water," Miriam said, pressing a cup into Jesus's hands during a brief lull. "You need to drink. And eat. You're pouring yourself out like wine at a wedding."

He accepted the water gratefully. "This is why I came. To bind up the brokenhearted. To proclaim freedom for the captives. To comfort all who mourn."

"Isaiah again," Andrew said. He'd been helping organise the crowds, his energy seemingly inexhaustible. "But you're not just proclaiming it. You're doing it. Right here. Right now."

A commotion at the door drew their attention. The Pharisees from the synagogue had arrived, along with several Herodians and what looked like an official scribe. They pushed through the crowd with the authority of those used to deference.

"By what authority do you do these things?" the lead Pharisee demanded. "Healing on the Sabbath is work, forbidden by the Law of Moses!"

"The sun has set," Peter pointed out. "The Sabbath ended an hour ago."

"But the healings began before sunset," the Pharisee countered. "We have witnesses. This man—" he pointed at Jesus like he was identifying a criminal—"has broken the Sabbath law repeatedly."

Jesus set down his cup, turning to face his accusers. The crowd grew quiet, sensing confrontation.

"Tell me," Jesus said mildly, "if one of you has a sheep that falls into a pit on the Sabbath, don't you take hold of it and lift it out? How much more valuable is a human being than a sheep? Therefore, it is lawful to do good on the Sabbath."

"You twist the law to suit yourself," another Pharisee spat. "First you eat with tax collectors and sinners. Then you claim authority to forgive sins. Now you break the Sabbath openly. What next? Will you tear down the Temple itself?"

"I will raise it up," Jesus said quietly, but something in his tone made everyone lean in. "Destroy this temple, and I will raise it again in three days."

The Pharisees recoiled as if slapped. "Now he speaks blasphemy openly! The Temple took forty-six years to build, and he claims he could raise it in three days?"

"You search the Scriptures because you think that in them you have eternal life," Jesus said, his voice gaining strength. "Yet it is they that bear witness about me. But you refuse to come to me that you may have life. You load people down with burdens you yourselves wouldn't touch with a finger. You tithe mint and cumin but neglect justice and mercy. You clean the outside of the cup, but the inside is full of greed and self-indulgence."

Each word hit like a hammer blow. The religious leaders' faces went from red to purple with rage.

"How dare you!" the lead Pharisee sputtered. "We are sons of Abraham! We have kept the law since youth! We—"

"Are whitewashed tombs," Jesus finished. "Beautiful on the outside but full of dead bones within. You shut the door of the kingdom of heaven in people's faces. You neither enter yourselves nor allow those who would enter to go in."

The crowd gasped at the directness of the assault. No one spoke to the religious authorities this way. No one challenged their position, their piety, or their power.

One of the Herodians, more politically minded than his religious companions, stepped forward with a calculating smile. "Teacher, we know you are sincere and teach the way of God truthfully. Tell us then—is it lawful to pay taxes to Caesar or not?"

It was a trap, and everyone knew it. Say yes, and he'd lose the people who groaned under Roman taxation. Say no, and he'd be guilty of sedition and arrested before dawn.

Jesus looked at the man with something almost like pity. "Show me the coin used for the tax."

Someone produced a denarius. Jesus held it up, the torchlight catching Caesar's profile. "Whose likeness and inscription is this?"

"Caesar's," they answered.

"Then render to Caesar the things that are Caesar's," Jesus said, flipping the coin back to them. "And to God the things that are God's."

The Herodian's smile faltered. It was a perfect answer—unassailable legally but subversive in its implications. If Caesar's image on the coin meant it belonged to Caesar, then humans, made in God's image, belonged to...

"We'll be watching you," the lead Pharisee said, gathering his robes about him. "Every word. Every action. Every violation of the law. The people may be fooled by your tricks, but we see what you are—a deceiver, a blasphemer, a threat to everything holy."

"No," Jesus said sadly. "You don't see at all. That's the tragedy. You have eyes but don't see, ears but don't hear. The kingdom of God is breaking in around you, and you're so busy defending your traditions that you're missing the very thing you've prayed for."

They left in high dudgeon, pushing through the crowd that parted reluctantly. But their departure didn't dampen the atmosphere. If anything, it energised it. The common people had watched religious authorities get a verbal thrashing and had seen their pretensions punctured and their traps turned against them.

"Did you see their faces?" someone laughed. "Like they'd swallowed sour wine!"

"Render to Caesar the things that are Caesar's," another repeated admiringly. "Brilliant!"

But Jesus wasn't celebrating. He looked tired suddenly, the weight of confrontation showing in his shoulders. "They'll be back," he told Peter quietly. "With more traps, more accusations. They won't stop until..."

He didn't finish, but Peter heard the unspoken ending. Until they kill me.

The healing continued late into the night. By the time the last supplicant had been seen, the last demon cast out, the last fever broken, the moon was high and the city slept. Jesus sat in the courtyard, surrounded by the debris of miracle—discarded crutches, abandoned bandages, and the detritus of transformation.

"You need to rest," Miriam said firmly. She'd been a tireless helper all evening, organising food for the hungry, water for the thirsty, and comfort for the waiting. "Even prophets need sleep."

"Not yet," Jesus said. "I need to pray. To be alone with my Father. To prepare for what's coming."

He rose, moving toward the door, but Peter stopped him. "Where will you go? It's dangerous to be out alone. The Pharisees weren't making idle threats."

"To the mountain," Jesus said. "Don't worry, Peter. It's not my time yet. There's still so much to do. Disciples to call. Truth to teach. A kingdom to proclaim."

"Let me come with you," Peter offered. "To watch your back."

Jesus smiled, the expression transforming his tired face. "Not tonight. But soon, Peter. Very soon, I'll call you to leave your nets and follow me. You and Andrew and others. Twelve in all, like the tribes of Israel. You'll be my witnesses, my friends, and my family in ways blood could never make."

"Twelve?" Peter's mind raced. "Who else?"

"You'll see. Some will surprise you. One will break your heart. But all are necessary. Even the one who..." Again, the unfinished sentence. Again, the shadow of future sorrow.

Jesus slipped out into the night, leaving Peter standing in his own courtyard feeling like a stranger in his own life. Everything had changed in a single day. This morning he'd been a fisherman with a family and a routine and a life that made sense. Tonight he stood at the threshold of something vast and terrible and wonderful.

"Come to bed," Miriam said softly, taking his arm. "Tomorrow will bring its own challenges."

But Peter couldn't sleep. He lay beside his wife, staring at the ceiling, replaying the day's events. The demon recognising Jesus. The boy's arm was made whole. The Pharisees routed. The endless stream of broken people made whole.

"What have we gotten ourselves into?" Miriam whispered in the darkness.

"I don't know," Peter admitted. "But I can't turn back now. Can't unknow what I know. Can't unsee what I've seen."

"I know." She found his hand and squeezed it. "I saw it too. The way he looked at people. Not just the surface but all the way down to who they really are. He looked at me that way when he promised the kingdom wouldn't break our family. " A pause. "I believed him."

"So did I," Peter said. "God help me, so did I."

Outside, Capernaum slept fitfully. In a hundred homes, healed bodies rested in wonder. In the synagogue, Pharisees plotted through the night. In the streets, rumours spread like wine from a broken jar.

The kingdom of heaven had come to the Village of Comfort. And nothing would ever be the same.

On a mountain overlooking it all, Jesus prayed alone, wrestling with the Father about the path ahead. The choosing of the twelve. The teachings that would confound. The miracles that would amaze. The opposition would grow until it flowered into crucifixion.

But also the joy. The wonder in children's eyes. The tears of the healed. The moment when understanding dawned in a disciple's face. The kingdom breaking in like dawn, unstoppable despite all the darkness could do.

"Your will be done," he finally whispered to the stars. "In Capernaum as it is in heaven."

The wind carried his words down to the sleeping city, where they settled like seeds in the hearts of dreamers. Tomorrow, some would wake and return to old patterns, the miracle already fading into memory. But others would wake changed, carrying kingdom fire in their bones.

And from a fisherman's house by the shore, the revolution would spread. Not with swords but with love. Not with force but with invitation. Not conquering but transforming, until the whole world would know that the kingdom of heaven had come near.

But that was tomorrow's work. Tonight, there was only this—a teacher praying on a mountain, a city sleeping in ignorance of its destiny, and the quiet movement of God through ordinary lives, making all things new.

The chosen city slept. But it would not sleep much longer.

Dawn was coming.

And with it, the kingdom.

Chapter 2: Authority in the Synagogue

The Sabbath horn echoed across Capernaum as the sun touched the western hills, its mournful note calling the faithful to prepare. In doorways and courtyards throughout the fishing town, women lit their lamps with practiced efficiency, the day's labour giving way to holy rest. Men hurried from the docks, still reeking of fish and brine, to wash themselves clean for the evening prayers. Children were scrubbed and scolded into their best clothes, their protests falling on deaf ears—the Sabbath waited for no one.

Jesus stood on the flat roof of Peter's house, watching the transformation. Yesterday, these same streets had pulsed with commerce—merchants hawking their wares, fishermen mending nets, and tax collectors tallying their gains. Now, as shadows lengthened and the last rays of sunlight painted the limestone walls gold, a different energy took hold. Sacred time approached, demanding its due.

"Master?" Peter's head appeared at the top of the ladder, his beard still damp from washing. "The sun sets soon. We should go."

Jesus nodded but didn't immediately move. His gaze swept across the town that would become his base of operations, this crossroads where Jewish faith met Roman commerce, where fishermen and tax collectors, zealots and collaborators, all gathered under one roof to hear the law of Moses. Tomorrow, the divisions would reassert themselves. But tonight, in the synagogue, they would stand shoulder to shoulder, united in their proclamation that the Lord their God was one.

"Tell me about your synagogue," Jesus said as they descended to the courtyard where Andrew, James, and John waited.

Peter's chest swelled with provincial pride. "It's not Jerusalem, of course, but we had a centurion—Roman, if you can believe it—who paid for the whole building. Said he loved our nation." He shook his head at the memory. "Strange days when Gentiles build houses of prayer for Jews."

"Perhaps not so strange," Jesus murmured, but Peter was already launching into descriptions of the synagogue's features—the carved stone lintel, the ark containing the Torah scrolls, and the seat of Moses where the rabbi sat to teach.

They joined the stream of people moving through the narrow streets. Jesus had covered his head with his prayer shawl, but several still recognised him from the previous day's healings. Whispers followed in their wake.

"That's him—the teacher from Nazareth."

"My cousin says he healed her fever with just a word."

"Another wonderworker, probably. They never last long."

James fell into step beside Jesus, his voice low. "They're curious about you. After what happened yesterday at Peter's house..."

"Let them be curious," Jesus replied. "Curiosity opens doors that certainty would keep locked."

The synagogue rose before them, its stone facade modest compared to Jerusalem's grandeur but impressive enough for a fishing town. Oil lamps already burnt in the windows, casting warm light into the gathering dusk. The last stragglers hurried up the steps, adjusting prayer shawls and smoothing robes.

Inside, the familiar scent of oil and aged wood enveloped them. The room was nearly full, with men on one side and women separated by a wooden partition on the other. Children fidgeted between their parents' legs, already restless despite their mothers' warning glares. At the front, the ark stood closed, its embroidered curtain concealing the precious scrolls within.

The synagogue ruler, a thin man named Jairus whom Peter had pointed out, stood near the ark, surveying the crowd with the harried expression of someone trying to maintain order in barely controlled chaos. His eyes found Jesus, narrowed slightly in assessment, then moved on. A visiting rabbi was nothing unusual—teachers often travelled between synagogues, bringing fresh perspectives on familiar texts.

Jesus and his companions found space near the middle of the room. Around them, the men of Capernaum arranged themselves according to some invisible hierarchy—the wealthy merchants near the front, common labourers toward the back, with fishermen like Peter occupying the fluid middle ground. The air hummed with subdued conversation, neighbours catching up on the week's events, debating points of law, and gossiping about whose son was courting whose daughter.

The hazzan—the synagogue attendant—struck a small bell, and conversations died. Jairus stepped forward, his reedy voice carrying surprising authority. "Hear, O Israel: The Lord our God, the Lord is one." The response rose from two hundred throats, the ancient words binding them across all divisions of class and occupation: "You shall love the Lord your God with all your heart and with all your soul and with all your strength."

The familiar rhythm of the service washed over them—prayers and benedictions worn smooth by centuries of repetition. Jesus's lips moved with the words, but his eyes remained alert, studying the gathered faces. Here was Israel in miniature: the devout and the doubters, the passionate and the merely dutiful, all going through motions that had become as natural as breathing.

When the time came for the Torah reading, the hazzan carefully removed the scroll from the ark, unwrapping it with reverence. The portion for the week was from Deuteronomy, Moses's final instructions to Israel before they entered the Promised Land. Seven men were called up to read, their voices rising and falling in the ancient chant.

Jesus listened to the familiar words with fresh ears. Choose life, Moses had urged. Follow God's commands that you may live and multiply in the land. But as Jesus watched the readers—one stumbling over the Hebrew, another racing through as if late for dinner—he saw how the life-giving words had calcified into religious performance. The commands meant to free had become chains. The relationship intended to bring joy had devolved into a transaction.

After the Torah portion came the reading from the Prophets. The hazzan looked to Jairus, who scanned the room with the air of a man making calculations. His gaze settled on Jesus.

"We have a visiting teacher among us," Jairus announced. "From Nazareth, I'm told. Perhaps he would honour us by reading from the Prophets and offering a word of instruction?"

It was phrased as an invitation, but Jesus heard the challenge beneath. A carpenter's son from Nazareth, claiming to teach? Let him prove himself in front of those who knew scripture from childhood, who could debate the finest points of law, and who wouldn't be impressed by a few healing tricks.

Jesus rose, making his way to the front. The hazzan handed him the scroll of Isaiah, and Jesus unrolled it carefully, his carpenter's hands sure on the ancient parchment. He found the passage he wanted—not the assigned portion for the week, which raised a few eyebrows, but no one objected. Visiting rabbis were granted certain liberties.

"The Spirit of the Lord is upon me," Jesus read, his voice filling the synagogue with an authority that made conversations in the back rows cease, "because he has anointed me to proclaim good news to the poor. He has sent me to proclaim liberty to the captives and recovery of sight to the blind, to set at liberty those who are oppressed, and to proclaim the year of the Lord's favour."

He rolled up the scroll, handed it back to the hazzan, and sat down in the seat of Moses. Every eye fixed on him, waiting. The tradition was clear—after reading, the teacher would explain the passage, drawing out its meaning for the people's edification.

Jesus let the silence stretch, feeling the weight of expectation. When he finally spoke, his voice was conversational, almost intimate, as if addressing each person individually rather than the crowd.

"You're waiting for me to explain this scripture," he said. "To tell you what Isaiah meant, what historical context shaped his words, and how many interpretations the sages have offered." A slight smile played at his lips. "But what if I told you something different? What if I told you that today—right now, in this room—this scripture is being fulfilled in your hearing?"

A ripple ran through the congregation. Someone in the back coughed. Women behind the partition leaned forward, straining to hear. Jairus's face had gone very still.

"You know these words," Jesus continued, standing now, moving away from the seat to walk among them. "You've heard them read year after year. Beautiful words. Comforting words. Words about someday, somewhere, when God acts to restore Israel. But what if someday is today? What if somewhere is here?"

He paused near a group of fishermen, men whose hands were permanently stained with scales and salt. "Good news to the poor. How many of you barely scraped together the temple tax this year? How many nights have you wondered if your nets would bring enough fish to feed your children?"

Uncomfortable shifting. These weren't things discussed in polite synagogue teaching.

Jesus moved on, stopping near a cluster of merchants. "Liberty to the captives. You follow the law, you keep the Sabbath, and you tithe mint and cumin. But how many of you feel truly free? How many are captive to fears you can't name, to emptiness that all your religious observance can't fill?"
His circuit brought him to a corner where the town's less respectable elements clustered—men who worked on the Sabbath when desperate enough, women whose reputations had been tarnished by whispers or worse. "Recovery of sight to the blind. Not just physical blindness, though that too. But the blindness keeps us from seeing God's kingdom breaking in all around us. The blindness that makes us think God's favour belongs only to the righteous, the pure, the ones who've never stumbled."
An elderly Pharisee named Eleazar stood abruptly. "Young man, these are bold words. Are you claiming to be the Messiah? Are you saying Isaiah's prophecy—a prophecy about the restoration of Israel—is about you?"
Jesus turned to face him, and something in his gaze made the older man take a half-step back. "I'm saying the kingdom of God doesn't arrive the way you expect. It doesn't come with armies or upheaval or the restoration of David's throne—at least, not in the way you imagine. It comes like seed scattered on soil, growing secretly. It comes like yeast worked through dough, transforming from within. It comes in a synagogue in Capernaum, on an ordinary Sabbath, when people discover that God's favor isn't something to be earned but something to be received."
"Blasphemy," someone muttered, but others were leaning forward, hungry for more.

Jesus spread his hands, encompassing the whole assembly. "You've made God's word into a burden too heavy to bear. You've turned relationship into regulation, love into law, and freedom into bondage. But the Lord's favor—his year of jubilee when debts are forgiven and slaves go free—is not a distant promise. It's a present reality for anyone with ears to hear."

"And who are you to interpret the law?" Eleazar pressed, his face flushed. "By what authority do you speak?"

Before Jesus could answer, a sound cut through the tension—a laugh, but not of joy. It was the broken cackle of madness, rising from the back of the room where a man had been sitting quietly throughout the service. Now he stood, his eyes wild, spittle flecking his beard.

"Ha!" The laugh came again, but the voice that followed it seemed to come from somewhere deeper, darker. "What have you to do with us, Jesus of Nazareth?"

The synagogue erupted. Women pulled their children close. Men stepped back, creating a circle of space around the disturbed man. He'd been a fixture in Capernaum for years—Matthias the potter, once a respectable craftsman until something had broken in his mind. Most days he was harmless, muttering to himself at the market, sleeping in doorways. The synagogue tolerated his presence on the principle that even the mad deserved to hear God's word.

But this was different. The voice coming from his throat didn't sound like Matthias at all.

"Have you come to destroy us?" The man's body contorted, his hands clawing at the air as if fighting invisible restraints. "I know who you are—the Holy One of God!"

The declaration rang off the stone walls. Holy One of God. It was a title from the Psalms, a designation for the coming Messiah. But hearing it from the mouth of a madman—or whatever spoke through the madman—sent ice through the veins of everyone present.

Jairus stepped forward, his face pale. "Matthias, please. Sit down. You're disturbing the service."

The man's head snapped toward the synagogue ruler, and the laugh came again. "Service? You call this service? You sit here week after week, mouthing prayers to a God you've made small enough to fit in your little boxes. And now He's here—the Holy One himself—and you want me to sit down?"

Jesus had remained still during the outburst, but now he moved. The crowd parted before him like water, and he walked straight toward the possessed man. No hesitation, no fear, just purposeful steps that seemed to shake the very air.

The man saw him coming and fell to his knees, his body convulsing. "No! Don't—we know who you are! Why have you come? It's not time yet! The agreement—"

"Be silent," Jesus said, and his voice carried an authority that made the earlier teaching seem like whispers. "Come out of him."

The words were simple, spoken without drama or ritual. No incantations, no calling on higher powers, no elaborate exorcism rites. Just a command, delivered with the casual certainty of someone who expected to be obeyed.

The man's body went rigid. A sound emerged from his throat—not quite a scream, not quite a roar, but something that seemed to contain all the rage and fear and twisted hunger of whatever had taken residence in Matthias's broken mind. He convulsed once, violently, his back arching impossibly before he collapsed to the stone floor.

Silence.

Then Matthias drew a shuddering breath and opened his eyes. Clear eyes. Sane eyes. He looked around in confusion, as if waking from a long nightmare.

"Where... where am I?" His voice was hoarse but recognisably his own. "How did I get to the synagogue?"

Two men helped him sit up, their hands trembling. Around the room, people stood frozen, trying to process what they'd just witnessed. They'd heard of exorcisms—lengthy rituals involving special prayers, blessed objects, and the invocation of Solomon's name. But this? A simple command and instant obedience?

"What is this?" someone whispered. "What kind of teaching is this?"

"He commands even the unclean spirits," another replied, awe and fear mingling in his voice, "and they obey him."

Eleazar the Pharisee found his voice, though it shook. "This... this proves nothing. The prince of demons can cast out demons. We need to examine—"

"Examine what?" Peter stepped forward, his fisherman's bluntness cutting through religious pretence. "We all saw it. We all heard it. Matthias has been mad for years, and now look at him."

Indeed, Matthias was struggling to his feet, supported by neighbours who'd avoided him for years. Tears streamed down his face as awareness returned—not just of where he was, but of where he'd been. The lost years, the darkness that had consumed him, the things he'd done and said under its influence.

"I remember," he whispered. "Oh God, I remember all of it." He looked at Jesus, and fresh tears came. "Rabbi, I... what I said... I didn't mean—"

"I know," Jesus said gently. "It wasn't you speaking. Go home, Matthias. Rest. Tomorrow, return to your wheel and your clay. Create beautiful things again."

The potter nodded, unable to speak. Friends led him out, their arms around him like a protective wall. As the door closed behind them, the synagogue exploded in discussion.

"Did you see—"

"The demon knew him!"

"Called him the Holy One—"

"But how? By what power?"

"No one teaches like this—"

Jairus clapped his hands sharply. "Please! We're still in the middle of service. Let us... let us complete our prayers."

But the heart had gone out of formal worship. People mumbled through the remaining benedictions, their minds clearly elsewhere. When the final "Amen" was spoken, the congregation surged toward the doors, eager to spread the news of what they'd witnessed.

Jesus found himself surrounded by a core of protectors—Peter and Andrew, James and John—who guided him through the press of bodies. Questions flew at him from all directions.

"Rabbi, how did you know?"

"Will Matthias stay healed?"

"Can you help my son? He has fits—"

"My daughter sees things that aren't there—"

"Please, Rabbi, my mother hasn't spoken in years—"

The needs crashed over him like waves, each person's desperation adding to the tide. Jesus felt the weight of their hope, their pain, and their hunger for someone—anyone—who could make sense of their suffering.

Outside, the cool night air provided momentary relief. The Sabbath stars had emerged, painting the sky in patterns that had guided travellers since Abraham's time. But the crowd followed, spilling out of the synagogue and into the courtyard.

"Tomorrow," Jesus said, his voice carrying despite its quietness. "Bring your sick tomorrow. Tonight is for rest, for pondering what you've seen. Tomorrow we'll speak of healing."

Reluctantly, the crowd began to disperse. Family groups walked home in animated discussion, their Sabbath meal conversations already decided. The news would spread through Capernaum like wildfire—the teacher from Nazareth had authority over unclean spirits. He taught as no one had taught before. Maybe, just maybe, he was the one they'd been waiting for.

As Jesus and his disciples made their way back to Peter's house, Andrew fell into step beside him. "Master, what you did in there... I've seen exorcists work. They struggle for hours, sometimes days. But you just spoke, and it obeyed. How?"

Jesus was quiet for a moment, considering his answer. "The kingdom of God isn't established by committee, Andrew. It doesn't arrive through proper channels and religious protocol. It breaks in with power, unexpected and undeniable. That spirit recognised what the religious leaders are still debating—that God's kingdom has come near."

"The demon called you the Holy One of God," John said quietly. "Is that... are you...?"

"I am who you will discover me to be," Jesus replied. "But discovery takes time. You can't learn to see in a moment what's been hidden for ages."

They reached Peter's house to find it already bustling with preparation. Peter's mother-in-law, miraculously recovered from her fever just the day before, had prepared a Sabbath meal that filled the courtyard with savoury aromas. She fussed over Jesus like a grandmother, pressing food on him, insisting he looked too thin.

"Eat, eat," she urged. "How can you heal others if you don't take care of yourself? And you boys"—she turned her attention to the disciples—"when was the last time you had a proper meal? Fishing all night, wandering all day. Sit. Eat. The kingdom of God can wait for full stomachs."

The normalcy of it—the domestic bustle, the ordinary kindness—provided a strange counterpoint to what had just occurred. Less than an hour ago, Jesus had commanded a demon in the synagogue. Now he sat breaking bread like any other Sabbath guest, listening to Peter's mother-in-law complain about the price of grain at the market.

But even in the midst of ordinary conversation, the disciples kept stealing glances at him. Who was this man they'd chosen to follow? John the Baptist had pointed him out and called him the Lamb of God. They'd seen him turn water to wine at a wedding and watched him cleanse the temple courts with a whip of cords. And now this—authority over evil spirits, teaching that made the scribes look like children reciting lessons they didn't understand.

As the meal progressed, neighbours began arriving. Word had already spread through the tight-knit community. They came with cautious curiosity, bringing wine or bread as pretence for their visit.

"Is it true?" Miriam from next door whispered to Peter's wife. "Did he really cast out Matthias's demon?"

"With just a word," Peter's wife confirmed, her own awe evident. "My husband saw the whole thing."

"My daughter has nightmares," Miriam said hesitantly. "Terrible dreams where she wakes screaming. Do you think…?"

"Bring her tomorrow," Peter's wife said gently. "He said he'd see the sick tomorrow."

Similar conversations rippled through the courtyard. Hope—that dangerous, beautiful thing—was kindling in hearts that had learnt to expect little from life. A teacher with authority over demons? If that were true, what else might be possible?

Jesus watched it all from his place at the table, seeing both the hope and the danger in it. They wanted a miracle worker, someone to solve their problems with a wave of his hand. They weren't wrong—he had come to heal, to restore, and to set free. But the freedom he offered went deeper than they imagined. Casting out demons was just the beginning, the attention-grabbing sign that pointed to a greater reality.

"You're troubled," John observed, sliding onto the bench beside him. Of all the disciples, the young fisherman had the keenest eye for Jesus's moods.

"Not troubled. Thoughtful." Jesus accepted a cup of wine from a passing servant. "They see the signs but miss their meaning. They want the gifts but not the giver."

"But they're listening now," John pointed out. "After what happened in the synagogue, they'll hang on your every word."

"For a time," Jesus agreed. "Until I say something that challenges their assumptions or asks more than they're willing to give. Then we'll see how deep their listening goes."

The evening wore on, marked by the rhythm of shared meals since time immemorial. Stories were told, children played between the adults' legs, and the wine loosened tongues and laughter alike. But beneath the ordinary Sabbath celebration ran an undercurrent of expectancy. Something had shifted in Capernaum's synagogue. A new kind of teacher had emerged, one whose words carried the weight of action, whose authority extended beyond human institutions into the realm of the spirit itself.

As the night deepened and guests began to take their leave, Jesus stepped out into the courtyard alone. The stars wheeled overhead, the same stars that had witnessed his birth in Bethlehem, his boyhood in Nazareth, and his baptism in the Jordan. Soon enough, they would witness darker moments—betrayal and denial, mockery and crucifixion. But tonight, they shone on the beginning of something new.

"Thank you for the sign," he prayed quietly. "For Matthias's freedom and the doors it opened. Give me wisdom for what comes next. They're hungry for bread, but they need to learn they're starving for righteousness. They want healing for their bodies, but their spirits are the deeper wound."

A footstep behind him. Peter was unable to sleep, his mind churning with the day's events.

"Master? Sorry to disturb you. I just... I can't stop thinking about what happened. That demon—it knew you. It was afraid of you."

Jesus turned to face his impetuous disciple. "What frightens you more, Peter? That the demon knew me, or that you don't?"

Peter's mouth opened, then closed. The question cut deep, exposing the gap between following and truly knowing.

"I want to know you," Peter said finally. "But every time I think I understand, you do something that shows me I've barely scratched the surface."

"Good," Jesus said with a slight smile. "The moment you think you have God figured out, you've created an idol. Keep wrestling, Peter. Keep questioning. It's the ones who think they see clearly who are truly blind."

They stood in companionable silence, teacher and student, while the night sounds of Capernaum washed over them—dogs barking, babies crying, and the eternal whisper of waves against the shore. Ordinary sounds of an ordinary town where something extraordinary had begun.

"They'll all come tomorrow, won't they?" Peter said. "Every sick person in Capernaum. Maybe from the surrounding villages too, once word spreads."

"Yes."

"Can you heal them all?"

Jesus looked at him steadily. "What do you think?"

Peter wrestled with the implications. A man who could command demons with a word—what were human ailments to such power? But there was something in Jesus's expression that suggested the question went deeper than ability.

"I think," Peter said slowly, "that you could. But I also think there's more to this than just fixing what's broken. Otherwise you'd have healed everyone in Nazareth."

"You're learning," Jesus said. "Miracles without a message are just magic tricks. Healing without transformation is just postponing the inevitable. I've come to heal, yes—but more than that, I've come to make all things new."

A cool breeze swept in from the lake, carrying the scent of fish and distant rain. Peter shivered, though not entirely from cold. He was beginning to grasp the edges of something vast, a purpose that made their fishing partnership seem like children's games.

"Get some sleep," Jesus advised. "Tomorrow will test us all."

Peter nodded and turned to go, then paused. "Master? What you said in the synagogue about the scripture being fulfilled... did you mean...?"

"I meant what I said. The year of the Lord's favour has begun. Good news for the poor, sight for the blind, and freedom for the captives. But Peter?" Jesus's eyes held depths of compassion and sorrow. "Not everyone will recognise it as good news. Not everyone wants to be free."

With that cryptic warning, Jesus returned to his prayers, and Peter to his bed. But sleep came slowly to the fisherman's house that night. In room after room, minds replayed the scene in the synagogue—the teaching that bypassed the mind to grip the heart, the demon's recognition and terror, and the simple command that shattered years of bondage.

By morning, the entire town would know. By evening, the surrounding villages. Within a week, all of Galilee would be talking about the teacher from Nazareth who spoke with authority and backed his words with power.

But that was tomorrow's challenge. Tonight, Matthias the potter slept peacefully for the first time in years, his mind his own again. Tonight, children who'd witnessed the exorcism whispered to each other about the man who made demons flee. Tonight, religious leaders lay awake wrestling with implications that threatened everything they thought they knew about how God worked.

And in Peter's courtyard, Jesus prayed on, preparing for the flood of human need that would arrive with the dawn. He'd shown them a glimpse of the kingdom's power. Now came the harder task—teaching them what that kingdom demanded, what it offered, and what it would ultimately cost.

The authority demonstrated in the synagogue was just the beginning. Like a pebble thrown into still water, the ripples would spread outward—through Capernaum, through Galilee, through Judea, and eventually through the whole world. But it started here, in a modest synagogue on an ordinary Sabbath, with a carpenter's son teaching with authority and a broken potter made whole.

The revolution had begun. Not with swords or political manifestos, but with a word of power that shattered the chains of spiritual bondage. The kingdom of God had come near, and nothing would ever be the same.

As the night deepened toward dawn, Capernaum slept fitfully, dreaming of demons fleeing and kingdoms arriving, of teachers who spoke with heaven's authority and healings that might finally answer years of prayer. Tomorrow would bring its own challenges, its own revelations.

But tonight, the echo of that commanding voice lingered in the synagogue's empty hall: "Be silent and come out of him."

Simple words. World-changing words. The first volleys in a war that would be won not through force but through surrender, not through hatred but through love that was stronger than death itself.

The Sabbath ended as the first stars faded toward dawn. And with it ended an old way of understanding God's interaction with His people. The teacher had come. The kingdom had arrived. The revolution of grace had begun.

All because a carpenter from Nazareth had dared to speak with authority in a Capernaum synagogue, and heaven itself had backed his words.

Chapter 3: Follow Me

The sun had not yet broken the horizon when Simon Peter pushed his boat into the dark waters of the Sea of Galilee. The familiar slap of waves against the hull, the creak of oars in their locks, the smell of fish and tar and wet rope—these were the sounds and scents of his life, as constant as breathing. His massive hands, scarred from countless nights of hauling nets, gripped the oars with practiced ease as he pulled toward the fishing grounds.
Behind him, his brother Andrew worked to prepare the nets, his movements efficient despite the darkness. They had fished these waters since boyhood, knew every current and depth, and knew every place where the shoals gathered. Their father had taught them, as his father had taught him, back through generations of Galilean fishermen who wrested their living from these unpredictable waters.
"Storm coming," Andrew said quietly, reading the signs in the feel of the air and the behaviour of the waves. "Maybe tomorrow, maybe the day after."
Peter grunted acknowledgement. After the strange events in the synagogue yesterday, a storm seemed almost fitting. That teacher from Nazareth—Jesus, they called him—had spoken with such authority that even the demons obeyed. Peter had seen the possessed man convulse and shriek and had watched the unclean spirit flee at a word from the teacher's lips. The whole town was still buzzing with it.
"There," Andrew pointed to a spot where the water showed a different texture in the pre-dawn gloom. "Cast there."

They worked in the rhythm born of long partnership, Peter positioning the boat while Andrew cast the net in a perfect circle. The weighted edges sank quickly, and they waited, hope and experience warring in their hearts. Some nights the lake gave generously. Other nights, she hoarded her treasures like a miser.

Tonight seemed to be one of the miserable nights. The first cast brought up nothing but some seaweed and a piece of waterlogged wood. They moved to another spot and cast again. Nothing. A third spot, a fourth. The eastern sky began to lighten, grey fading to pearl, and still their nets came up empty.

"The fish have ears tonight," Andrew muttered, using the old fisherman's expression for nights when the catch eluded them. "Or perhaps they too went to hear the teacher speak."

Peter didn't laugh at the weak joke. His mind kept returning to the synagogue, to that voice that had commanded the demon with such ease. He'd heard many teachers over the years—Pharisees who buried the truth under layers of rules, Sadducees who turned faith into politics, and revolutionaries who confused the kingdom of God with the kingdom of swords. But this Jesus was different. He spoke of God as if he knew Him personally, intimately, like a son knows a father.

"Peter." Andrew's voice was sharp with warning. "Company."

Peter looked where his brother pointed. Another boat was approaching, the Zebedee fishing vessel with James and John at the oars. The brothers were their partners in the fishing cooperative, sharing costs and splitting profits. Like Peter and Andrew, they'd been on the water all night.

"Any luck?" James called across the water, though the empty nets draped over Peter's gunwales already gave the answer.

"The lake is stubborn tonight," Peter replied. "You?"

John held up a basket with perhaps a dozen small fish. "Barely enough to feed our own families, let alone sell in the market."

The two boats drifted closer, the fishermen commiserating over their poor fortune. It happened sometimes—nights when despite all their skill and knowledge, the fish simply weren't there. Or were there but wouldn't bite. It was the uncertainty that made fishing both maddening and addictive. You never knew when the next cast might bring up a net-breaking haul.

"We should head in," James said practically. "The morning merchants will be setting up their stalls soon. Maybe we can at least sell these few for breakfast money."

Peter was about to agree when movement on the shore caught his eye. A figure walked along the beach, barely visible in the dawn light. There was something about the way he moved, purposeful yet unhurried, that seemed familiar.

"Is that...?" Andrew leaned forward, squinting.

It was. Jesus of Nazareth, the teacher from yesterday, walked along the shoreline as if he were taking a casual morning stroll. He paused near where their boats would beach, and even from this distance, Peter could see he was watching them.

"The teacher," John said unnecessarily. "What's he doing out so early?"

"We are the same thing, perhaps," James suggested. "Looking for breakfast."

They rowed toward shore, curiosity overcoming the disappointment of their failed night. As they drew closer, Peter could see Jesus more clearly. He wore the simple tunic of a workman, travel-stained but clean. His feet were bare, sandals carried in one hand. But it was his eyes that caught and held attention—dark eyes that seemed to see everything, understand everything, and still somehow invite you closer.

"Peace be with you," Jesus called when they were within earshot. "How was the fishing?"

"The peace is yours, Teacher," Peter replied formally, then added with fisherman's honesty, "The fishing was terrible. We've worked all night and caught nothing."

Jesus smiled, and there was something in that smile that made Peter's heart skip. "Put out into deep water," Jesus said, his voice carrying easily across the water. "Let down your nets for a catch."

Peter felt his jaw tighten. Here was a carpenter's son from a hill town telling a veteran fisherman how to fish. Everything in him wanted to explain that they'd just spent all night trying every spot, every depth. That the fish weren't running. That nets cast in daylight, when the fish could see them, were even less likely to succeed than those cast in darkness.

But something in those eyes stopped him. Instead, he heard himself saying, "Master, we've worked hard all night and haven't caught anything. But because you say so, I will let down the nets."

Andrew shot him a look of disbelief. James and John exchanged glances that clearly questioned Peter's sanity. But Peter was already turning the boat, rowing back toward deeper water. After a moment's hesitation, Andrew began preparing the nets again.

"This is foolishness," Andrew muttered, but he cast the net with his usual skill when Peter gave the signal.

For a moment, nothing happened. The net sank into the green depths, and Peter could almost hear the sceptical thoughts of his companions. Then the water exploded.

Fish—hundreds, thousands of them—boiled to the surface. The net, designed to hold a good catch, stretched and strained under the weight. Peter grabbed the ropes, feeling them burn against his palms as the catch tried to escape.

"Andrew! Help me!" He threw his weight against the pull, muscles developed over decades of fishing straining to their limit. Andrew joined him, and together they fought to control the impossible haul.

"The net's tearing!" Andrew shouted. "It can't hold this many!"

"James! John!" Peter bellowed to the other boat. "Come help us!"

The Zebedee brothers didn't need to be asked twice. They rowed over quickly, and soon all four men were working frantically to salvage the catch. They managed to distribute the fish between both boats, but even so, the vessels sat dangerously low in the water, gunwales nearly awash.

Peter stood in his dangerously laden boat, staring at the mass of silver bodies that filled it from stem to stern. His hands were bloody from the ropes, his tunic soaked with sweat and lake water. This was impossible. In all his years of fishing, in all the stories passed down from his father and grandfather, he'd never heard of anything like this.

He looked toward shore, where Jesus stood watching, that same knowing smile on his face. And suddenly, Peter understood. This wasn't about fish. This had never been about fish. This was about power—the same power that had cast out the demon yesterday, the same authority that made even the creatures of the deep obey.

The realisation hit Peter like a physical blow. He stumbled through the fish filling his boat and fell to his knees in the shallow water near shore, not caring that he was ruining the catch beneath him.

"Go away from me, Lord!" The words tore from his throat. "I am a sinful man!"

Because he was. Oh, he was. Peter knew his own heart—the pride, the anger, and the dozen small compromises made every day. The fish he'd sold, claiming they were fresh when they were a day old. The weights he'd used weren't quite honest. The harsh words to his wife when the fishing was poor. The doubts about God that plagued him in the dark hours before dawn.

And here was holiness incarnate, power that commanded nature itself. Peter felt exposed, naked, and unworthy to be in the presence of such authority. He pressed his face to his bloody hands, unable to look at the teacher.

A hand touched his shoulder. Gentle, calloused from years of working wood. "Don't be afraid, Simon."

Peter looked up through his fingers. Jesus had waded into the water and stood beside him, unconcerned about his wet robes. Those eyes—how could eyes hold such power and such kindness simultaneously?

"From now on," Jesus said, his voice carrying a weight that seemed to press into Peter's very bones, "you will fish for people."

Fish for people. Peter's mind struggled with the image. What did that mean? How did one fish for people? But even as the questions formed, he felt something shift inside him, like a boat changing direction in response to the rudder. This was a calling. A commissioning. An invitation to something far greater than hauling fish from the lake.

Jesus turned to the others—Andrew still standing stunned in the boat, James and John staring at the impossible catch that threatened to swamp their vessel. "Follow me," he said simply.

Two words. That was all. No explanation of where they were going, what they would do, or how they would live. No contract negotiated, no terms discussed. Just "Follow me."

Peter watched his brother's face and saw the same recognition dawning there. Andrew had always been the thoughtful one, the one who considered carefully before acting. But now he climbed out of the boat without hesitation, wading through the fish-filled water to stand beside Jesus.

"What about the catch?" James asked, ever practical. "This is more wealth than we've seen in months. We can't just leave it."

"Bring the boats to shore," Jesus said. "There are others who need to eat today. The widows, the orphans, those who have no boats of their own. Let them have the fish."

Give away the catch? Peter's fisherman's heart rebelled at the thought. This haul could feed their families for weeks and could be sold for enough money to repair nets, fix boats, and maybe even expand their business. But even as the protests formed, he knew they didn't matter. Something infinitely more valuable than fish was being offered here.

They struggled to beach the overladen boats, water sloshing over the sides with each pull of the oars. Word had already begun to spread—it always did in a town where everyone watched everyone else's business. People came running to see the miraculous catch, to help pull the boats ashore, and to marvel at the sheer impossibility of it.

"Simon's boat is full to sinking!" "Where did all these fish come from?" "The teacher told them where to cast!" "Impossible! No one can command the fish!"

Peter barely heard the excited chatter. His eyes were fixed on Jesus, who stood calmly amidst the chaos, directing the distribution of fish to those who needed them most. An elderly widow received a basket full. A family with too many children and not enough food walked away with laden arms. Former lepers, still bearing the social stigma of their healing, were given the choicest fish without anyone daring to object in Jesus's presence.

"You're really going to do this?" The voice belonged to Zebedee, James and John's father, who had arrived to see what the commotion was about. His weathered face showed a mixture of pride and loss as he looked at his sons. "Leave the family business? Follow this teacher?"

James looked at his father, then at Jesus, then back. "Abba, I don't fully understand it myself. But when he says, 'Follow me,' it's like... like the whole world shifts. Like everything I thought was important becomes secondary to those two words."

"It's like the stories of Elijah calling Elisha," John added softly. "When the prophet's mantle falls on you, you don't ask questions. You just go."

Zebedee's eyes glistened with unshed tears, but he nodded slowly. "Then go with my blessing, my sons. But remember where you came from. Remember that you're fishermen, no matter what else you become."

"We'll take care of the business," one of the hired workers assured him. "The boys have taught us well."

Peter thought of his own wife, probably just waking up, expecting him to return with the night's catch and the day's wages. How could he explain this to her? How could he make her understand that he was leaving everything to follow a teacher who might lead them anywhere, promising them nothing except the cryptic offer to make them fishers of people?

As if reading his thoughts, Jesus said, "Come to your homes first. Say what needs to be said. Arrange what needs to be arranged. Then meet me at the house where I'm staying—you know the one. We have much to discuss."

The crowd was growing larger, people drawn by rumours of the miraculous catch and the even more miraculous decision of four established fishermen to abandon their trade. Peter saw faces he knew—merchants he dealt with, religious leaders who would surely have opinions about this irregular teacher, and fellow fishermen wondering if he'd lost his mind.

"Peter, what are you doing?" One of them, a rival named Matthias, pushed through the crowd. "You can't just walk away from all this! You have contracts and obligations. You have a wife to feed!"

Peter found himself grinning, surprising himself with the joy that bubbled up from somewhere deep inside. "I've been catching fish my whole life, Matthias. Maybe it's time I caught something else."

"Caught what? Dreams? Empty promises from another would-be Messiah? How many have we seen come and go?"

"How many commanded the fish to jump into our nets?" Andrew countered, his quiet voice carrying surprising authority. "How many spoke and demons fled?"

Matthias had no answer to that. The crowd parted as Jesus began walking back toward town, and Peter found himself following without conscious decision. His feet moved of their own accord, drawn by something stronger than habit or reason.

Behind him, he could hear James organising the distribution of the remaining fish and John explaining to questioners what had happened. But Peter's attention was fixed on the man walking ahead of him, this carpenter who commanded nature, this teacher who saw straight through to a person's heart.

They walked through the narrow streets of Capernaum, past Peter's own house, where his wife, Miriam, stood in the doorway, dish towel in hand, mouth open in surprise at seeing him in the middle of a crowd instead of cleaning his nets after a night's work.

"Simon?" she called, confusion clear in her voice. "What's happening? Where are the fish?"

"Given away," he said, pausing at their gate. "All of them. Miriam, I need to tell you something..."

She looked from him to Jesus, who had stopped to wait, to the crowd that watched with avid curiosity. "Inside," she said firmly. "Whatever madness has taken you, we'll discuss it inside, not as entertainment for the neighbours."

Peter followed her into their modest courtyard, acutely aware of Jesus waiting outside and of the magnitude of what he was about to say. Miriam set down her dish towel with the careful precision of someone trying very hard not to throw something.

"Start from the beginning," she said. "And it had better be good, Simon bar Jonah. We have bills to pay and mouths to feed. You can't just give away a night's catch on a whim."

So Peter told her. About the empty nets all night. About Jesus appearing on the shore. About the command to cast into deep water and the impossible catch that followed. As he spoke, he watched her face change from anger to confusion to something that might have been wonder.

"Show me your hands," she said when he finished.

He held them out, palms up. The rope burns were red and raw, some still seeping blood. She traced them gently with one finger.

"These aren't from normal fishing," she said softly. "I've seen your hands after good catches. This... this is something else."

"I have to follow him, Miriam. I can't explain it better than that. When he says, 'Follow me,' it's like... like the whole universe bends toward those words. Like everything I've ever done was just preparation for hearing them."

She was quiet for a long moment, then sighed. "I married a fisherman. Steady work, predictable income, home every morning. Now what am I getting? A follower of teachers? A dreamer of dreams?"

"I don't know," Peter admitted. "I only know I have to go."

She studied his face, then nodded slowly. "Then go. But Peter..." She gripped his hands, ignoring the blood. "Don't forget us. Whatever this teacher leads you to, don't forget you have a home, a family, and people who love you even when you're just Simon the fisherman, not Simon the miracle witness."

He kissed her, tasting tears—his or hers, he wasn't sure. "I could never forget. How could I forget the woman who married a loud-mouthed fisherman with more muscles than sense?"

"By following teachers who tell you to throw nets where fish can see them," she retorted, but there was a smile in it. "Go. Before I change my mind and tie you to the grinding stone."

Peter left his house feeling like he was walking in a dream. The crowd had dispersed somewhat, though Jesus still waited, now in conversation with an elderly woman Peter recognised as one of the town's widows. He was promising to visit her son, who was sick with a fever.

"I'm ready," Peter said when Jesus looked up.

"No," Jesus said gently. "You're not. None of us are ever ready for what God calls us to. But you're willing, and that's enough for now."

They collected Andrew, who had made his own explanations to their household. The brothers had lived together since their father's death, Andrew's quiet steadiness balancing Peter's impulsiveness. Now they would follow this teacher together into whatever unknown future awaited.

James and John joined them at the designated house, both looking slightly stunned by their own decisions. James kept running his hands through his hair, a nervous gesture he'd had since childhood. John, younger and usually more adaptable, seemed to be processing everything internally, his eyes distant and thoughtful.

The house belonged to a widow named Susanna, who had opened her home to Jesus during his stay in Capernaum. It was modest but clean, with a small courtyard where they could gather away from curious eyes. Jesus sat on a simple wooden bench—did he notice the craftsmanship, Peter wondered, being a carpenter himself?—and gestured for them to sit.

"You're wondering what you've gotten yourselves into," Jesus began without preamble. "You're wondering if you've made a terrible mistake, leaving everything to follow someone you barely know."

"The thought had crossed my mind," James admitted with characteristic honesty.

Jesus smiled. "Good. I don't want followers who don't think, who don't question, who don't count the cost. What I'm offering isn't easy. It's not comfortable. It's not safe."

"Then what is it?" Andrew asked in his quiet way.

"It's true," Jesus said simply. "It's the kingdom of God breaking into the world. It's sight for the blind and freedom for the captives. It's good news for the poor and the year of the Lord's favour. It's everything the prophets spoke of, everything your hearts have longed for even when you didn't have words for the longing."

Peter felt that shifting sensation again, like standing in a boat when a large wave passed underneath. "But why us? We're not scribes or Pharisees. We're not trained in the law. We're fishermen. We smell like fish more often than not."

"Exactly," Jesus said, and his eyes held that mixture of authority and mirth that Peter was beginning to recognise. "The kingdom of God isn't built on human wisdom or religious credentials. It's built on transformed hearts, on people willing to leave their nets and follow. You know how to work hard. You know how to work together. You know how to persist when the catch seems impossible. These are the skills I need."

"For fishing for people," John said slowly, testing the phrase. "What does that mean, exactly?"

Jesus leaned forward, his voice taking on the teaching tone they'd heard in the synagogue. "What do you do when you fish?"

"Cast nets," Peter said promptly.

"Before that."

Peter thought. "We go where the fish are. We watch the water, the weather, and the signs. We learn their patterns."

"And?"

"We work together," Andrew added. "One boat alone can't handle a large catch. We need partners."

"We mend our nets," James contributed. "Check our equipment. Make sure everything is ready."

"We persist," John said. "Even when the nights are long and the nets are empty."

"All of these things," Jesus said, "you'll do with people. You'll go where they are—not wait for them to come to you. You'll watch for the signs of hearts ready to hear. You'll work together, because the harvest is too great for any one person. You'll prepare yourselves, maintaining your spiritual equipment. And you'll persist, even when it seems like no one is listening."

"But to what end?" Peter pressed. "What's the catch, so to speak?"

Jesus's face grew serious. "Lives transformed. Hearts turned back to God. The broken made whole. The lost was found. The kingdom of God isn't just words, Simon. It's power. Their lives changed so dramatically that the person might as well have been born again."

"Like the demon-possessed man yesterday," Andrew said with sudden understanding. "He was one person when the demon had him, another after you freed him."

"The first catch of many," Jesus confirmed. "But that was just the beginning. What you'll see, what you'll do..." He paused, and for a moment Peter thought he saw something deep in the teacher's eyes—knowledge of things yet to come, wonderful and terrible in equal measure. "The miracles are signs, pointing to something greater. The true miracle is a heart of stone becoming a heart of flesh, a life of darkness becoming a life of light."

"When do we start?" Peter asked, already knowing the answer.

"You already have. The moment you left your nets, you became fishers of men. But there's much to learn first. You'll stay with me, watch what I do, and listen to what I teach. You'll see things that will challenge everything you thought you knew about God, about righteousness, about what's possible when heaven touches earth."

"All four of us?" James asked. "Just the four?"

"For now. There will be others—twelve in the inner circle eventually. Each chosen for specific reasons, each bringing different gifts. But you four are the first. The foundation stones, you might say."

Peter felt the weight of that, the responsibility. Foundation stones. What was being built on them? And were they strong enough to bear it?

As if reading his thoughts—and Peter was beginning to suspect Jesus could do exactly that—the teacher said, "Don't worry about being strong enough. God doesn't call the qualified; He qualifies the called. Your weakness will become the stage for His strength."

"Speaking of strength," Susanna appeared in the doorway, "you all need to eat. Miracle-working and life-changing decisions require food."

She brought out bread and olives, cheese, and watered wine. Simple fare, but after a night of fruitless fishing and a morning of world-shaking decisions, it tasted like a feast. They ate in companionable silence for a while, each lost in their own thoughts.

"Teacher," John finally said, "in the synagogue yesterday, the demon called you 'the Holy One of God.' What did it mean?"

Jesus paused with bread halfway to his mouth. "What do you think it meant?"

"I... I'm not sure. The Holy One—that's a title for God Himself. But you're..." John trailed off, unable or unwilling to complete the thought.

"I'm what?" Jesus prompted gently.

"You're a man," James said bluntly. "You eat bread. You get tired. You have dust on your feet like the rest of us. How can you be...?" He too couldn't finish.

"This is one of the mysteries you'll come to understand," Jesus said. "Not all at once—your minds and hearts need time to expand enough to hold the truth. But yes, I eat bread. Yes, I get tired. Yes, my feet get dusty on these Galilean roads. And yet..."

He left the sentence hanging, but Peter felt the weight of that 'yet.' Yet he commanded fish, and they obeyed. Yet he spoke to demons, and they fled. Yet when he said, "Follow me," grown men left everything to obey.

"My mother will have questions," Andrew said suddenly, breaking the philosophical tension. "She always said I think too much. Now I'm following a teacher who speaks in riddles."

Jesus laughed, a rich, warm sound that made them all smile. "Your mother sounds wise. And yes, I do speak in riddles sometimes. The kingdom of God is too large for plain speech. It requires parables, metaphors, and stories that work on the heart while the mind is still catching up."

"Will you teach us to understand?" Peter asked.

"I'll do better than that. I'll teach you to see. There's a difference between understanding with your mind and seeing with your spirit. One produces knowledge; the other produces transformation."

They finished their meal as the sun climbed toward noon. Outside, they could hear the normal sounds of Capernaum going about its business—merchants calling their wares, children playing, and women chatting at the well. But inside this modest courtyard, Peter felt they had stepped outside normal life into something extraordinary.

"What now?" he asked when the last crumb had been eaten.

"Now we visit the sick woman's son," Jesus said, standing and brushing crumbs from his robe. "The kingdom of God isn't just words, remember. It's a demonstration. You're about to see what fishing for people really looks like."

They followed him out into the noon heat, four fishermen who had traded their nets for something they couldn't yet define. Peter walked beside Jesus, close enough to see the dust on his sandals, the sweat on his brow, and all the evidence of shared humanity. And yet...

And yet when they reached the sick woman's house and Jesus laid his hand on her fevered son, speaking a quiet word of command, the fever fled like morning mist before the sun. The boy sat up, clear-eyed and hungry, while his mother wept with joy and the fishermen stood speechless.

"This," Jesus said quietly, turning to his new followers, "this is why I've called you. Not just to witness miracles, but to participate in them. To be my hands and feet and voice in places I cannot go alone."

"You mean we'll...?" Peter couldn't finish the thought. It was too audacious.

"In time, yes. You'll heal the sick, cast out demons, and proclaim the kingdom. But first, you must learn. You must see. You must be transformed yourselves before you can transform others."

They left the rejoicing household and walked through Capernaum's streets. Everywhere they went, people noticed. Some pointed and whispered about the morning's miraculous catch. Others, who had heard about the healing, pressed closer hoping for their own miracle. Jesus moved through them all with patient grace, touching this one, speaking to that one, leaving a wake of wonder behind him.

"It's like watching a lamp walking through darkness," John murmured to his brother. "Everywhere he goes, the shadows flee."

"Pretty words from a fisherman," James teased, but gently. "Though I suppose we're not fishermen anymore. What are we now?"

"Disciples," Andrew said firmly. "Learners. Students of... of what? What do we call you, Teacher?"

Jesus turned back to them with that knowing smile. "Call me Rabbi for now. Master, if you prefer. In time, you'll understand more fully who I am. But for now, Rabbi is enough."

They were approaching the lake shore again, and Peter could see their boats pulled up on the beach, empty now of their miraculous catch. Other fishermen were working on their nets nearby, some of whom called out greetings or questions.

"Simon! Andrew! Back already? Where's your catch?"

"Given to the poor," Peter called back, surprising himself with the pride in his voice. Yesterday he would have been ashamed to admit giving away profit. Today it felt like a badge of honour.

"Given away?" The fisherman, an old friend named Nathaniel, came closer, his weathered face sceptical. "Have you lost your minds? How will you feed your families?"

"The same way the birds are fed," Jesus interjected gently. "By a father who knows what they need."

Nathaniel's scepticism deepened. "Birds don't have to pay Roman taxes or buy bread in the market."

"No," Jesus agreed. "But neither do they store up treasures that rust and rot. Neither do they lose sleep worrying about tomorrow's catch. Tell me, Nathaniel—in all your years of fishing, of careful planning and storing up, have you found peace?"

The old fisherman's mouth opened, then closed. Peter could see him thinking, remembering nights of worry and days of grinding labour that never quite produced enough.

"I thought not," Jesus said, but his voice was kind, not condemning. "The kingdom of God offers a different way. Not easy, but free. Not safe, but true. These men," he gestured to the four disciples, "have chosen to seek first the kingdom. Everything else will be added as needed."

"Pretty words," Nathaniel muttered, but Peter could see uncertainty in his eyes. "We'll see how pretty they are when winter comes and the pantries are empty."

"We will see," Jesus agreed peacefully. "And when that time comes, remember this conversation. The door to the kingdom is always open for those willing to enter."

They left Nathaniel standing on the shore, staring after them with troubled eyes. Peter wondered how many such conversations lay ahead, how many sceptics they would meet, and how many would think them fools for following this unconventional rabbi.

"Doubt is natural," Jesus said, once again seeming to read Peter's thoughts. "Even you will doubt sometimes. There will be storms that make you question, failures that make you wonder if you heard correctly when I said, 'Follow me.' But doubt isn't the opposite of faith—it's often the refining fire that makes faith stronger."

"Have you ever doubted?" Andrew asked, then immediately coloured. "I'm sorry, that was presumptuous—"

"It's honest," Jesus corrected. "And honesty is always welcome. Yes, I've known... not doubt exactly, but the weight of choosing the Father's will over easier paths. You'll understand more about that later. For now, know that I don't ask you to do anything I haven't done or won't do myself."

They spent the afternoon walking through the surrounding villages. In each place, the pattern repeated—teaching that made hearts burn, healings that made bodies whole, and demonstrations of power that left witnesses stammering. And through it all, Jesus included his new disciples, explaining privately what he taught publicly, showing them not just what he did but why.

"The power isn't the point," he explained as they rested under an olive tree between villages. "Anyone given authority from heaven could heal bodies. But healing the division between God and humanity—that's the true work. The miracles are just doorways, creating openings for hearts to believe, to turn, to be made new."

"But why does there need to be healing at all?" James asked. "Why does God allow sickness, suffering, and demons to torment people?"

Jesus was quiet for a moment, his eyes distant. "You're asking about the fall, about the breaking that happened in the garden. Why does a good God allow evil to exist? It's the question every generation asks."

"And the answer?" John prompted.

"The answer can't be spoken, only demonstrated. Watch what I do. See how heaven invades earth through acts of compassion, healing, and restoration. The kingdom of God isn't a philosophical argument—it's a living reality breaking into a broken world. Evil exists because free will exists. But love exists too, and love is stronger."

"Stronger how?" Peter asked. "Evil seems pretty strong from where I sit. Roman swords, Herod's prisons, sickness that wastes children away..."

"All temporary," Jesus said firmly. "All passing shadows. But every act of love, every choice for good, every heart turned toward the Father—these echo in eternity. You'll see, Simon. You'll see power that makes Roman legions look like children playing with sticks. But it won't look like power as the world understands it."

As evening approached, they returned to Capernaum. The town was buzzing with news of the day's healings, and a crowd had gathered at Susanna's house, bringing sick relatives, hoping for miracles. Jesus sighed but didn't turn them away.

"Watch closely," he told his disciples. "See how the kingdom comes—not with fanfare and trumpets, but with a touch, a word, a moment of genuine compassion."

For the next two hours, they witnessed a parade of human suffering transformed. A blind beggar received sight and immediately began describing the colours of the sunset he'd never seen. A woman with a withered hand watched in wonder as it straightened and filled out. Children with fever were cooled, adults with chronic pain were freed, and minds tormented by unseen forces were liberated.

But it was what happened between the miracles that Peter found most instructive. The way Jesus really looked at each person, seeing them as individuals, not just problems to solve. The questions he asked seemed to heal hearts even before he healed bodies. The way he touched lepers without flinching, spoke to women as equals, and treated Roman servants with the same compassion as Jewish neighbours.

"He's rewriting all the rules," Andrew murmured to Peter during a brief break. "Everything we were taught about clean and unclean, worthy and unworthy—he's ignoring it all."

"Not ignoring," John corrected, overhearing. "Fulfilling. The rules were supposed to point to God's holiness and love. But we turned them into walls. He's showing what they were always meant to be—bridges."

As the last supplicant left, healed and rejoicing, Jesus slumped with exhaustion. It was the first time Peter had seen him show physical weakness, and it was oddly reassuring. Whatever else he was, Jesus was also genuinely human, subject to the same limits they all faced.

"You need rest, Rabbi," Peter said. "And food. When did you last eat a real meal?"

Jesus smiled tiredly. "This morning, with you. But you're right. The spirit may be willing, but the flesh has limits. One of the paradoxes of the incarnation."

Peter didn't understand the last comment, but he understood exhaustion. "Come to my house. Miriam will feed us all. She's probably cooked enough for an army, expecting me to bring half the fishing fleet home as usual."

"An imposition—" Jesus began, but Peter cut him off with a gesture learnt from years of Jewish hospitality.

"An honour. Please. Let me offer what I can."

Jesus studied him for a moment, then nodded. "Very well. But I warn you—once you start hosting travelling rabbis, it becomes a habit."

They walked through the evening streets, the disciples flanking Jesus like an impromptu honour guard. People called out greetings, blessings, and requests for just one more healing. Jesus acknowledged them all but kept moving, and Peter felt a fierce protectiveness rise in him. The teacher had given all day. He needed rest.

80

Miriam met them at the door, and Peter could see her quickly counting heads and calculating food quantities. "Six for dinner," she said with the resignation of a fisherman's wife used to unexpected guests. "I suppose you'll all want to wash first?"

She'd set up the washing basin in the courtyard, and they took turns cleaning the dust from their feet and hands. Peter watched Jesus perform the simple ritual and was struck again by the ordinariness of it. Hands that had healed dozens today now washed dirt from between toes like any traveller. The meal Miriam produced was simple but abundant—fish stew (from yesterday's catch, before the miraculous morning), fresh bread, olives, cheese, and figs from their small tree. She served with quiet efficiency, and Peter caught her studying Jesus when she thought no one was looking.

"So," she said finally, setting down the last dish, "you're the one who convinced my husband to give away a fortune in fish and abandon his livelihood."

Peter tensed, but Jesus met her gaze calmly. "I am. Does that anger you?"

"It terrifies me," she said with typical directness. "Simon is many things—loud, impulsive, quick to speak, and slow to think. But he's also faithful, hard-working, and a good provider. Now he wants to follow you, and I don't even know where you're leading him."

"Neither does he," Jesus said gently. "Faith often means walking without seeing the whole path. But I can promise you this—what Simon loses in fishing for fish, he'll gain a hundredfold in fishing for people. And you, Miriam, brave wife who speaks her mind—you too have a part to play in the kingdom that's coming."

"I'm just a fisherman's wife," she protested. "What part could I play?"

"The kingdom of God is built on 'just' people," Jesus replied. "Just fishermen, just tax collectors, just housewives, just carpenters. God delights in using the ordinary to accomplish the extraordinary. Your hospitality tonight is kingdom work. Your support of Simon's calling is kingdom work. Never diminish the holy in the mundane."

Miriam blinked rapidly, and Peter saw tears she was too proud to shed. "You speak like no rabbi I've ever heard," she said finally.

"That's what I said," Peter added, reaching for his wife's hand. "He teaches with authority, not like the scribes who just quote other scribes who quote other scribes."

"It's because I speak of what I know," Jesus said simply. "Not theories about God, but the reality of Him. Not speculation about the kingdom, but its actual presence. You'll understand more as time goes on."

They ate in comfortable silence for a while, the warmth of good food and fellowship filling the modest room. Peter found himself studying his companions—Andrew thoughtful as always, processing the day's events; James practical and direct, already thinking about tomorrow's logistics; John younger and more mystical, seeing layers of meaning in everything; and Jesus tired but peacefully present, fully engaged with the simple pleasure of a shared meal.

"Teacher," Miriam said suddenly, "will you say the blessing? I mean, the after-meal blessing? I'd like to hear how you pray."

Jesus smiled and lifted his hands. But instead of the formal Hebrew prayers they all knew, he spoke in Aramaic, the common tongue, as if talking to someone in the room:

"Abba, Father, we thank you for this food, for the hands that prepared it, and for the fellowship that seasons it. Bless this house that has welcomed strangers. Bless Miriam, who feeds not just bodies but souls with her hospitality. Bless these men who have stepped out in faith today, not knowing where the path leads but trusting the One who calls. May your kingdom come in this house, in this town, and in all the world. May your will be done here as perfectly as in heaven. Amen."

"Abba," Andrew repeated softly. "You called the Creator of the universe 'Daddy.'"

"Is He not?" Jesus asked. "Is not the truest thing about God that He is Father? Not a distant sovereign but an intimate parent? This too you'll come to understand—that the God who spoke galaxies into existence also counts the hairs on your head."

"All twelve of them," Peter joked, running a hand over his thinning scalp. But the joke couldn't hide the wonder in his eyes. Abba. It changed everything if you could approach the Almighty like a child approaching a loving father.

"I should check on the boats," James said suddenly. "Make sure they're properly secured, the nets hung to dry. Just because we're... whatever we are now... doesn't mean we should be poor stewards of the equipment."

"I'll come with you," John offered.

"We all will," Jesus said, standing. "I'd like to see these tools of your former trade. And the walk will do us good after Miriam's excellent meal."

They made their way back to the shore, where the boats rested on the sand like beached whales. Other fishermen were preparing for the night's work, and Peter felt a strange disconnection. Just this morning, this had been his world—nets and boats and the endless rhythm of casting and hauling. Now it felt like something from another lifetime.

"Second thoughts?" Jesus asked quietly, coming to stand beside him.

"No. Maybe. I don't know." Peter picked up a piece of net, running his fingers over the familiar knots. "This I understand. Fishing. It's hard work, but it's comprehensible. Cast the net, haul it in, sell the fish, and repeat. But fishing for people..."

"It's the same principle with eternal stakes," Jesus finished. "You still cast—but with words of hope instead of woven rope. You still haul—but hearts instead of fish. You still work through the night when the catch seems impossible. And sometimes, like this morning, you see the miraculous when you cast where it makes no sense."

"Will it always be miraculous?" Andrew asked, joining them. "The healings, the authority over demons—will we see this every day?"

"You'll see what each day requires," Jesus said. "Some days will overflow with miracles. Others will be ordinary—travelling, teaching, facing rejection. The kingdom comes both ways—in power and in patience, in demonstration and in duration. Both are necessary."

James and John finished checking the boats and joined the group. "All secure," James reported. "The hired men know what to do. Father says to tell you he's praying for us. And for you, Teacher."

"Your father is a good man," Jesus said. "It's not easy to release sons to an uncertain future. His blessing means more than you know."

They stood there as darkness gathered, four fishermen and their rabbi, watching the lake that had defined their lives prepare for another night of labour. Out on the water, lamps were beginning to flicker as the night fishermen set out.

"We should return," Jesus said finally. "Tomorrow we travel to the surrounding villages. The kingdom message must go out, and you must learn by watching before you're sent to do it yourselves."

"Where will we sleep?" practical James asked. "If we're travelling with you, we need to know about provisions, lodging—"

"Remember the birds," Jesus said with that mysterious smile. "They don't sow or reap or store in barns, yet your heavenly Father feeds them. How much more valuable are you than birds? Each day's worries are sufficient for that day. Tomorrow will take care of itself."

It wasn't really an answer, Peter thought, but somehow it was enough. They walked back through the darkened streets, and at Susanna's house, they found she'd prepared sleeping spaces for all of them—simple pallets, but clean and welcoming.

"The teacher can have my son's room," she said. "He's grown and gone to Jerusalem. The rest of you can sleep in the main room. It's not much, but—"

"It's perfect," Jesus assured her. "Thank you for your hospitality. The kingdom of God rests on such kindness."

As they prepared for sleep, Peter found himself too energised to rest immediately. The day had been too full, too transformative. This morning he'd been a fisherman. Tonight he was... what? A disciple. A follower. A future fisher of men, whatever that truly meant.

"Can't sleep either?" John whispered from his nearby pallet.

"Too much to think about," Peter admitted. "My mind keeps going over everything. The fish, the healings, the teachings. It's like trying to drink from a flood."

"'Deep calls to deep,'" John quoted from the psalms. "I feel like something deep in me is responding to something deep in him. Like recognition, but of what, I don't know."

"The Holy One of God," Andrew murmured from his pallet. "That's what the demon called him. What if... what if it's true? Not metaphorically, but literally?"

"Then we're in for more than we bargained for," James said practically. "Following a teacher is one thing. Following the Holy One of God... that's something else entirely."

"But would it change anything?" Peter asked. "We've already left everything. We've already said yes. Whether he's a prophet or... or something more... we're committed now."

"Are we?" Jesus's voice came softly from the doorway. He stood silhouetted against the lamplight from the courtyard. "Commitment is tested, not declared. You've made a good beginning today, but it's only the first step of a long journey. There will be times when you want to return to your nets, when the familiar seems safer than the miraculous."

"Will you blame us if we do?" Andrew asked with his characteristic honesty.

"I'll understand," Jesus said, coming to sit among them like a brother rather than a teacher. "The flesh is weak even when the spirit is willing. But I've prayed for you—yes, already—that your faith won't fail. And when you stumble, which you will, remember that falling isn't failing unless you refuse to get back up."

"You make it sound like we're going to war," James observed.

"Aren't we?" Jesus's eyes reflected the distant lamplight. "The kingdom of God advances, and the kingdom of darkness resists. Every healing is a victory, every transformed life a territory reclaimed. But the enemy doesn't yield ground easily. You saw that today with the demons—they know who I am and why I've come. The battle is real, even if the weapons are different than swords and spears."

"What are our weapons then?" Peter asked, fisherman-practical as always.

"Truth. Love. Faith. Prayer. The word of God. Compassion that breaks through hardened hearts. Forgiveness that disarms hatred. These sound weak to those who trust in iron and bronze, but they're more powerful than all the legions of Rome."

"Will we... will we learn to use them?" John asked hesitantly. "Will we heal like you do? Cast out demons?"

"In time, yes. But first, you must be healed yourselves. The demons in your own hearts must be cast out—the demons of pride, of fear, of unforgiveness, and of doubt. Only the free can set others free. Only the whole can bring wholeness. This is why you're with me now, watching, learning, being transformed."

"I don't feel very transformed," Peter admitted. "I feel like the same loud fisherman who left his nets this morning."

Jesus smiled, that warm expression that made you feel known and loved despite all your flaws. "Transformation is like dawn, Simon. It happens so gradually you don't notice until suddenly the whole world is light. Trust the process. Trust the One who called you."

They talked a while longer, voices soft in the darkness, questions and answers flowing like a gentle tide. Finally, Jesus stood. "Sleep now. Tomorrow brings its own adventures, and you'll need strength for them."

He returned to his room, and gradually the disciples settled into sleep. But Peter lay awake a bit longer, staring at the ceiling beams barely visible in the darkness. This morning he'd been Simon the fisherman. Tonight he was Simon the disciple. Someday, Jesus had hinted, he'd be something else—Peter, the rock, though what that meant remained a mystery.

"Lord," he prayed silently, "I don't understand what you're doing." I don't know why you chose me. But something in my deepest heart recognises something in him. Help me follow well. Help me learn what it means to fish for people. Help me become whatever you're calling me to become.

Outside, he could hear the night sounds of Capernaum—dogs barking, a baby crying, and the distant splash of oars as fishermen worked the lake. Ordinary sounds of an ordinary town. But in this house slept four men whose lives had become extraordinary simply by saying yes to two words: "Follow me."

Peter smiled in the darkness. Whatever tomorrow brought, it wouldn't be ordinary. When you followed someone who commanded fish and cast out demons and spoke of God as Abba, ordinary was the one thing you could never expect.

As sleep finally took him, he dreamed of nets. But these nets were different—woven not of rope but of light, cast not into water but into crowds of people. And when they were hauled in, they were full not of fish but of faces, each one shining with the same light he'd seen in the teacher's eyes.

"Fishers of men," he murmured in his sleep. And somewhere in the adjoining room, Jesus smiled and continued his night-long prayers for these four who'd left everything to discover everything, who'd given up catching fish to learn to catch something infinitely more precious—human souls turning toward the light.

Chapter 4: Through the Roof

The morning sun hadn't yet burnt off the mist rising from the Sea of Galilee when Matthias first heard the voices. He lay on his mat, as he had every morning for the past eight years, listening to the world wake up around him while his own body remained a prison of stillness. The voices grew louder—excited, urgent, carrying that particular quality that meant something extraordinary was happening in Capernaum.

"He's back," his sister Ruth said, bursting through the doorway with such energy that the water jar on her hip sloshed. "Jesus of Nazareth. He's at Simon Peter's house."

Matthias closed his eyes. He'd heard about the teacher, of course. Who in Capernaum hadn't? The man who spoke with authority made the synagogue leaders look like children reciting half-remembered lessons. The one who'd cast out demons with a word, healed Peter's mother-in-law of fever, and cleansed a leper with a touch. Stories upon stories, each more incredible than the last.

"Don't," he said, knowing what was coming next.

"Matthias—"

"I said don't." He turned his face to the wall, the only movement he could manage without help. "I've heard enough about miracle workers."

Ruth set down the water jar with more force than necessary. "This is different. You didn't see what happened in the synagogue. The demon knew him and called him the Holy One of God before Jesus cast it out. And Simon's mother—she was burning with fever one moment, serving dinner the next."

"Then let him heal those who can get to him," Matthias said bitterly. "Unless he makes house calls to forgotten paralytics, it doesn't concern me."

Ruth knelt beside his mat, her work-roughened hand gentle on his shoulder. "Brother, please. After everything we've tried—"

"Everything we've tried has failed." The words came out harsher than he intended. Eight years of failed remedies had worn his hope down to nothing. Physicians who took their money and left him worse than before. Holy men who blamed his condition on hidden sin. Supposed healers whose potions did nothing but turn his stomach. "I'm tired, Ruth. Tired of hope that leads nowhere."

His sister was quiet for a long moment. When she spoke again, her voice carried that stubborn tone he knew too well. "Then it's good you have friends who aren't."

Before Matthias could ask what she meant, she was gone, leaving him alone with the ceiling he'd memorised down to every crack and stain. He could hear the crowd now, distant but growing, like thunder rolling in from the lake. Whatever was happening at Peter's house, it was drawing half of Capernaum.

The door burst open again, but this time it wasn't Ruth. Four men crowded into the small room, their faces flushed with exertion and something else—determination, perhaps, or faith. Matthias recognised them all: Tobias the fisherman, whose boats worked alongside Peter's; young Daniel, who helped his father in the marketplace; Eli the tanner; and Jacob, whose olive groves stretched up the hillside.

"No," Matthias said, understanding immediately why they'd come. "Whatever you're thinking, no."

"We're not thinking," Tobias said, already moving to one corner of the mat. "We're doing."

"The teacher is here," Daniel added, grabbing another corner. "The house is already packed, but we'll find a way."

"You'll find a way to humiliate me, you mean." Matthias tried to sound angry, but fear leaked through. "Dragging a paralytic through the streets like a spectacle—"

"Like a friend," Eli corrected, taking the third corner. "Like a brother who deserves a chance at healing."

Jacob took the final corner, his grip steady. "On three. One, two—"

"Wait!" Matthias's protest was lost as they lifted him, mat and all. The world tilted sickeningly. He hadn't been upright in so long that the change in perspective made him dizzy. "Please, I can't—"

"You can't," Tobias agreed, navigating carefully through the doorway. "That's why we're here."

The street hit Matthias like a physical blow. People everywhere, more than he'd seen in eight years of staring at the same walls. Children darting between legs, women balancing water jars, merchants hawking their wares. And all of them staring as his friends carried him past, a grown man helpless as an infant on a mat that had become his entire world.

Shame burnt hot in his chest. He closed his eyes, but that only made the swaying worse as his friends picked up their pace. He could hear whispers following them—recognition, pity, curiosity. "Isn't that Matthias? The paralytic? Where are they taking him?"

"Almost there," Daniel panted. The young man was struggling with his corner, sweat beading on his forehead despite the morning cool.

Matthias opened his eyes to see they were approaching Peter's house, and his heart sank. The crowd was impossible—bodies pressed together so tightly that not even air could slip between them. People stood on tiptoes, craning their necks, straining to see or hear something of what was happening inside. The doorway was completely blocked, as were the windows.

"We'll never get through," Matthias said, relief and disappointment warring in his chest.

Tobias set down his corner of the mat carefully, studying the situation with the same intensity he brought to reading weather patterns on the lake. "No," he said slowly. "We won't. Not through the door."

"Then let's go home," Matthias urged. "You tried. I appreciate it, but—"

"The roof," Tobias said suddenly. "We'll go through the roof."

The other three men looked at him as if he'd suggested they sprout wings and fly.

"Have you lost your mind?" Eli demanded. "That's Peter's house!"

"And Peter's a fisherman who understands that sometimes you have to cast your nets in unexpected places," Tobias replied. He was already moving, testing the wooden ladder that leaned against the side of the house. "Jacob, you and Daniel take Matthias up first. Eli and I will follow with tools."

"Tools?" Matthias's voice cracked. "You can't seriously be thinking of—"

"Tearing through a roof to get you to Jesus?" Tobias grinned, the expression making him look decades younger. "That's exactly what I'm thinking. Unless you have a better idea?"

Matthias didn't. He lay helpless as his friends lifted him again, this time toward the ladder. Jacob went up first, backwards, while Daniel pushed from below. Each rung was a small agony of swaying and vertigo. Matthias bit his lip to keep from crying out, tasting blood.

The roof, when they finally reached it, was typical of Capernaum's architecture—flat, made of wooden beams covered with branches and packed mud, and sturdy enough to serve as an extra room during good weather. Several other people had already claimed spots up here, trying to hear the teaching from above. They scrambled aside as Jacob and Daniel hauled Matthias onto the surface.

"This is insane," Matthias whispered, but his friends were beyond listening. Tobias and Eli had appeared with tools—a saw, a hammer, and a prying bar. Without hesitation, they went to work on the roof directly above where the sound of voices was loudest.

"Hey!" someone shouted. "You can't do that!"

"Watch us," Tobias grunted, prying up a section of hardened mud.

The crowd below must have heard the commotion. Matthias could imagine the scene—debris beginning to fall, sunlight breaking through where no sunlight should be. The voices grew louder, some angry, some merely curious. And then, cutting through it all, a voice that made Matthias's skin prickle with something he couldn't name.

"Let them come."

Just three words, but they carried such authority that all other voices fell silent. Even Tobias paused in his work, meeting Matthias's eyes with something like awe.

"He knows we're here," Daniel whispered. "He's waiting for us."

They worked faster now, enlarging the hole until it was wide enough for a man and his mat. Matthias could see down into the house—packed with bodies, the air thick with the scent of too many people in too small a space. Scribes in their fine robes sat near the front, having claimed the positions of honour. Pharisees from Jerusalem, their phylacteries broad and tassels long, watched with expressions of barely concealed scepticism. And in the centre, sitting with a casualness that seemed to mock the tension in the room, was Jesus.

He wasn't what Matthias had expected. No golden glow, no otherworldly beauty. Just a man in a workman's tunic, hands that showed the calluses of his trade, and a face weathered by sun and wind. But his eyes—when he looked up through the hole in the roof, meeting Matthias's gaze directly, those eyes held depths that made Matthias forget how to breathe.

"The ropes," Tobias said urgently. "Quick now."

They'd come prepared. Four ropes, one for each corner of the mat. Matthias wanted to protest again—the indignity of it, being lowered like cargo through a roof—but that gaze held him silent. There was no judgement in it, no pity. Just a recognition that went soul-deep, as if this teacher could see every broken thing inside him and loved him anyway.
"Ready?" Jacob asked.
Matthias nodded, not trusting his voice. The world tilted again as they lifted him and positioned him over the hole. For a moment he hung suspended between heaven and earth, the crowd below gasping as they realised what was happening. Then, slowly, carefully, his friends began to lower him. Dust rained down. Matthias could hear coughing, complaints, and the scrape of people moving aside to make room. The ropes creaked ominously. His mat swayed like a boat in rough waters. But those eyes never left his, drawing him down like an anchor.
The descent seemed to last forever and end too soon. His mat touched the floor with a soft thump, and suddenly Matthias was in the centre of the room, surrounded by a sea of faces. Some showed annoyance at the interruption. Others displayed the vivid curiosity of those witnessing the spectacle. The religious leaders looked scandalised, their dignity affronted by such crude methods.
But Jesus smiled.
It wasn't mockery or condescension. It was the smile of someone who'd been expecting this exact moment, who found joy in the lengths to which friendship would go. He looked up at the four faces peering anxiously through the hole in the roof.

"Your faith is beautiful," he said simply. Then, turning his attention to Matthias: "Friend, your sins are forgiven."

The words dropped into the room like stones into still water, sending ripples of shock in all directions. Matthias felt them hit his chest with physical force. His sins? He'd expected—hoped for, dreaded—words about his legs, his useless body. Not this intimate speaking to the deeper paralysis he'd never voiced aloud.

Because he was paralysed inside, wasn't he? Eight years of bitterness had locked his heart as surely as whatever injury had locked his spine. Eight years of rage at God, at fate, at his own body's betrayal. Eight years of sharp words to those who loved him, of jealousy toward those who could walk, of the slow poison of self-pity. His friends had torn through a roof to bring him healing, and all he'd done was complain.

"Who is this who speaks blasphemies?" The voice belonged to a Pharisee, his Jerusalem accent sharp with indignation. "Who can forgive sins but God alone?"

Murmurs of agreement rippled through the religious delegation. Matthias saw hands moving to phylacteries, as if touching the scripture boxes could ward off whatever heresy was unfolding. The common people pressed closer, sensing confrontation.

Jesus turned his gaze to the Pharisee who'd spoken, and Matthias saw something shift in the teacher's expression. Still gentle, but now carrying an edge like a well-honed blade.

"Why do you question this in your hearts?" Jesus asked. The room fell silent again, because somehow he'd known their thoughts before they voiced them. "Which is easier: to say to this paralyzed man, 'Your sins are forgiven,' or to say, 'Get up, take your mat, and walk'?"

The question hung in the air like incense, its implications staggering. Anyone could claim to forgive sins—the results were invisible, unprovable. But to command paralysed legs to work? That would require actual power, actual authority.

One of the scribes opened his mouth, perhaps to argue the theological point, but Jesus didn't give him the chance. He turned back to Matthias, and now those eyes held something that made every hair on Matthias's body stand on end. Power, yes, but power in service of love. Authority, but authority wielded with the gentleness of a shepherd with a wounded lamb.

"But so that you may know that the Son of Man has authority on earth to forgive sins—" He paused, letting the title sink in. The Son of Man. The figure from Daniel's prophecy, coming with the clouds of heaven. Here, in a fisherman's house in Capernaum, speaking to a paralytic who'd been lowered through the roof.

Jesus leaned forward slightly, his voice carrying clearly through the room. "I tell you, get up, take your mat, and go home."

The command hit Matthias like lightning. Not harsh, not forceful, but inevitable as sunrise. Get up. As if it were that simple. As if eight years of paralysis could be undone with three words. As if—

Fire raced down his spine. Not painful fire, but life, pure and shocking as cold water on a sleeping face. Matthias gasped, his back arching. Sensation flooded into limbs that had been dead so long he'd forgotten they existed. Pins and needles, then warmth, then strength, impossible strength.

His toes moved. He stared at them in wonder, these parts of himself that hadn't obeyed his will since that terrible day when the scaffolding collapsed and his world went dark. His ankles flexed. His knees bent. Muscles that should have been atrophied to nothing responded as if they'd never forgotten their purpose.

"I—" Matthias's voice broke. He was crying, he realised, tears streaming down his face. "I can feel—"

"Then stand," Jesus said gently. "Your friends went to a lot of trouble to bring you here. Don't you think you should walk out on your own?"

Stand. Such a simple word for such an impossible action. But his body was already moving, responding to a will greater than his own. Matthias rolled to his side—when had he last been able to do that?—and pushed himself up on arms that trembled not with weakness but with overwhelming emotion.

The crowd had backed away, giving him room. He could see their faces—awe, fear, confusion, joy. The religious leaders looked as if they'd swallowed something bitter. His friends' faces still peered down through the hole in the roof, Tobias openly weeping, the others shouting praises to God.

Matthias got his feet under him. The floor felt strange, solid in a way he'd forgotten. He straightened slowly, muscles remembering their old cooperation. Eight years of perspective from a mat, and suddenly he was standing, the world at its proper height again.

He took a step. Then another. His legs held, not just held but rejoiced in their rediscovered purpose. A laugh bubbled up from somewhere deep in his chest—joy too large for his body to contain. He bent, picked up his mat—the prison that had held him for so long now just a piece of fabric and rope—and took another step.

"Matthias!" "Ruth's voice," from somewhere in the crowd. She must have followed and must have forced her way inside. He turned, saw her face transformed by wonder, and walked to her. Walked. On legs that moved at his command. Through a crowd that parted like the Red Sea.

He reached his sister, dropped the mat, and pulled her into an embrace that eight years of paralysis had denied them. She sobbed against his chest, her tears soaking his tunic. Around them, the crowd erupted. Shouts of praise glorifying God, voices raised in chaotic joy. "We've never seen anything like this! God has visited His people! Blessed be the God of Israel!"

But Matthias turned back to Jesus, needing to see him again, to thank him, and to ask him how and why and what came next. The teacher was watching him with that same smile, but now Matthias understood it better. It wasn't just joy at a body healed. It was joy at a soul set free.

"Your sins are forgiven," Jesus had said first. Before the healing, before the miracle, everyone could see. Because he'd known, somehow, that the paralysis of the heart was the greater affliction. The bitterness, the rage, the self-pity—all of it washed away in those three words. And only then, with his soul free, could his body follow.

"Thank you," Matthias said, the words pitifully inadequate. "Master, I—thank you."

Jesus nodded, accepting the gratitude with grace. But his eyes had already moved to the religious leaders, who were huddled together in fierce whispered conference. The miracle was undeniable, but their faces showed no joy, only the hard calculation of those whose authority had been challenged.

"Go home," Jesus told Matthias gently. "Tell your story. Let them know what God has done for you today."

Home. He could walk home. Matthias picked up his mat again, holding it like a trophy. The crowd parted for him, some reaching out to touch him as if his healing might be contagious. He moved toward the door, each step a small miracle of coordination and strength.

At the threshold, he paused and looked up. Four faces still peered down through the damaged roof, tears and laughter mingling on their features. His friends, who'd loved him enough to carry him, to tear through a roof, to refuse to accept that his story was over.

"The drinks are on me at the tavern tonight!" Matthias called up to them. "And every night for a month!"

"Just fix Peter's roof first!" Tobias called back, and the laughter that followed was as bright as the morning sun.

Matthias stepped out into the street, into a world that had become new in the space of moments. His legs carried him forward with steady purpose, but his mind reeled with the implications of what had happened. The Son of Man had authority to forgive sins. The same authority that commanded paralysed legs to walk could speak absolution to paralysed souls.

Behind him, he could hear the crowd spilling out of Peter's house, the story already spreading like fire through Capernaum. By nightfall, everyone would know. The paralytic who'd been lowered through a roof had walked out carrying his mat. The teacher from Nazareth had claimed the authority of heaven itself.

Ruth walked beside him, her hand on his arm as if she needed the physical contact to believe it was real. "Eight years," she kept murmuring. "Eight years, and then in a moment—"

"In a moment, everything changes," Matthias finished. He thought of Jesus's eyes, that deep knowing, that recognition of every broken place. "He saw me, Ruth. Not just my legs. Me."

They passed the synagogue where Matthias had once studied Torah, before the accident, when he'd dreamed of becoming a teacher himself. The building looked the same, but how could anything look the same when the world had shifted on its axis?

"Will you follow him?" Ruth asked quietly. "This is Jesus?"

Matthias considered the question. Inside Peter's house, something new was being born. A kingdom, Jesus called it, where paralytics walked and sins were forgiven and friends tore through roofs for love. A kingdom where the last became first and the broken were made whole.

"How can I not?" he replied. "My legs work because he commanded it. But more than that—" He paused, searching for words. "My heart works again. The anger, the bitterness—Ruth, it's gone. Like it was the real paralysis all along."

They turned the corner onto their own street, and Matthias saw neighbours beginning to gather. Word was already spreading. Old Samuel, who'd often sat with him on the worst days, sharing stories and wine. Miriam, who'd brought food when Ruth was too exhausted to cook. David the merchant, who'd always had a kind word despite Matthias's surly responses.

"Is it true?" Samuel called out, his ancient voice trembling. "Did the teacher heal you?"

Matthias set down his mat in the dust of the street and stood on it, arms spread wide. "See for yourself! These legs that were dead now live. This heart that was stone now beats with joy. The teacher—" He paused, overwhelmed. "The teacher has authority I don't understand, but I know it's from God."

More neighbours appeared, drawn by the commotion. Children who'd been warned not to stare at the paralytic now gaped openly as he walked, jumped, and even attempted a small dance that made everyone laugh. Their parents wept, praising God, reaching out to touch Matthias as if to confirm the miracle.

"Tell us everything," Miriam demanded. "Every word, every detail."

So Matthias told them, standing on the mat that had been his prison, his voice growing stronger with each word. He told them about his friends who wouldn't give up, about the hole in Peter's roof, about being lowered into the presence of a man whose eyes saw straight through to the soul. He told them about sins forgiven before legs healed, about authority claimed and proven, and about religious leaders scandalised and common people amazed.

"But who is he?" David asked. "This Jesus of Nazareth—is he a prophet? Something more?"

Matthias thought of how Jesus had called himself the Son of Man, how he'd claimed the right to forgive sins, and how the Pharisees had accused him of blasphemy. He thought of the power that had raced through his dead limbs, divine electricity that spoke of creation itself.

"I don't know everything about who he is," Matthias admitted. "But I know this—he has power over both body and soul. He speaks, and paralysed men walk. He forgives, and eight years of bitterness vanish like morning mist. If that's not God at work, I don't know what is."

The crowd murmured, processing this testimony. Some looked sceptical—miracles were easy to claim, harder to prove. Others showed the hunger of those who'd waited too long for hope. A few were already turning, heading toward Peter's house to see for themselves.

"Will he heal others?" Old Samuel asked, leaning heavily on his walking stick. His joints had pained him for decades, leaving him twisted and slow. "Or was this favour only for you?"

"The house was full of sick people when I left," Matthias said. "And the teacher showed no signs of stopping. But Samuel—" He paused, remembering. "He healed my soul first. Whatever else you seek from him, seek that above all."

As the crowd began to disperse, some to spread the news, others to seek out Jesus for themselves, Matthias finally entered his own home. It looked exactly as it had that morning—the same rough walls, the same simple furnishings, the same mat in the corner where he'd lain for eight years. But everything was different.

He walked to the mat—walked!—and stood looking down at it. Such a simple thing, woven reeds and rope. It had been his world, his prison, his identity. Matthias the paralytic. Matthias bore the burden. Matthias the bitter.

Now it was just a mat.

"What will you do with it?" Ruth asked from the doorway.

Matthias bent and rolled it up carefully. "Keep it," he decided. "As a reminder. Of what I was, and what grace can do." He smiled at his sister. "And to show my grandchildren someday, when I tell them about the day their grandfather was lowered through a roof to meet the Messiah."

"Grandchildren?" Ruth laughed, the sound bright with possibility. "You're getting ahead of yourself. First you need to find a wife who can tolerate your terrible jokes."

"My jokes will improve," Matthias said with mock seriousness. "Everything improves when you can walk."

But even as they laughed, his mind returned to Peter's house, to what was undoubtedly still unfolding there. Jesus had looked at the religious leaders with such sadness, knowing they would reject what their eyes had seen. The battle lines were being drawn—those who would accept this radical authority, this claiming of divine prerogative by a Galilean carpenter, and those who would oppose it with every fiber of their being.

A knock at the door interrupted his thoughts. Tobias stood there, dusty and dishevelled from his roof-breaking adventure, grinning like a man who'd found treasure.

"Thought you might want to know," he said. "After you left, the teacher kept teaching. The Pharisees tried to trap him with questions, but every answer left them more frustrated. And the healing—Matthias, I've never seen anything like it. The blind seeing, the deaf hearing, demons cast out with a word."

"And Peter's roof?" Matthias asked, suddenly feeling guilty.

Tobias waved a hand dismissively. "Already being repaired. Half the city wants to help, just to be part of the story. By tomorrow, Peter will have the finest roof in Capernaum." His expression grew more serious. "But Matthias, you should know—the teacher is gathering followers. Not just crowds, but disciples. People who'll walk with him learn from him."

"And you're thinking of joining them?"

"I'm thinking of it," Tobias admitted. "After what I saw today, after what he did for you—how can I go back to just fishing? There are nets, and then there are nets, if you understand me."

Matthias did understand. He'd been caught in a net today, pulled from the depths of despair by friends who wouldn't let him drown. And now he was being invited into a different kind of fishing altogether.

"When?" he asked simply.

"He's staying at Peter's tonight, but tomorrow he'll likely move on. Another village, another synagogue, another crowd of desperate people." Tobias paused. "You could come. Both of you could come. See what else this kingdom he speaks of might hold."

Ruth spoke before Matthias could. "We'll think about it. My brother has been horizontal for eight years. Perhaps he should try being vertical for a day or two before making life-changing decisions."

Tobias laughed. "Fair enough. But don't think too long. Something tells me this teacher won't be staying in one place. The religious leaders are already sending messages to Jerusalem. They don't like their authority challenged."

After Tobias left, Matthias and Ruth sat in companionable silence as evening settled over Capernaum. The sounds of the city filtered through their window—merchants closing shop, mothers calling children home, fishermen preparing their nets for the night's work. Ordinary sounds of ordinary life, made extraordinary by the fact that Matthias could stand and walk to the window to hear them better.

"I want to follow him," he said finally. "Not just tomorrow or the next day, but truly follow. Learn from him. Serve him. Tell others what he's done." He turned to Ruth. "But I won't leave you alone. You've carried enough burden for one lifetime."

Ruth stood and joined him at the window. "Who says I'd let you go alone? If this Jesus can make my bitter, paralysed brother dance badly in the street, I want to see what else he can do." She smiled. "Besides, someone needs to make sure you don't try to climb through any more roofs."

They laughed, but underneath the humour lay a current of decision. The safe, small life they'd known—Ruth caring for her paralysed brother, Matthias imprisoned in his bitterness—was over. Something new was beginning, as unprecedented as dead legs suddenly alive.

That night, Matthias lay on his mat by choice rather than necessity. He flexed his feet, bent his knees, and marvelled at the simple miracle of voluntary movement. But more than that, he marvelled at the lightness in his chest where anger had lived for so long. Forgiven. The word echoed through him like a bell, clear and true.

He thought of Jesus, probably still teaching despite the late hour, surrounded by seekers and sceptics alike. Tomorrow there would be more villages, more crowds, and more confrontations with religious authorities who couldn't accept what their theology couldn't contain. The path of anyone who followed this teacher would not be easy.

But then, Matthias reflected, he'd never expected easy. He'd expected to die on a mat, paralysed and bitter. Instead, he'd been given a second chance at life—not just physical life, but something deeper and truer. A chance to be part of whatever kingdom Jesus was building, where the last became first and the broken were made whole.

Outside, he could hear voices in the street. The story was still spreading, rippling out from Peter's damaged roof like waves on the sea. By morning, all of Capernaum would know. By week's end, the tale would reach other villages. The paralytic who'd been lowered through a roof. The teacher who forgave sins and made the lame walk.

Matthias smiled in the darkness. Let them tell the story. Let them wonder and debate and argue about what it meant. He knew what it meant. It meant that God hadn't forgotten the broken ones. It meant that mercy could break through any barrier, even if it had to tear a hole in the roof to do it. It meant that sometimes, when human help and divine power worked together, the impossible became possible.

Tomorrow, he decided, he would find Jesus. He would kneel—because he could kneel now, could choose to lower himself rather than being forever lowered—and he would ask to follow. To learn. To serve. To spend whatever life he'd been given back in service to the one who'd given it.

But tonight, he would simply lie on his mat and wiggle his toes, a man made new by grace that came through a hole in a roof. It was, he thought, a very good way to begin again.

The stars were bright over Capernaum, and somewhere in the city, Jesus of Nazareth was likely still awake, praying or teaching or healing yet another desperate soul. The kingdom of God was breaking in, one miracle at a time, and Matthias had been caught up in its advance. His friends had carried him to Jesus, but from now on, he would walk there himself.

It was enough to make even a former paralytic believe that anything was possible.

As sleep finally claimed him, Matthias thought he heard singing—whether from the street or from his own grateful heart, he couldn't tell. It didn't matter. Joy had come through a roof today, and nothing would ever be the same.

In the morning, he would rise and walk. But more than that, he would rise and follow. The teacher who had authority to forgive sins and heal bodies was building something new in the world, and Matthias wanted to be part of it. Eight years of paralysis had ended with four friends and a hole in a roof. Whatever came next, it had to be better than lying still.

The mat beneath him was just a mat now, not a prison. And tomorrow, when he rolled it up and slung it over his shoulder, it would become something else—a testimony, a reminder, a sign that pointed to the power of the one who'd said, "Rise and walk."

Matthias slept, and his dreams were full of movement.

Chapter 5: Nets Breaking with Abundance

The pre-dawn air hung thick with failure over the Sea of Galilee. Simon Peter's hands, raw from hauling empty nets all night, mechanically sorted the tangled mess of rope and weights. Beside him, his brother Andrew worked in similar silence, their usual morning banter crushed under the weight of another fruitless night.

"Nothing," James ben Zebedee called from the other boat, his voice carrying across the still water. "Not even minnows for bait."

Peter grunted in response, not trusting his voice. Three nights running they'd caught nothing. Three nights of perfect conditions—calm seas, no moon, and the water temperature that usually brought the fish schooling. Yet their nets had come up empty each time, as if the sea itself had turned against them.

The financial pressure sat on Peter's shoulders like a millstone. Taxes were due—both to Rome and to the temple. His mother-in-law needed medicine for her persistent fever. The roof leaked. And now this—the fish had simply vanished.

"Maybe we should try the eastern shore," Andrew suggested quietly. "Where the Gentiles fish."

Peter's jaw tightened. Fish from Gentile waters would require special purification before selling to observant Jews, cutting into already slim profits. But empty nets earned nothing at all.

"Simon!" The voice carried clearly across the water, and Peter's head snapped up. Jesus stood on the shore, barely visible in the grey pre-dawn light. Already a crowd was gathering around him—how did people always know where to find the teacher?

"Rabbi," Peter called back, trying to keep the exhaustion from his voice. Jesus had healed his mother-in-law just days ago, and Peter owed him courtesy at minimum. "You're up early."

"As are you," Jesus replied, walking closer to the water's edge. "How was the fishing?"

Peter and Andrew exchanged glances. "The fish have apparently decided to observe an extended Sabbath," Peter said dryly.

Jesus smiled at that, but his eyes held something deeper—understanding, perhaps, or anticipation. The crowd behind him was growing, pressing closer, eager for his teaching. Peter watched as Jesus glanced around, assessing the situation, then looked directly at their boat.

"Simon, may I use your boat? Push out a little from shore so everyone can hear."

Peter hesitated. The nets still needed cleaning and mending. The boat reeked of a night's worth of sweat and discouragement. But those eyes held his—those strange, compelling eyes that seemed to see straight through to his soul.

"Of course, Rabbi." Peter began pushing the boat back into the shallows. "Andrew, finish with the nets. I'll be back shortly."

But Jesus was already climbing aboard, settling himself at the bow. "Bring the nets," he said casually. "We're not finished with them yet."

Something in his tone made Peter pause, but he nodded to Andrew. Together they loaded the still-tangled nets back into the boat, though Peter couldn't imagine why. The sun would be up soon—no fisherman worth his salt tried to catch fish after dawn.

Peter pushed them out perhaps twenty cubits from shore, just far enough that Jesus's voice would carry across the water to the crowd. He dropped the small anchor and settled back, trying to stay awake as Jesus began to teach.

The teacher's voice rolled across the water like gentle thunder, painting pictures with words. He spoke of God's kingdom as a treasure hidden in a field, a pearl of great price, and a net cast into the sea that gathered fish of every kind. That last image made Peter shift uncomfortably. Their own nets had gathered nothing but seaweed and disappointment.

"The kingdom of heaven," Jesus was saying, "is like a master who went out early to hire workers for his vineyard..."

Peter found himself drawn into the story despite his exhaustion. Jesus had a way of taking the familiar—vineyards, fishing, farming—and turning them inside out until you saw God's fingerprints all over ordinary life. The crowd on shore listened with rapt attention, some sitting, others standing knee-deep in the water to get closer.

As Jesus taught, Peter's mind wandered to their first real encounter. He and Andrew had been disciples of John the Baptiser, drawn by the wild prophet's call to repentance. When John had pointed to Jesus and declared, "Behold, the Lamb of God," something had stirred in Peter's chest. They'd followed, spent a day with him, and life had never quite returned to normal since. Yet here he was, still fishing, still struggling, still failing. If Jesus was truly the Messiah, why were his followers pulling empty nets from barren waters?

"Do you see, Simon?" Jesus's voice pulled him from his reverie. The teaching had apparently ended; the crowd was beginning to disperse. Jesus turned to face him fully. "Do you see how hungry they are? Not for bread—though that hunger is real enough—but for hope. For truth. For the assurance that God has not forgotten them."

"I see hungry people every day, Rabbi," Peter replied, perhaps more shortly than intended. "I see tax collectors taking food from children's mouths. I see Romans treating us like dogs. I see—" He gestured at the empty nets. "I see a creation that no longer provides for those who work it."

Jesus studied him for a long moment, and Peter felt exposed, as if all his doubts and frustrations were written on his face like Hebrew script.

"Put out into the deep water," Jesus said quietly, "and let down your nets for a catch."

Peter stared at him. The words made no sense. Every fisherman knew the fish went deep during daylight, far beyond the reach of nets. The sun was already painting the eastern hills gold. The time for fishing had passed hours ago.

"Master," he said carefully, using the title of respect despite his scepticism, "we've worked all night and caught nothing. The fish aren't running. And now with the sun up..." He trailed off, seeing something shift in Jesus's expression. Not anger, exactly, but a kind of patient expectation that was somehow harder to resist than any command.

"Nevertheless," Peter heard himself saying, "at your word, I will let down the nets."

His arms protested as he pulled up the anchor. Everything in his professional experience screamed that this was foolishness. But something in Jesus's eyes—that same something that had made him leave John's side to follow this rabbi—compelled obedience.

Peter rowed toward deeper water, his back to Jesus, grateful for the excuse not to meet those penetrating eyes. Behind him, he could hear Jesus humming softly—a psalm, perhaps, or one of the ancient fishing songs. The familiar slap of oars against water, the creak of the boat's timbers, the cry of gulls beginning their morning hunt—all of it felt surreal, as if he were moving through a dream.

"Here?" he asked when they reached the deep fishing grounds.

"Here," Jesus confirmed.

Peter stood, taking up the nets with practiced efficiency despite his exhaustion. Andrew had done good work—the tangles were gone, and the weights were properly distributed. Peter kissed the edge of the net according to custom, murmured the blessing his father had taught him, and cast.

The net sailed out in a perfect arc, spreading like a bird's wing before hitting the water with a satisfying splash. The weights pulled it down quickly in the deep water. Peter began counting slowly, giving it time to sink, to spread, to—

The rope went taut so suddenly it nearly pulled him overboard.

"What in the name of—" Peter braced himself, wrapping the rope around his forearms. The boat lurched, tilting dangerously. "Rabbi, help me!"

But Jesus remained seated, watching with that same calm expectation. Peter hauled on the rope, his muscles screaming. The net was fighting him—no, not the net. The fish. The net was full of fish, fuller than he'd ever felt it, so heavy he couldn't budge it.

"Andrew!" he bellowed toward shore. "James! John! Come quickly!"

He saw his brother's head snap up and saw the moment of hesitation before Andrew started running for the other boat. Within moments, both boats were rowing hard toward them.

"What is it?" Andrew called as they approached. "What's wrong?"

"Nothing's wrong," Peter gasped, still fighting to hold the net. "Everything's right. Help me!"

It took all four of them to haul in the net, and even then they barely managed. As it broke the surface, Peter's breath caught. Fish—countless fish, silver bodies flashing in the morning sun, so many the net began to tear under the weight. Tilapia, sardines, and carp—species that never schooled together, all thrashing in impossible abundance.

"The other net!" James shouted. "Quick, before we lose them!"

They worked frantically, transferring fish to both boats, but there were too many. Water sloshed over the sides as the boats sank lower and lower. Peter found himself laughing—wild, uncontrolled laughter born of exhaustion and amazement. A night's work, a week's work, and a month's work filled both boats until they threatened to founder.

And through it all, Jesus sat calmly, a slight smile playing at his lips, as if he'd expected nothing less.

It was that calm certainty that broke something in Peter. As the immediate frenzy of securing the catch passed, as his brother and friends exclaimed over the impossible haul, Peter truly looked at Jesus for the first time. Not as a teacher, not as a healer, not even as a prophet.

He saw power. Raw, creative power, the kind that spoke worlds into existence and commanded the very fish of the sea. The kind of power that knew where every fish swam, that could gather them with a word, that could provide abundance where there had been only emptiness.

Peter's knees gave out. He fell hard, heedless of the fish flopping around him, heedless of the water sloshing in the overloaded boat. The wood bit into his knees, but he barely noticed. All he could see was his own darkness next to this man's light.

"Depart from me, Lord," the words tore from his throat, raw and desperate. "For I am a sinful man."

Every selfish thought, every harsh word, and every moment of doubt crashed over him like a wave. How many times had he cheated on weights at the market? How many times had he looked at his neighbour's wife with desire? How many times had he cursed God himself for empty nets and empty bellies?

And here sat holiness itself, casual as you please, in his reeking fishing boat. "I am a sinful man," he repeated, unable to lift his eyes. "You don't know—you can't know what I am."

A hand touched his shoulder, warm and calloused—a working man's hand, not so different from his own. "Simon, son of Jonah," Jesus said softly. "Look at me."

Peter couldn't. Wouldn't. To meet those eyes would be to be consumed, surely. He'd seen what happened when the unholy touched the holy—hadn't Uzzah died for merely steadying the Ark? Hadn't Isaiah cried out in terror when he saw the Lord's glory?

"Simon," Jesus said again, and now there was gentle amusement in his voice. "I'm not going anywhere. And neither are you. Look at me."

Slowly, like a man approaching a lion, Peter raised his head. Jesus's face was kind, amused even, but behind the human features, Peter sensed depths that made the sea look shallow. This was the One who knew the location of every fish, who could command them to swim into nets, and who could look at a man and see every secret thing.

"Do not be afraid," Jesus said, and the words carried weight beyond their simplicity. "Yes, you are a sinful man. So is Andrew. So are James and John. So is every person who pressed close to hear my teaching. But Simon—" He paused, ensuring Peter was truly listening. "From now on, you will catch people."

"I don't understand," Peter whispered.

Jesus gestured at the boats, so full of fish they could barely float. "What did you do to catch these fish?"

"Nothing. I just... obeyed your word."

"Exactly." Jesus smiled fully now. "You let down your nets at my word, despite your experience, despite your exhaustion, despite your certainty of failure. And see what happened?"

Peter looked around at the miraculous catch, his mind reeling. "But Rabbi, I know how to catch fish. I don't know how to catch people."

"Did you know how to catch these fish?" Jesus asked. "Did your knowledge help you last night? Or the night before?"

"No," Peter admitted.

"Then perhaps it's time to learn a new kind of fishing. One that depends not on your skill but on my word. One that fills nets with eternal souls rather than temporary sustenance." Jesus stood, somehow maintaining perfect balance in the rocking boat. "The harvest is plentiful, Simon. But the workers—the real fishermen—are few."

Peter felt Andrew's hand on his back, steady and supportive. His brother had moved closer during the exchange, and now Peter could see the same awe, the same recognition, in Andrew's eyes. They had known Jesus was special and had followed him casually, returning to their nets when practical needs demanded. But this—this was different. This was a line in the sand, a moment of decision.

"All these fish," Peter said slowly, "they'll feed many families. Pay many debts."

"Yes," Jesus agreed. "Your last catch as a fisherman will provide for those you leave behind. Your father's business will not suffer. Your families will not go hungry. I know you, Simon—I know you couldn't follow if you thought others would pay the price."

The knowing in those words broke Peter's last resistance. This man—this more-than-man—truly saw him. Not the bluster he showed the world, not the competent fisherman or the devoted son, but the real Simon beneath it all. And still he called.

"Where you lead, Lord," Peter said, the title coming naturally now, carrying new weight, "I will follow."

Jesus helped him to his feet, and Peter was surprised to find his legs steady despite the rocking boat. Around them, James and John were securing the incredible catch, their movements efficient but their eyes constantly drawn back to Jesus. The sun had fully risen now, painting the sea gold and crimson, and the sight of the two overladen boats seemed like something from a prophet's vision.

"We should get these to shore," Andrew said practically. "Before we sink."

"Always the practical one," Peter said, finding his voice again. But he didn't move to take the oars. "What about you?" he asked James and John. "What about your father's business?"

The two brothers exchanged a long look. Their father, Zebedee, ran one of the most successful fishing operations on the lake. They had hired servants, multiple boats, and contracts with merchants as far away as Jerusalem. Following Jesus would mean abandoning all of that.

"The night we met him," James said slowly, "when he called us from mending nets, I thought it was just for a day. Maybe a week. An adventure before returning to real life." He looked at the miraculous catch surrounding them. "But this isn't about adventure, is it? This is about the kingdom of heaven breaking into our world."

"Father will be furious," John added, but he was smiling. "He's been planning to expand and buy more boats. He had us learning Greek to deal with Gentile merchants."

"And now?" Jesus asked, though Peter suspected he already knew the answer.

"Now we learn a different language," John replied. "The language of the kingdom you speak of."

They rowed to shore slowly and carefully, the boats so low in the water that Peter held his breath with each small wave. A crowd had already gathered—word of the miraculous catch spreading faster than wildfire. Peter saw his wife Miriam among them, her face cycling through emotions too quickly to read.

123

As they approached the shallows, willing hands waded out to help. The story was already spreading, growing with each telling. By nightfall, Peter knew, it would be said they caught every fish in the sea, that the boats had flown rather than sailed, and that angels had helped haul the nets.

But the truth, Peter thought, was more staggering than any embellishment. The teacher they'd been following casually, returning to whenever convenient, had just revealed himself as master over creation itself. And he wanted them—simple, sinful, struggling fishermen—to be his closest companions.

Zebedee stood at the water's edge, his weathered face unreadable as he watched his sons secure the boats. Peter saw the moment understanding dawned and saw the older man's shoulders slump slightly before straightening with resigned pride.

"So," Zebedee said as James and John waded ashore. "The teacher has shown his hand at last."

"Father," James began, but Zebedee raised a hand.

"I have eyes, boy. I see what no natural explanation can account for." He looked past his sons to Jesus, who was helping distribute fish to the gathering crowd. "I've heard him teach. I've seen the healings. And now this." He gestured at the impossible catch. "A man would be a fool to stand in the way of the Almighty."

"We'll help you find good workers," John offered quickly. "Train them before we—"

"Before you follow him to wherever this leads," Zebedee finished. "I know. Your mother saw this coming before I did. She's already been preparing."

He pulled both sons into a rough embrace, and Peter had to look away from the private moment. His own father was long dead, but he remembered the pride in those eyes when Peter had first cast a net successfully. What pride would there be in abandoning the family trade?

"Peter." Miriam's voice cut through his thoughts. His wife stood ankle-deep in water, her practical tunic hiked up, her face a mask of controlled emotion. "We need to talk."

He followed her a little apart from the crowd, acutely aware of the fish scales covering his clothes and the smell of his trade that he would soon leave behind.

"I know what you're going to say," Miriam began before he could speak. "I saw it in your eyes the moment the nets came up full. You're leaving."

"Miriam—"

"Let me finish." Her voice was steady, but her hands trembled. "My mother owes her life to him. Half the town has a healing story. And now this—commanding the very fish of the sea. I would be a fool not to see what you see."

"I don't want to leave you," Peter said honestly. "Or your mother. Or our home. But Miriam, when he spoke to me in the boat, when he looked at me—" He struggled for words. "It was like standing before the throne of God himself. How can I not follow?"

She touched his face gently, her fingers tracing the lines that sun and worry had carved there. "You've never done anything by half measures, Simon bar Jonah. Why would following the Messiah be different?"

"You believe that's who he is?"

"I believe my mother was dying, and now she lives. I believe you fished empty waters all night, and now we have provisions for months. I believe—" She paused, choosing her words carefully. "I believe God is doing something new, and you're being called to be part of it. How could I stand in the way of that?"

Peter pulled her close, heedless of the fish scales and wet clothes. "I don't deserve you."

"No," she agreed, and he could hear the smile in her voice. "But you're stuck with me anyway. Now go. He's waiting."

Peter looked back to where Jesus stood surrounded by people, his hands moving as he taught, occasionally pointing to the boats and their miraculous catch. Even from a distance, Peter could see the way people leaned in, hungry for every word.

"From now on, you will catch people," Jesus had said. Peter still didn't fully understand what that meant, but he thought of the crowd on the shore that morning, pressing close to hear about God's kingdom. He thought of empty hearts like empty nets, waiting to be filled with something they didn't even know they were missing.

Andrew appeared at his elbow. "Ready, brother?"

"No," Peter admitted. "But when has that ever stopped us?"

Together they walked back to where Jesus waited. James and John were already there, their farewells complete. The four of them stood before the teacher, covered in fish scales and sweat, reeking of their trade, as unlikely a group of world-changers as ever existed.

"So," Jesus said, and that amused smile was back. "Ready to learn a new kind of fishing?"

"Teach us, Lord," Peter said, and meant it with every fibre of his being.

Jesus looked at each of them in turn, and Peter felt again that sense of being truly seen, truly known. "The first lesson," Jesus said, "is the same as today's catch. When I give the word, you act—even when it makes no sense, even when experience says otherwise, even when everyone thinks you're fools. Can you do that?"

"We can try," Andrew said carefully.

"Trying isn't enough," Jesus replied, but his tone was gentle. "You'll fail—oh, how you'll fail. You'll doubt. You'll run. You'll deny you ever knew me." His eyes lingered on Peter at that last statement, and Peter felt a chill despite the warming sun. "But after the failure will come restoration. After the denial, affirmation. After the fear, courage you never knew you possessed."

"I don't understand," John said.

"You will," Jesus promised. "For now, it's enough that you're willing to follow. The understanding will come with the journey."

He turned and began walking along the shore, not back toward Capernaum but south, toward the wilderness areas where John had baptised. Without hesitation, the four fishermen followed, leaving behind boats and nets and the biggest catch of their lives.

As they walked, Peter looked back once at the scene they were leaving—the crowd still exclaiming over the miraculous catch, Zebedee organising the distribution with his hired servants, and Miriam standing apart, watching him go with eyes that held both sorrow and pride.

"Second thoughts?" Jesus asked, though he didn't turn around.

"Many thoughts," Peter admitted. "But no doubts. Not after today."

"Good. Because where we're going, doubts are a luxury you can't afford. The kingdom of heaven is breaking into this world, Simon, and the powers of darkness won't yield without a fight. You've seen me command fish. Before this is over, you'll see me command storms, cast out demons, and raise the dead. And you'll do the same in my name."

"We will?" Andrew sounded sceptical.

"You will. But first, you must learn who I really am. Not just a teacher. Not just a prophet. Not even just the Messiah you're expecting. You must learn to see the Father through me, to understand that when you've seen me, you've seen Him."

The words should have sounded blasphemous. Any other man claiming such things would have been stoned or dismissed as mad. But Peter had seen the fish come at his word and had felt the divine authority in his presence. If this man claimed unity with the Father, who was Peter to argue?

They walked in silence for a time, the sounds of the lake fading behind them. Other followers began to appear—some Peter recognised from the crowds that regularly gathered to hear Jesus teach. Mary of Magdala was there, the woman Jesus had freed from seven demons. Several other women followed at a respectful distance, along with men Peter didn't recognise.

"How many follow you, Lord?" James asked.

"Today? Perhaps seventy who are serious and hundreds who are curious. By the end?" Jesus paused, looking toward Jerusalem's distant hills. "Twelve who will change the world. Though not in the way they expect."

"Only twelve?" John sounded disappointed.

"Twelve is enough," Jesus said. "Twelve tribes came from one man's faith. Twelve apostles will carry that faith to the ends of the earth. But you four—you'll be special among the twelve. The inner circle. You'll see things the others won't and bear burdens the others can't. Can you accept that responsibility?"

Peter thought of the fish, of the net breaking with abundance, of the moment he'd recognised the divine in his boat. "After what we've seen today, how can we not?"

Jesus stopped walking and turned to face them fully. The morning sun created a halo effect around his head, and for a moment Peter saw him transfigured—not the carpenter from Nazareth but something ancient and terrible and beautiful.

"Because," Jesus said softly, "following me will cost you everything. Your trades, your reputations, your families' understanding. Eventually, it will cost most of you your lives. I call you friends, not servants, and I will never deceive you about the price of friendship with me."

A cold wind blew off the lake despite the warming day. Peter shivered, but not from the temperature. He was remembering old stories—prophets sawn in two, martyrs stoned for their faith, the price always demanded of those who stood for God in a world that preferred darkness.

"Tell us plainly, Lord," he said. "Will you restore the kingdom to Israel? Will you drive out the Romans?"

Jesus's expression was unreadable. "I will establish a kingdom, yes. But not the kind you imagine. Not with swords and armies but with truth and sacrifice. The Romans are not your true enemy, Simon. The darkness in men's hearts—that's the occupying force I've come to overthrow."

"But King David—" James began.

"David was a man of war because that was what his time required," Jesus interrupted. "But the kingdom I bring is not of this world. It can't be defended with swords or expanded by force. It grows like yeast in dough, like seeds in soil—quietly, invisibly, until suddenly it's everywhere."

Peter exchanged glances with the others. This wasn't the triumphant Messiah they'd been taught to expect. Yet the man who could command fish with a word surely had the power to command armies. Why choose the harder path?

"You're thinking too small," Jesus said, reading their expressions. "You're imagining a Jewish kingdom free from Rome. I'm talking about a kingdom that includes Romans and Greeks, slaves and free, men and women, and every tribe and tongue under heaven. The net I cast catches fish of every kind."

"The Gentiles?" Andrew couldn't hide his shock. "But they're unclean—"

"Nothing God has made clean can be called unclean," Jesus said firmly. "But that's a lesson for another day. For now, it's enough that you're willing to follow, even without understanding everything. Faith often means moving forward in the dark, trusting the one who holds the light."

They resumed walking, but the atmosphere had changed. Peter felt the weight of the decision, the gravity of what they'd committed to. This wasn't going to be the glorious revolution he'd imagined. It would be harder, stranger, and more demanding than anything he'd prepared for.

Yet when he looked at Jesus, striding confidently ahead, he felt that same pull that had made him drop everything and push the boat out for one more cast. This man held secrets of the kingdom and wielded power over creation itself. Whatever the cost of following, the cost of not following would be greater—a life spent wondering what might have been, what miracles he might have seen, and what purpose he might have served.

"Lord," he called out, surprising himself with the firmness in his voice. "Whatever you ask, wherever you lead, I will follow. I may fail—you seem certain I will—but I'll get back up and follow again. This I swear."

Jesus stopped and turned back, and the smile that spread across his face was like sunrise after a long night. "Oh, Simon," he said, and there was such affection in the words that Peter felt tears prick his eyes. "You have no idea how much those words mean to me. Or how much I'll remind you of them in days to come. But yes—you'll fall, and you'll rise, and in the end, you'll be the rock upon which I build my church."

"Church?" The word was unfamiliar in this context.

"The gathering of those who follow me. The new Israel, not bound by blood or law but by faith and love. But come—we have much to do before any of that comes to pass. There are sick to heal, hungry to feed, and lost to find. The fish was just the beginning. Ready to see what comes next?"

They were. As they followed Jesus away from the lake that had defined their lives, Peter felt he was crossing an invisible boundary. Behind lay everything familiar—family business, predictable days, manageable problems. Ahead lay mystery, challenge, and the unknown adventure of following a man who commanded fish and spoke of kingdoms not of this world.

The sun climbed higher, burning off the morning mist. Somewhere behind them, their families were dealing with the miraculous catch, their lives changed by the abundance. But for Peter, Andrew, James, and John, the real abundance lay ahead—in the words of eternal life their teacher carried, in the kingdom he proclaimed, and in the calling to catch not fish but human souls.

"No turning back," Andrew murmured beside him.

"No turning back," Peter agreed. And despite the uncertainty, despite the warnings of suffering to come, he found he was smiling. He'd spent his life pulling empty nets from dark water. Now he would learn to cast nets into human hearts, trusting the one who knew where the fish swam to fill those nets with eternal catch.

The boats grew small behind them. Ahead, the road stretched toward destiny. And Peter, who would become Cephas, who would become the Rock, walked forward into his calling, leaving wet footprints that would soon dry in the morning sun but whose impact would ripple through centuries to come.

Chapter 6: Healing by Sacred Waters

The journey from Capernaum to Jerusalem always unsettled Jesus's disciples. It meant leaving the familiar shores of Galilee, where their master's reputation provided some protection, and venturing into the viper's nest of Temple politics and Roman occupation. But when Jesus announced they would travel south for the unnamed feast, none dared protest. They had learnt that their rabbi's timing followed rhythms they couldn't always perceive.

Peter walked beside his brother Andrew, both men unconsciously checking the placement of the concealed blades they'd taken to carrying since the threats against Jesus had intensified. Behind them, James and John muttered about lodging arrangements, while Matthew calculated the group's dwindling funds. The other disciples spread out along the dusty road, some engaged in theological debate, others simply enjoying the break from the crushing crowds that now followed Jesus everywhere in Galilee.

"Which feast is it, do you think?" Thomas asked Philip as they navigated a particularly rocky stretch of road. "Passover isn't for months, and we just celebrated Tabernacles."

Philip shrugged. "Does it matter? When the Master says we go to Jerusalem, we go."

But Jesus heard the question, as he seemed to hear everything these days, even when walking several paces ahead. He turned, his eyes holding that peculiar mixture of weariness and purpose that had become familiar to them.

"The feast matters less than the work my Father has prepared," he said, his voice carrying despite the distance. "There are prisoners waiting to be freed, though their chains are not what men expect."

The disciples exchanged glances. Another cryptic saying to add to their growing collection. Sometimes following Jesus felt like trying to understand thunder—you felt its power long before you comprehended its source.

They traveled for three days, stopping in villages where Jesus couldn't help but heal the sick who were brought to him, despite his intent to pass quietly. Word of his presence spread like wildfire, and by the time they reached Jerusalem's outskirts, a modest crowd had attached itself to their group.

"So much for arriving unnoticed," Judas grumbled, clutching the money bag closer as beggars pressed in from all sides.

Jesus dismissed the crowd gently but firmly at the city gates, promising to teach in the Temple courts during the feast days. As the masses dispersed, he turned to his disciples with an unexpected announcement.

"Go into the city and find lodging," he instructed. "I have business at the Pool of Bethesda."

"Master, let us come with you," Peter insisted, his hand instinctively moving to his concealed weapon. "The Pharisees have spies everywhere."

Jesus's smile held a touch of sadness. "Simon, Simon. Still trying to protect me with steel and strength. But today's battle requires different weapons. Go. I'll find you before evening."

They wanted to protest, but something in his tone brooked no argument. Reluctantly, the twelve headed toward the city proper, while Jesus turned northeast, toward the Sheep Gate and the famous pool beyond.

The Pool of Bethesda sprawled before him like an open wound in the city's flesh. Five covered colonnades surrounded the double pool, their elegant architecture a mockery of the human misery they sheltered. The air hung thick with the stench of unwashed bodies, festering sores, and despair so tangible it seemed to have its own weight.

They called it the House of Mercy, these five porches, but Jesus saw little mercy here. Hundreds of broken bodies lay on mats and stretchers, some propped against the columns, others sprawled wherever they'd managed to claim space. The blind, the lame, the paralysed—Jerusalem's forgotten ones, gathered here in desperate hope of a miracle.

The legend was ancient and persistent: at certain times, an angel would trouble the waters, and the first person to enter the pool after the stirring would be healed. Whether divine truth or desperate superstition, the belief was strong enough to draw the sick from across Judea. They waited days, months, and some even years, watching for the slightest ripple that might signal their deliverance.

Jesus moved slowly through the crowd, his carpenter's hands clenched at his sides. Each face told a story of shattered dreams. A young mother, blind from birth, clutching a baby she'd never seen. An old soldier, his legs withered by some Syrian spear, still wearing the remnants of his uniform with pathetic pride. Children with twisted limbs, their parents' eyes hollow with exhausted hope.

The religious leaders walked past this place daily on their way to the Temple, their phylacteries broad and their prayers loud, but their eyes carefully averted. After all, sickness was often seen as punishment for sin. Better to leave God's judgement undisturbed.

But Jesus saw differently. Where others saw divine punishment, he saw humanity crushed beneath the weight of a broken world. Where others saw hopeless cases, he saw children of Abraham waiting to dance.

His attention was drawn to a man lying near the pool's edge, but not too near. While others jostled for position, ready to throw themselves into the water at the first sign of movement, this man lay still, his mat worn thin from decades of use. His legs were like dried sticks beneath a ragged blanket, and his face bore the peculiar resignation of one who had outlasted hope itself.

Jesus knew without asking—thirty-eight years. Thirty-eight years of watching others claim the healing he sought. Thirty-eight years of being too slow, too weak, too alone. The man no longer even watched the water. He simply existed, sustained by the occasional coin from guilty passersby and the bitter bread of broken dreams.

"Do you want to be healed?"

The words cut through the ambient misery like a blade. The invalid's eyes snapped open, focusing with difficulty on the figure standing above him. Just another religious tourist, probably, come to gawk at the desperate. But something in the voice...

"Sir," the man replied, his own voice rusty from disuse, "I have no one to help me into the pool when the water is stirred. While I am trying to get in, someone else goes down ahead of me."

Thirty-eight years of disappointment condensed into those few words. No family left to help him. No friends who hadn't grown weary of his need. Just an old man on a mat, forever watching others receive what he could never quite grasp.

Jesus felt the familiar fire kindle in his chest—part righteous anger at the systems that abandoned the weak, part divine compassion that demanded action. The Sabbath laws pressed against his consciousness, warning of consequences. He could almost hear the Pharisees' future accusations: healing on the Sabbath, breaking the hedge around the Torah, and leading the people astray.

But the Kingdom of God would not be constrained by human interpretations of divine law. Mercy would triumph over sacrifice. Love would shatter the chains that religious tradition had forged.

"Get up," Jesus commanded, his voice carrying an authority that made nearby conversations cease. "Pick up your mat and walk."

The words hung in the air like lightning about to strike. Those close enough to hear turned to stare. The invalid's eyes widened, confusion warring with something that might have been hope if it hadn't been crushed so many times before.

But even as his mind struggled to process the impossible command, his body began to respond. Warmth flooded through limbs that hadn't felt anything for nearly four decades. Muscles that had atrophied to nothing suddenly swelled with strength. Nerves that had been dead so long they'd turned to dust sparked back to life in a cascade of sensation so intense it nearly brought tears.

The man gasped, his hands flying to his legs. He could feel them. Not just the phantom sensations that had tormented him for years, but real, solid, living flesh. Trembling, he pushed himself up on arms that suddenly bore his weight without protest.

Around them, the crowd began to murmur. Some had seen Jesus in Galilee and had heard whispers of miracles by the sea. But this was Jerusalem, the holy city where prophets came to die, not to heal.

The invalid stood on legs that had been useless for thirty-eight years. He swayed for a moment, muscle memory returning like a forgotten language. Then he took a step. Another. His face transformed from shock to wonder to a joy so pure it was almost painful to witness.

"My legs," he whispered. Then louder, "My legs! I can feel my legs!"

He bent to pick up his mat—that hated, precious mat that had been his world for so long—and clutched it to his chest like a trophy. Tears streamed down his weathered face as he turned in circles, testing his newfound strength, hardly daring to believe.

"Who?" he started to ask, but when he looked for his healer, Jesus had already melted back into the crowd. The Son of Man had not come to gather acclaim but to proclaim the Kingdom's arrival through acts of restoration. The healed man stood in the centre of a growing circle of amazement. Other invalids pressed closer, hope kindling in eyes that had been dead for years. But the religious authorities were already pushing through the crowd, their faces dark with suspicion.

"You there," one of them barked, pointing at the man holding his mat. "What are you doing? It's the Sabbath! The law forbids you to carry your mat."

The joy on the man's face flickered. Of course. In his overwhelming happiness, he'd forgotten the web of regulations that governed every aspect of Jewish life. Carrying a burden on the Sabbath was work, and work was forbidden.

"The man who healed me said to me, 'Pick up your mat and walk,'" he replied, his voice a mixture of defiance and uncertainty.

The Pharisees' eyes narrowed. "Who is this fellow who told you to pick it up and walk?"

But the healed man could only shrug helplessly. His benefactor had disappeared as suddenly as he'd appeared, leaving only the impossible miracle as evidence of his presence.

The religious leaders withdrew, muttering among themselves. Another violation to add to their growing list. The Galilean teacher was becoming more than a nuisance—he was becoming a threat to the very foundations of their authority.

Meanwhile, Jesus had made his way to the Temple courts. He moved through the Court of the Gentiles, past the money changers and dove sellers, his heart heavy with the knowledge of what was coming. The healing at Bethesda would not go unchallenged. The battle lines were being drawn ever clearer.

He found a quiet corner in Solomon's Colonnade and sat, drawing his cloak around him. Soon his disciples would find him here, full of questions about his solitary expedition. Soon the crowds would gather, hungry for teaching and miracles. But for now, he had a few moments of solitude to prepare for what must come next.

The invalid—former invalid, Jesus corrected himself with a small smile—would be looking for him. The man deserved to know who had transformed his life. More importantly, he needed to understand that physical healing was only the beginning of what God offered.

As if summoned by his thoughts, Jesus spotted the man entering the Temple courts, still carrying his mat, still walking with the careful wonder of one who had received an impossible gift. Their eyes met across the crowded courtyard, and the man's face lit up with recognition.

He hurried over, weaving between pilgrims and merchants, and fell to his knees before Jesus. "Master! It was you. You're the one who healed me."

Jesus helped him to his feet, studying the face marked by decades of suffering. "See, you are well again," he said, his voice gentle but serious. "Stop sinning, or something worse may happen to you."

The words were not a threat but a warning. Physical healing without spiritual transformation was like painting over rotted wood—it might look better temporarily, but the underlying decay remained. This man had been given a second chance at life. What he did with it would determine whether he found true freedom or simply exchanged one form of bondage for another.

The man nodded slowly, understanding dawning in his eyes. He clutched his mat tighter, as if it were a diploma from a school of suffering. "I understand, Master. For thirty-eight years I waited for the water to heal my body. But you... you've offered to heal my soul."

"The pool could only offer temporary relief to one person at a time," Jesus said. "But the living water I offer springs up to eternal life for all who thirst."

Before the man could respond, a commotion arose near the temple entrance. The religious authorities had arrived in force, their faces set in lines of righteous indignation. They'd found their target.

"There he is," one of them announced, pointing at Jesus. "The Sabbath-breaker who incites others to sin."

Jesus stood, placing himself between the authorities and the healed man. The confrontation he'd anticipated was here. But this was why he'd come to Jerusalem—not just to heal one man at a pool, but to challenge the very systems that kept God's people in bondage.

"You search the Scriptures because you think that in them you have eternal life," Jesus said, his voice carrying across the courtyard with supernatural clarity. "Yet these are the very Scriptures that testify about me, and you refuse to come to me to have life."

The Pharisees recoiled as if slapped. This Galilean carpenter dared to suggest that their lifetime of study had missed the point? That their careful observance of every jot and tittle of the law had somehow led them away from God rather than toward Him?

"My Father is always at his work to this very day," Jesus continued, his eyes blazing with divine authority, "and I too am working."

A gasp ran through the crowd. He'd done it again—called God his Father in that intimate way that implied equality. The religious leaders' faces purpled with rage. This was blasphemy of the highest order.

"He makes himself equal with God," one of them hissed to another. "The penalty is death."

But Jesus wasn't finished. The crowd pressed closer, sensing that something momentous was happening. His disciples had found him now, forming a protective circle, though they looked as bewildered as everyone else.

"Very truly I tell you," Jesus declared, "the Son can do nothing by himself; he can do only what he sees his Father doing, because whatever the Father does the Son also does. For the Father loves the Son and shows him all he does."

The healed man stood transfixed, his mat forgotten in his hands. This teacher who had restored his legs was claiming to be... what? The Son of God? The Messiah? The implications were staggering.

"Just as the Father raises the dead and gives them life," Jesus continued, each word falling like a hammer blow on religious pretence, "even so the Son gives life to whom he is pleased to give it. Moreover, the Father judges no one but has entrusted all judgement to the Son, that all may honour the Son just as they honour the Father. Whoever does not honour the Son does not honour the Father, who sent him."

The religious authorities were nearly apoplectic now. This wasn't just healing on the Sabbath—this was a direct assault on everything they held sacred. This carpenter was claiming divine prerogatives, placing himself at the very centre of God's redemptive plan.

One of the scribes, his voice trembling with fury, stepped forward. "By what authority do you say these things? What sign do you show us?"

Jesus turned his penetrating gaze on the man. "You have Moses, in whom you put your hope. But if you believed Moses, you would believe me, for he wrote about me. Since you do not believe what he wrote, how are you going to believe what I say?"

The crowd stirred uneasily. This was dangerous territory. Moses was the lawgiver, the friend of God, and the greatest prophet Israel had known. To claim that Moses had written about him...

"There is one who accuses you," Jesus said, his voice dropping to a conversational tone that somehow made it more threatening. "Moses, on whom your hopes are set. Your accuser is not some foreign god or pagan philosophy. It's the very law you claim to defend."

He turned to address the wider crowd, his voice rising again. "Do not think I have come to abolish the Law or the Prophets. I have not come to abolish them but to fulfil them. Every stroke of the pen will be accomplished, but not in the way you expect. You strain out gnats while swallowing camels. You tithe mint and cumin while neglecting justice, mercy, and faithfulness."

The healed man felt his knees go weak again, but not from paralysis. The spiritual authority radiating from Jesus was almost physical in its intensity. This was no ordinary rabbi debating fine points of theology. This was something—someone—else entirely.

"You study the Scriptures diligently," Jesus continued, his eyes sweeping across the assembled religious leaders, "because you think that in them you have eternal life. These are the very Scriptures that testify about me, yet you refuse to come to me to have life."

One of the younger Pharisees, his face flushed with indignation, burst out, "You are not yet fifty years old, and you claim Abraham has seen you?"

Jesus's response was immediate and devastating. "Very truly I tell you, before Abraham was born, I am."

The silence that followed was absolute. Even the merchants stopped hawking their wares. Even the doves ceased their cooing. "I AM" was the sacred name, the name God had revealed to Moses at the burning bush, the name no devout Jew would even pronounce.

Several of the religious leaders began tearing their robes—the traditional response to blasphemy. Others scrambled for stones, the prescribed punishment for such sacrilege. The crowd began to scatter, some in fear, others in confusion.

But Jesus stood calm in the centre of the storm, his disciples forming a protective wall around him. Peter's hand was on his sword hilt, but Jesus placed a restraining hand on his arm.

"My time has not yet come," he said quietly. "And no one takes my life from me. I lay it down of my own accord."

The healed man watched in amazement as Jesus and his followers moved through the crowd. The religious authorities seemed frozen, their stones held but not thrown, as if an invisible force restrained them. The teacher who had healed his legs passed close by, and their eyes met one final time.

"Remember," Jesus said softly, meant for his ears alone. "Your healing is a sign pointing to something greater. Don't stop at the sign. Follow where it leads."

Then he was gone, disappearing into the labyrinthine streets of Jerusalem with his disciples, leaving behind a Temple court in uproar and a man whose life had been transformed in ways he was only beginning to understand. The healed man stood there, still clutching his mat, as the crowd swirled around him. Some looked at him with awe, others with suspicion. He had become evidence in a trial that was only beginning, a living testimony to power that challenged every assumption about God, law, and human limitation.

Slowly, he made his way out of the Temple courts. His legs, so recently useless, carried him with growing confidence. But it was his heart that felt the greatest change. For thirty-eight years he had waited by a pool, hoping for an angel to trouble the waters. But the healing he'd received was so much more than physical restoration.

As he walked through Jerusalem's narrow streets, he began to understand what Jesus meant about something worse than paralysis. To be physically whole but spiritually dead—wasn't that the condition of the religious leaders who had confronted the Lord? They could walk, run, or dance if they chose, but their souls were more paralysed than his legs had ever been.

He paused at a street corner, a decision crystallising in his mind. He could return to the pool and share his testimony with those still waiting for their miracle. Or he could do what his heart was telling him—follow this Jesus, learn more about the living water he offered, and discover what it meant to be truly, completely whole.

The choice, he realised, was the same one facing everyone who encountered Jesus. Stop at the miracle, or follow where it led. Accept physical healing alone, or embrace the transformation of the soul.

He thought of the religious leaders, so angry that healing had happened on the wrong day. He thought of Jesus, willing to break their traditions to set one man free. He thought of thirty-eight years of waiting and how, in one moment, everything had changed.

The man looked down at his mat—that symbol of his former life, his decades of paralysis and despair. Then, with deliberate intention, he walked to the nearest refuse heap and threw it away. He wouldn't need it anymore. He was walking now, in more ways than one.

Back at the pool of Bethesda, the other invalids continued their vigil. They'd seen one of their own healed and had heard whispers of the controversial teacher who'd done it. Some redoubled their efforts to be first into the water. Others began to wonder if perhaps they'd been waiting by the wrong pool all along.

The five porches still sheltered the desperate. The water still lay placid, waiting for an angel's touch that might or might not come. But something had shifted in the spiritual atmosphere. Hope, that most dangerous of emotions, had been kindled.

Word spread through the community of the broken. The teacher from Galilee had healed on the Sabbath. He'd told a thirty-eight-year-old paralytic to rise and walk, and the man had obeyed. More than that, he'd claimed to be doing his father's work, had spoken of judgement and eternal life, and had made claims that either marked him as divine or dangerously deluded.

An old blind woman, her fingers forever working at her begging bowl, lifted her face toward where she imagined the sky must be. "Perhaps," she whispered to no one in particular, "the Prophet, like Moses, has finally come."

Her neighbor, a man whose legs had been crushed by a Roman wagon, snorted in derision. "The Messiah will come with armies and glory, not sneaking around healing people and running from the authorities."

"But he healed Ezra," the woman insisted. "Thirty-eight years, and the man walks. That's not nothing."

"One healing doesn't make a Messiah," the crippled man replied. "Wake me when he overthrows Rome and restores David's throne."

But the blind woman continued to ponder. She'd heard the teachings that sometimes drifted over from the Temple courts. She knew the prophecies of a Suffering Servant, of one who would bear their infirmities and carry their sorrows. What if the Messiah's kingdom wasn't what they expected? What if it started not with military might but with mercy to the marginalised?

The debate continued around the pool as evening shadows lengthened. Some sided with the blind woman, wondering if perhaps God was moving in unexpected ways. Others held fast to traditional expectations, unwilling to accept a Messiah who seemed more interested in healing bodies than raising armies.

Meanwhile, Jesus and his disciples had found lodging in the lower city, in the home of a sympathiser who asked no questions about their hasty departure from the Temple. The twelve were buzzing with questions and concerns, their voices overlapping in their eagerness to understand what had just happened.

"Master, they were ready to stone you," Peter said, pacing the small room like a caged lion. "We should leave Jerusalem tonight and return to Galilee, where you have support."

"The religious leaders will not forget this," Matthew added, his tax collector's mind already calculating the political cost. "You've challenged their authority publicly. They'll make you a target."

Jesus sat calmly in their midst, breaking bread for their evening meal. "Did you notice the man I healed?" he asked, seemingly ignoring their concerns.

The disciples exchanged glances. "Of course, Master," John replied. "Thirty-eight years paralysed. It was miraculous."

"Was it?" Jesus asked, his eyes twinkling with something that might have been amusement. "Or was it simply the Kingdom of God breaking into the kingdom of this world? When the reign of God comes near, the lame walk, the blind see, and the dead are raised. This is not exceptional—it's to be expected."

"But the Sabbath controversy..." Thomas began.

"The Sabbath was made for man, not man for the Sabbath," Jesus interrupted gently. "Do you think my Father ceases to sustain the universe every seventh day? Does he stop loving, stop caring, and stop healing because of a human calendar? The religious leaders have turned a gift into a burden, a day of rest into a prison of regulations."

Judas, ever practical, voiced what several were thinking. "But surely it would be wiser to avoid unnecessary confrontation. You could have healed the man any other day."

Jesus's expression grew serious. "Judas, if you wait for a convenient time to do good, you'll wait forever. That man had been waiting thirty-eight years. Should I have made him wait one day more to avoid offending those who care more about rules than people?"

The room fell silent, each disciple wrestling with the implications. Following Jesus, they were beginning to understand meant abandoning not just their nets and tax booths but their very understanding of how God worked in the world.

"There's something else," Jesus continued, his voice taking on the teaching tone they'd come to recognise. "The healing was a sign, but not the kind of sign the Pharisees demanded. They want spectacle—fire from heaven, armies of angels. But the Kingdom comes like a mustard seed, small and seemingly insignificant, yet containing the power to transform everything."

"So the man's healing..." Philip began slowly.

"Is a parable in flesh and bone," Jesus finished. "Thirty-eight years of paralysis ended in a moment. How long has Israel been paralyzed by empty religion, by leaders who bind heavy burdens but won't lift a finger to help carry them? The healing of one man points to the healing I offer to all."

Andrew, always thoughtful, asked, "What did you mean when you told him to stop sinning or something worse might happen? Was his paralysis caused by sin?"

Jesus shook his head. "Not all suffering comes from personal sin. This world is broken, groaning under the weight of humanity's rebellion. Rain falls on the righteous and unrighteous alike, and tragedy visits both. But I warned him because physical healing without spiritual transformation is incomplete. What good is it to have working legs if you use them to walk away from God?"

The disciples pondered this as they shared their simple meal. Outside, they could hear the city settling into evening routines. Somewhere, the religious authorities were likely meeting, plotting their next move. Somewhere, a formerly paralysed man was learning to navigate life on legs that worked.

"Master," Peter finally asked, "what happens now? The confrontation today—it felt like a declaration of war."

Jesus's smile was sad but determined. "It was, in a way. But not the kind of war you're thinking of, Simon. This is a battle for the hearts and souls of God's people. The weapons are truth and love, mercy and justice. The enemy is not Rome or even the Pharisees, but the spiritual forces that keep people in bondage."

"And we're your army?" James asked, trying to understand.

"You're my witnesses," Jesus corrected. "You've seen what the Kingdom looks like—the lame walking, the hungry fed, the outcasts welcomed. Soon, I'll send you out to proclaim this good news, to heal in my name, and to announce that the reign of God has come near."

"But we're just fishermen and tax collectors," Andrew protested. "The religious leaders have studied the law their entire lives. How can we stand against them?"

Jesus reached out and placed a hand on Andrew's shoulder. "The same way David stood against Goliath—not in your own strength, but in the power of the Lord. The Kingdom doesn't come through human wisdom or might, but through the Spirit of God working in ordinary people who dare to believe."

The conversation continued late into the night, Jesus patiently answering questions, correcting misunderstandings, and preparing them for the trials ahead. They couldn't know that in a few short years, these same men would stand before councils and kings, boldly proclaiming the message of the Kingdom. They couldn't see how the healing of one paralysed man would ripple outward, inspiring faith in countless others who felt trapped by circumstances beyond their control.

But Jesus knew. As his disciples finally drifted off to sleep, he stepped out onto the flat roof of the house to pray. Jerusalem spread out below him, the Temple towering over all, its gold facade catching the last rays of moonlight. Somewhere in this city, religious leaders plotted his death. Somewhere, a healed man was discovering what it meant to walk in newness of life.

"Father," Jesus prayed, his voice barely above a whisper, "thank you for this day. For the opportunity to reveal your heart for the broken. For the chance to challenge systems that oppress rather than liberate. Give me strength for what lies ahead. Help these men understand that your Kingdom comes not through force but through suffering love. And watch over the one who was healed. May he find not just physical wholeness but the abundant life you desire for all your children."

A cool breeze stirred, carrying the scents of cooking fires and humanity. The city slept, unaware that the King walked among them, that the Kingdom of Heaven was breaking in through acts of mercy and words of truth.

Tomorrow would bring new challenges. The religious authorities would intensify their opposition. The crowds would continue to misunderstand, seeking signs and wonders while missing the Sign standing before them. The disciples would struggle to grasp a Messiah who came to serve rather than be served.

But tonight, a man who hadn't walked in thirty-eight years was probably still awake, marvelling at the sensation of working muscles and steady legs.

Tonight, the Kingdom of God had touched earth at the Pool of Bethesda, and one life had been forever changed.

The healing by sacred waters was more than a miracle—it was a declaration. The old ways of waiting for angels to trouble the water were passing away. The new had come in the person of Jesus, who troubled the waters of religious tradition and offered healing that went deeper than any pool could reach.

As Jesus stood on that rooftop, praying for the city that would soon cry for his crucifixion, he thought of all the paralysed souls waiting for someone to help them into pools of their own making. Religious pools, political pools, social pools—all promising healing but delivering only disappointment. He had come to offer something different. Not a pool that could heal one person occasionally, but living water that would become a spring welling up to eternal life. Not a system that favoured the strong and swift, but a kingdom where the last would be first and the weak would shame the powerful.

The confrontation at the Temple had indeed been a declaration of war, but not the kind the disciples imagined. This was war against every system that kept people paralysed—whether physically, spiritually, or socially. It was a war against religious hypocrisy that honoured God with lips while hearts remained far from him. It was war against the powers of darkness that convinced people their paralysis was permanent, their situations hopeless. And it was a war that would be won not through swords or political maneuvering, but through a cross. The healed man couldn't know it, but his restoration pointed forward to an even greater healing—the healing of the relationship between God and humanity, accomplished through the broken body and shed blood of the One who had commanded him to rise and walk.

For now, though, it was enough that one man had been set free. One man who had waited thirty-eight years for an angel now knew that God himself had come near. One man who had been defined by his paralysis now had to discover who he was when he could walk.

The ripples from this healing would spread outward, touching lives across Jerusalem and beyond. Some would believe, recognising in Jesus the fulfilment of prophecies they'd cherished for generations. Others would harden their hearts, clinging to traditions that had become more important than the God they claimed to serve.

But the Kingdom of God would not be stopped. It would advance one healed life at a time, one transformed heart at a time, and one act of mercy at a time. The pool of Bethesda would continue to attract the desperate, but word would spread of a Teacher who didn't wait for angels to trouble the water—who was himself the troubled water that brought healing to all who would receive it.

As the night deepened, Jesus finally returned to the room where his disciples slept. He looked at each face—Peter, impetuous and passionate; John, young and idealistic; Matthew, still learning to see people as more than economic units; and Judas, complex and conflicted. These were the men who would carry forward the message of the Kingdom, who would themselves become pools of healing water in a parched world.

They had so much to learn and so far to grow. But they had taken the first step—they had left everything to follow him. Like the paralysed man picking up his mat, they had responded to his call to rise and walk in newness of life.

Tomorrow would bring new challenges, new confrontations, and new opportunities to demonstrate the Kingdom's power. But tonight, it was enough to rest in the knowledge that the healing had begun. At the Pool of Bethesda, where desperate people waited for angels, God himself had appeared.

And he had declared, with authority that shook the foundations of religious power, that the waiting was over. The Kingdom had come. The healing could begin.

Rise up and walk. The words echoed through the night, a promise and a command, a challenge and an invitation. Rise up from whatever paralysis holds you. Walk in the freedom of the children of God.

The sacred waters had been troubled by a power greater than any angel. And anyone—anyone—who stepped in faith into that disturbance would find themselves forever changed.

Chapter 7: Mountains and Multitudes

The mountain called to him in the pre-dawn darkness, its bulk a deeper black against the star-scattered sky. Jesus stood at the edge of Capernaum, feeling the pull of solitude, the need for communion with his Father that had been building for days. Behind him, Peter's house lay quiet, the fisherman and his family still deep in sleep. But Jesus couldn't rest. Not tonight. Tomorrow would change everything.

He began the ascent alone, his feet finding the familiar path even in darkness. This wasn't Sinai or Zion, just one of the many hills that rose above the Sea of Galilee, but tonight it would become holy ground. Tonight, he would choose the men who would carry his message to the ends of the earth.

The irony wasn't lost on him. Moses had climbed a mountain to receive the Law. Now he climbed to give a new law, written not on tablets of stone but on human hearts. Moses had come down with commands that would govern a nation. He would come down with men who would transform the world.

As he climbed, Jesus thought of the crowds that had been following him. Word of the healings had spread like wildfire through Galilee. The paralytic is walking. The lepers were cleansed. The centurion's servant was healed with just a word. Every miracle brought more people, more desperation, and more hope placed on his shoulders.

But healing bodies was only the beginning. The sickness ran deeper—a soul-sickness that no amount of physical restoration could cure. They needed new hearts, new minds, and a completely new way of understanding God and his kingdom. And he couldn't do it alone. At least, he had chosen to not do it alone.

The path grew steeper, and Jesus paused to catch his breath. His body, fully human, felt the strain of the climb. Sweat beaded on his forehead despite the cool night air. His muscles protested the exertion. It would have been so easy to simply appear at the summit, to bypass the physical struggle. But that wasn't the way he had chosen. Every step, every breath, every ache was part of his identification with humanity.

He thought of the men sleeping below. Fishermen, tax collectors, zealots—an unlikely group to entrust with the kingdom of God. Peter, with his impulsiveness, is quick to speak and quicker to act. Andrew, quieter than his brother but no less devoted. James and John, the "sons of thunder," ambitious and fiery. Matthew is still adjusting to his new life after leaving his tax booth. Each one flawed, each one limited, each one chosen.

The summit was bare except for scattered rocks and scrub brush. Jesus found a relatively flat spot and knelt, his knees pressing into the thin soil. Above him, the stars wheeled in their ancient patterns—the same stars Abraham had counted, the same ones that had announced his birth to eastern sages. But tonight they seemed especially bright, as if creation itself leaned in to witness what was about to unfold.

"Father," he said aloud, his voice carrying on the mountain breeze. The word contained everything—intimacy, submission, trust. It was the word that scandalised the religious leaders, this claiming of God as Abba, as Daddy. But it was the truest word he knew.

Prayer for Jesus wasn't the formal recitation that many practiced, lips moving through memorised phrases while minds wandered. It was conversation, communion, a sharing of heart between Father and Son that had existed before the foundation of the world. Here on the mountain, with no human ears to hear, he could speak freely.

"The time has come," he continued. "They've seen enough to believe, but not so much that they follow for the wrong reasons. They're ready to be called out, set apart, marked as mine."

He thought of each man he would name when dawn came. Some had been with him from the beginning. Others had joined more recently. All had left something behind—nets, tax booths, political dreams, and family obligations. But leaving was only the first step. Now they needed to be formed, shaped, prepared for what was coming.

"Give me wisdom," Jesus prayed. "Let me choose not based on human standards but on your purposes. Not the wise, the powerful, or the naturally gifted—but those you have prepared, those whose hearts are ready even if their minds don't yet understand."

The eastern sky began to lighten almost imperceptibly, black fading to deepest blue. Jesus shifted position, his human body already stiff from kneeling. But he didn't rise. Not yet. There was too much to lay before his Father.

He prayed for each man by name, seeing not just who they were but who they would become. Peter—the rock who would crumble and be rebuilt stronger. John—the son of thunder who would become the apostle of love. Thomas—the sceptic whose doubt would lead to the greatest declaration of faith. Judas—

Jesus paused, his heart clenching with a pain that was both human and divine. Even now, knowing what would come, the betrayal was chosen. Free will, that terrible and glorious gift, meant that even those called could choose to turn away. But Judas too had a role to play, dark though it was.

"Your will be done," Jesus said, and meant it, though the words tasted of future sorrow. "In everything, your will be done."

As dawn approached, Jesus expanded his prayer beyond the twelve to the multitudes who would gather. They would come expecting a prophet, a teacher, maybe even the Messiah. But the kingdom he would describe would confound their expectations. Blessed are the poor? The meek inheriting the earth? Loving enemies? It went against every natural instinct, every cultural norm.

"Give them ears to hear," he prayed. "Open their hearts to receive what seems impossible. Let your Spirit move among them, translating my words into the language their souls understand."

The sky continued to brighten, pink and gold creeping above the eastern horizon. Below, the Sea of Galilee began to materialise from the darkness, its surface like polished bronze in the early light. Fishing boats were already out, dark specks on the water. Life was going on as normal, unaware that this day would mark a turning point in history.

Jesus rose, his knees protesting after the long vigil. He stretched, fully human in this moment, working out the kinks in his back and shoulders. But his spirit soared with the certainty that came from communion with the Father. The choices were clear. The message was ready. The time was now. He began the descent as the first birds started their morning songs. By the time he reached the lower slopes, he could see people already gathering. Word had spread that the teacher would be speaking today, and they came from all directions—farmers leaving their fields, merchants closing their shops, mothers carrying children, and old men leaning on staffs.

At Peter's house, he found his core group of disciples already awake and anxious. They had noticed his absence in the night and guessed where he had gone. Peter approached first, as usual, his weathered face creased with concern.

"Master, you were gone all night. We were worried."

Jesus placed a hand on the fisherman's shoulder. "I had to pray. Today is important, Simon. More important than you know."

"Are you going to teach?" Andrew asked. "The crowds are already gathering. There must be hundreds, maybe thousands."

"I will teach," Jesus confirmed. "But first, I must choose."

They looked at him with confusion, but Jesus didn't elaborate. Instead, he asked them to spread the word among all who had been following him closely. Not just the crowds, but those who had shown deeper commitment, who had lingered after the masses dispersed, hungry for more than just miracles.

Within an hour, about seventy people had gathered in the courtyard of Peter's house. Men mostly, but some women too—those brave enough to break social conventions for the sake of truth. Jesus knew each face, each story. The wealthy merchant who had liquidated his business to follow. The young scribe had been expelled from synagogue for asking too many questions. The former prostitute whose gratitude had transformed into discipleship. Each one precious, each one called to their own purpose. But from among them, twelve would be set apart.

Jesus stood on the steps leading to the flat roof, where he could see and be seen by all. The morning sun was behind him, and he knew his silhouette must appear dark and imposing. Good. What he was about to do required bravery.

"You have followed me," he began, his voice carrying clearly across the courtyard. "You have seen the works of God and heard the message of the kingdom. But the harvest is plentiful, and the workers are few. Today, I call some of you to a deeper commitment, a closer walk, and a heavier burden."

The crowd stirred, anticipation rippling through them like wind on water. Everyone wondered—would they be chosen? Did they want to be chosen? Being singled out by this controversial teacher could mean privilege, but it could also mean persecution.

"When I call your name, come forward."

Jesus paused, looking at each face, seeing past the external to the heart. Then he began.

"Simon, whom I call Peter."

The big fisherman stepped forward immediately, with no hesitation despite not knowing what he was agreeing to. That was Peter—impulsive, wholehearted, throwing himself into whatever lay ahead. His wife watched from the doorway, pride and worry warring in her expression.

"Andrew, brother of Simon."

Andrew moved to stand beside Peter, quieter but no less committed. The brothers exchanged a glance—whatever this was, they were in it together.

"James, son of Zebedee."

The older of the thunder brothers strode forward, confidence in every step. He had left a thriving fishing business for this. No turning back now.

"John, son of Zebedee."

Young John, barely out of his teens, joined his brother. There was something special about John—a capacity for both fire and tenderness that would serve the kingdom well.

"Philip."

The man from Bethsaida came forward, his analytical mind already working to understand what this selection meant. Philip never did anything without thinking it through, but once convinced, he was immovable.

"Nathanael, also called Bartholomew."

The sceptic who had wondered if anything good could come from Nazareth now stepped forward without hesitation. His initial doubt had transformed into unshakeable faith after their first encounter.

"Matthew, also called Levi."

A murmur ran through the crowd. The tax collector? Still? Even after these months, some struggled to accept that Jesus had called such a man. But Matthew came forward, head high, knowing he was chosen not despite his past but because of what it had taught him about grace.

"Thomas."

The twin moved forward slowly, thoughtfully. Everything about Thomas was deliberate and considered. His questions weren't doubts so much as a deep need to understand, to touch truth with his own hands.

"James, son of Alphaeus."

Another James, this one quieter, often overlooked in the shadow of more dominant personalities. But Jesus saw the depth there, the steady faithfulness that would endure when flash and charm failed.

"Thaddaeus, also called Judas son of James."

Not to be confused with the other Judas still to be named. This one had a heart for the oppressed, a passion for justice that would need to be channeled but never quenched.

"Simon the Zealot"

Another murmur from the crowd. A zealot and a tax collector in the same group? The political revolutionary who had fought Rome standing beside the collaborator who had collected for Rome? Only Jesus could imagine such a reconciliation.

Jesus paused before speaking the last name. He could feel the weight of future sorrow pressing on his chest. But it had to be done. Even this was part of the plan.

"Judas Iscariot."

The man from Kerioth—the only Judean among the Galileans—stepped forward. He was intelligent, capable, and trusted by the others. They would make him treasurer, never suspecting the darkness that would eventually consume him. Jesus looked at him with love and grief intertwined. Even knowing the end, he chose him. Love always chooses, always hopes, even when it knows the cost.

Twelve men stood before him now. Fishermen, tax collectors, zealots, sceptics and believers, impulsive and careful, young and old. Not a priest among them. Not a Pharisee or scribe or any of the religious elite. Just ordinary men called to an extraordinary purpose.

"You twelve," Jesus said, his voice carrying new authority, "I name apostles. Sent ones. You will be with me, learn from me, and eventually, I will send you out with authority to proclaim the kingdom and cast out demons. You will be my witnesses to Israel and beyond."

Peter, never able to stay silent long, asked, "Master, why us? There are others here who seem more qualified, more educated—"

"I choose not as the world chooses," Jesus interrupted gently. "Not based on wisdom or strength or nobility. I choose based on the Father's will and the readiness of the heart. You twelve have been given to me by the Father. You are my gift from him, and through you, the world will be blessed."

The weight of calling settled on twelve pairs of shoulders. Some stood straighter, embracing it. Others seemed to shrink slightly, already feeling inadequate. But all stayed. Whatever Jesus was calling them to, they would follow.

"Now," Jesus said, addressing the larger group again, "we go to the mountain. All of you. There are things that must be said, truths that must be proclaimed. The kingdom of God is at hand, but it's not what you think. It's not what anyone thinks. Come and hear."

The procession that formed was remarkable. Jesus led, with the twelve apostles close behind him in a group that was still learning its dynamics. Behind them came the other disciples, then the crowds that had been gathering all morning. By the time they reached the designated hillside—a natural amphitheatre where the acoustics would carry his voice to thousands—the multitude was vast.

They came from everywhere. Farmers with soil still under their nails. Fishermen smelling of the sea. Merchants with calculating eyes. Women with children clinging to their robes. Roman sympathisers and Jewish nationalists. The desperately poor and the cautiously wealthy. The sick were hoping for healing, and the healthy were curious about this teacher who spoke with such authority.

As Jesus looked out over them, he saw Israel in miniature. These were the lost sheep he had come to gather. These were the ones who hungered and thirsted, though they didn't yet know for what. These were the blessed ones, though the blessings he would pronounce would seem like reversals of everything they had been taught.

He found a natural platform of rock partway up the slope where everyone could see him. The twelve arranged themselves close by—not a barrier between Jesus and the people, but a bridge. They would be the ones to carry this message forward when he was gone.

The crowd gradually quieted, thousands of eyes fixed on the teacher from Nazareth. Mothers shushed children. Men stopped their discussions. Even the wind seemed to pause, as if creation itself leaned in to listen.

Jesus sat, the traditional posture of a rabbi about to teach. But what came from his mouth would be unlike any rabbinic teaching they had heard. He looked out over the sea of faces—expectant, sceptical, hopeful, desperate—and felt the familiar surge of compassion. These were sheep without a shepherd, and he had come to gather them.

When he spoke, his voice carried with supernatural clarity, reaching even those on the edges of the vast crowd.

"Blessed are the poor in spirit, for theirs is the kingdom of heaven."

A ripple of confusion ran through the crowd. Blessed are the poor in spirit? They had always been taught that blessing came from righteousness, from keeping the law, from God's favor manifested in prosperity and success. But Jesus was pronouncing blessings on those who knew their spiritual bankruptcy?

"Blessed are those who mourn, for they will be comforted."

Another reversal. Mourning was a curse, a sign of God's judgement or absence. How could mourners be blessed? But Jesus continued, his voice steady and sure.

"Blessed are the meek, for they will inherit the earth."

Now there were audible murmurs of disagreement. The meek inheriting the earth? It was the strong who inherited, the powerful, those who seized what they wanted. Rome hadn't conquered the world through meekness. Even David, their greatest king, had been a warrior.

"Blessed are those who hunger and thirst for righteousness, for they will be filled."

This made more sense to some. The Pharisees spoke often of hungering for righteousness. But Jesus's tone suggested he meant something different, something deeper than external law-keeping.

"Blessed are the merciful, for they will be shown mercy."

"Blessed are the pure in heart, for they will see God."

"Blessed are the peacemakers, for they will be called children of God."

Each beatitude built on the last, painting a picture of kingdom citizens that looked nothing like the zealot warriors many hoped for. This was not a call to arms against Rome but a call to a radically different way of being in the world.

"Blessed are those who are persecuted because of righteousness, for theirs is the kingdom of heaven."

Jesus paused, letting this sink in. Then he made it personal:

"Blessed are you when people insult you, persecute you, and falsely say all kinds of evil against you because of me. Rejoice and be glad, because great is your reward in heaven, for in the same way they persecuted the prophets who were before you."

The crowd was silent now, processing these upside-down blessings. Some faces showed dawning understanding—those who had suffered, who had been marginalized, who had never felt blessed by the religious system. Others looked troubled, especially among the more prosperous and powerful who had come to investigate this new teacher.

Peter leaned toward John and whispered, "He's turning everything upside down."

"Or right-side up," John whispered back, his young face alight with wonder.

Jesus continued, his metaphors shifting to images everyone could understand:

"You are the salt of the earth. But if the salt loses its saltiness, how can it be made salty again? It is no longer good for anything, except to be thrown out and trampled underfoot."

They knew salt—precious, preserving, flavouring. To be called salt was an honour. But salt that lost its purpose? That was a sobering warning.

"You are the light of the world. A town built on a hill cannot be hidden. Neither do people light a lamp and put it under a bowl. Instead they put it on its stand, and it gives light to everyone in the house. In the same way, let your light shine before others, that they may see your good deeds and glorify your Father in heaven."

Light of the world. Such an audacious claim for fishermen and farmers, tax collectors and housewives. Yet Jesus spoke it as a simple fact. They were light, whether they felt like it or not. The only question was whether they would shine or hide.

Then came the words that made the Pharisees in the crowd stiffen with alarm:

"Do not think that I have come to abolish the Law or the Prophets; I have not come to abolish them but to fulfil them. For truly I tell you, until heaven and earth disappear, not the smallest letter, not the least stroke of a pen, will by any means disappear from the Law until everything is accomplished."

A sigh of relief from the religiously conservative. He wasn't throwing out Moses after all. But then:

"For I tell you that unless your righteousness surpasses that of the Pharisees and the teachers of the law, you will certainly not enter the kingdom of heaven."

Gasps now. Surpass the righteousness of the Pharisees? These were the men who tithed their mint and cumin, who wouldn't walk too far on the Sabbath, and who had built hedge after hedge around the law to ensure they never broke it. How could anyone be more righteous?

But Jesus was just getting started. He began to reinterpret the law, not loosening it but tightening it beyond any external observance:

"You have heard that it was said to the people long ago, 'You shall not murder, and anyone who murders will be subject to judgment.' But I tell you that anyone who is angry with a brother or sister will be subject to judgement."

Murder began in the heart with anger. The law addressed actions; Jesus addressed attitudes.

"You have heard that it was said, 'You shall not commit adultery.' But I tell you that anyone who looks at a woman lustfully has already committed adultery with her in his heart."

Adultery too began internally, with the wandering eye and the fantasising mind. No one was innocent by this standard.

His hyperbole shocked them: "If your right eye causes you to stumble, gouge it out and throw it away... If your right hand causes you to stumble, cut it off and throw it away."

They understood he wasn't literally calling for self-mutilation, but the severity of the language drove home the point: sin was serious, and half-measures wouldn't suffice.

He challenged their easy acceptance of divorce, their oath-making that tried to create loopholes for lying, and their carefully calibrated system of limited retaliation.

"You have heard that it was said, 'Eye for eye, and tooth for tooth.' But I tell you, do not resist an evil person. If anyone slaps you on the right cheek, turn to them the other cheek also."

This was too much for some. Not resist evil? Let people strike you without retaliation? The zealots in the crowd shifted uncomfortably. This wasn't the military Messiah they hoped for.

But Jesus pressed further into the impossible:

"You have heard that it was said, 'Love your neighbor and hate your enemy.' But I tell you, love your enemies and pray for those who persecute you, that you may be children of your Father in heaven."

Love your enemies. Pray for persecutors. In a land occupied by Rome, where collaboration and resistance were the only options anyone could imagine, Jesus offered a third way that transcended both.

"He causes his sun to rise on the evil and the good and sends rain on the righteous and the unrighteous. If you love those who love you, what reward will you get? Are not even the tax collectors doing that? And if you greet only your own people, what are you doing more than others? Do not even pagans do that?"

Then the standard that took everyone's breath away:

"Be perfect, therefore, as your heavenly Father is perfect."

Perfect. Complete. Whole. Not just better than average, not just more religious than the next person, but perfect like God himself. It was an impossible standard—which was exactly the point. No one could achieve this through their own effort. Something else was needed, something Jesus would provide, though they didn't understand that yet.

The sun climbed higher as Jesus continued teaching. Children grew restless, but their parents hushed them, not wanting to miss a word. This wasn't like the teaching in the synagogues, where familiar passages were dissected and debated. This was fresh water to thirsty souls, even if it sometimes burnt going down.

Jesus addressed their religious practices—giving to the needy, prayer, fasting—stripping away the performance aspect that had crept in:

"Be careful not to practice your righteousness in front of others to be seen by them. If you do, you will have no reward from your Father in heaven."

No trumpet announcements when giving charity. No long prayers on street corners. No disfiguring faces to show off fasting. True righteousness was between the individual and God, not a show for human applause.

Then he taught them to pray, giving them words that were shockingly simple and intimate:

"Our Father in heaven, hallowed be your name, your kingdom come, your will be done, on earth as it is in heaven. Give us today our daily bread. And forgive us our debts, as we also have forgiven our debtors. And lead us not into temptation, but deliver us from the evil one."

No elaborate formulas. No special religious language. Just a child talking to a father about needs both physical and spiritual. The simplicity was revolutionary.

But that forgiveness clause—that was challenging. Jesus elaborated: "For if you forgive other people when they sin against you, your heavenly Father will also forgive you. But if you do not forgive others their sins, your Father will not forgive your sins."

Forgiveness wasn't optional. It was the evidence of having truly received God's forgiveness. In a culture built on honour and shame, where grudges could last generations, this was radical.

Jesus moved on to address their relationship with material possessions: "Do not store up for yourselves treasures on earth, where moths and vermin destroy, and where thieves break in and steal. But store up for yourselves treasures in heaven, where moths and vermin do not destroy, and where thieves do not break in and steal. For where your treasure is, there your heart will be also."

In a subsistence economy where one bad harvest could mean starvation, this call to not hoard seemed impractical. But Jesus wasn't finished:

"No one can serve two masters. Either you will hate the one and love the other, or you will be devoted to the one and despise the other. You cannot serve both God and money."

Choose. That was the recurring theme. Choose whom you would serve, what you would value, and where you would invest your life.

Then came words that spoke directly to the anxiety that plagued rich and poor alike:

"Therefore I tell you, do not worry about your life, what you will eat or drink, or about your body, what you will wear. Is not life more than food, and the body more than clothes?"

He pointed to the birds circling overhead and the wildflowers dotting the hillside.

"Look at the birds of the air; they do not sow or reap or store away in barns, and yet your heavenly Father feeds them. Are you not much more valuable than they? Can any one of you by worrying add a single hour to your life?"

"And why do you worry about clothes? See how the flowers of the field grow. They do not labour or spin. Yet I tell you that not even Solomon in all his splendor was dressed like one of these. If that is how God clothes the grass of the field, which is here today and tomorrow is thrown into the fire, will he not much more clothe you—you of little faith?"

The phrase stung gently—"you of little faith." Not "you of no faith," but little faith. They believed, but not enough to let go of anxiety. They trusted, but not enough to stop grasping.

"So do not worry, saying, 'What shall we eat?' or 'What shall we drink?' or 'What shall we wear?' For the pagans run after all these things, and your heavenly Father knows that you need them. But seek first his kingdom and his righteousness, and all these things will be given to you as well."

Seek first the kingdom. Let everything else be secondary. Trust that the Father who dressed the flowers and fed the birds would care for his children. It was a call to radical reorientation of priorities.

"Therefore do not worry about tomorrow, for tomorrow will worry about itself. Each day has enough trouble of its own."

Live in the present. Trust for today. Let tomorrow's worries wait for tomorrow's grace. Simple words, but how hard to live by.

Jesus shifted to addressing how they related to one another:

"Do not judge, or you too will be judged. For in the same way you judge others, you will be judged, and with the measure you use, it will be measured to you."

He used humour to drive home the point:

"Why do you look at the speck of sawdust in your brother's eye and pay no attention to the plank in your own eye? How can you say to your brother, 'Let me take the speck out of your eye,' when all the time there is a plank in your own eye? You hypocrite, first take the plank out of your own eye, and then you will see clearly to remove the speck from your brother's eye."

The image was absurd—someone with a beam protruding from their eye trying to perform delicate surgery on another. Some in the crowd actually laughed, but it was laughter that led to conviction. They all knew people like that. They all were people like that.

But Jesus balanced this with a warning against indiscriminate acceptance:

"Do not give dogs what is sacred; do not throw your pearls to pigs. If you do, they may trample them under their feet and turn and tear you to pieces."

Discernment was needed. Not judgmentalism, but wisdom to recognise when someone wasn't ready to receive truth. The twelve apostles glanced at each other, beginning to understand that their future mission would require both bold proclamation and careful discretion.

Then came encouragement:

"Ask and it will be given to you; seek and you will find; knock and the door will be opened to you. For everyone who asks receives; the one who seeks finds; and to the one who knocks, the door will be opened."

This wasn't a blank check for wish fulfilment. In context, it was about seeking the kingdom, asking for the ability to live by these impossible standards, and knocking on heaven's door for the resources to be citizens of this upside-down kingdom.

Jesus made it personal again:

"Which of you, if your son asks for bread, will give him a stone? Or if he asks for a fish, will he give him a snake? If you, then, though you are evil, know how to give good gifts to your children, how much more will your Father in heaven give good gifts to those who ask him!"

Even flawed human fathers generally tried to care for their children. How much more would the perfect heavenly Father provide for his? But note what Jesus assumed—"though you are evil." Not basically good people with some flaws, but evil people capable of good. It was a stark anthropology that contradicted cultural assumptions about their own righteousness.

Then the golden rule, stated positively rather than in the negative form familiar from other teachers:

"So in everything, do to others what you would have them do to you, for this sums up the Law and the Prophets."

Not just "don't do to others what you don't want done to you," but actively do good, take initiative, treat others as you wish to be treated. The entire law could be summed up in this principle of active love.

As the teaching moved toward conclusion, Jesus' tone grew more urgent:

"Enter through the narrow gate. For wide is the gate and broad is the road that leads to destruction, and many enter through it. But small is the gate and narrow the road that leads to life, and only a few find it."

Choose. Again, choose. The default path led to destruction. The kingdom path was narrow, difficult, and countercultural. Following Jesus wouldn't be a mass movement of easy believism but a costly choice to swim against the current.

He warned against false prophets who would come looking religious but seeking to devour. The metaphor was stark:

"By their fruit you will recognise them. Do people pick grapes from thornbushes or figs from thistles? Likewise, every good tree bears good fruit, but a bad tree bears bad fruit."

Look at results, not rhetoric. Judge teachers by what their teaching produces in people's lives, not by how impressive they sound.

Then the sobering warning:

"Not everyone who says to me, 'Lord, Lord,' will enter the kingdom of heaven, but only the one who does the will of my Father who is in heaven. Many will say to me on that day, 'Lord, Lord, did we not prophesy in your name and in your name drive out demons and in your name perform many miracles?' Then I will tell them plainly, 'I never knew you. Away from me, you evildoers!'"

Religious activity, even miraculous religious activity, wasn't enough. What mattered was relationship—being known by Jesus—and obedience—doing the Father's will. The crowds stirred uneasily. How many of them were following Jesus for the miracles, the excitement, and the possibility of political revolution? How many were ready to actually live by these radical teachings?

Jesus concluded with a parable that would echo through the ages: "Therefore everyone who hears these words of mine and puts them into practice is like a wise man who built his house on the rock. The rain came down, the streams rose, and the winds blew and beat against that house; yet it did not fall, because it had its foundation on the rock. But everyone who hears these words of mine and does not put them into practice is like a foolish man who built his house on sand. The rain came down, the streams rose, and the winds blew and beat against that house, and it fell with a great crash."

The message was clear: hearing wasn't enough. Even agreeing wasn't enough. Only those who built their lives on obedience to Jesus' words would stand when the storms came. And storms would come—Jesus didn't promise easy lives to his followers. He promised unshakeable foundations.

When Jesus finished speaking, the silence was profound. Thousands of people sat in stunned contemplation. This wasn't what they had expected. Where was the call to arms against Rome? Where was the promise of prosperity for God's chosen people? Where was the restoration of David's throne in all its military glory?

Instead, they had heard a vision of a kingdom built on humility, mercy, and purity of heart. A kingdom where enemies were loved, cheeks were turned, and crosses were carried. A kingdom that started in the heart and worked its way out, rather than being imposed from the top down.

Matthew, the former tax collector, found himself weeping. He had spent years building his life on sand—accumulating wealth through collaboration with Rome, justifying his choices as pragmatic necessity. Now he saw clearly that everything he had valued was worthless. Only what Jesus offered had lasting value.

Simon the Zealot sat rigid, his mind racing. Love your enemies? Pray for persecutors? Everything in him had been trained for resistance, for holy war against the occupiers. But Jesus offered a different kind of resistance—a refusal to let enemies define you, a love that overcame evil with good. It was harder than violence. It required more courage than picking up a sword.

Peter turned to his brother Andrew. "Did you understand all that?"

Andrew shook his head slowly. "Not all. But enough to know everything has changed."

"How can anyone live like that?" Peter wondered aloud. "Be perfect as God is perfect? It's impossible."

John, overhearing, said quietly, "Maybe that's the point. Maybe we can't, on our own. Maybe that's why we need him."

As the crowd began to disperse, the reactions were as varied as the people. Some left troubled, sensing that following this teacher would cost everything. Some left exhilarated, feeling like they had finally heard truth that resonated in their souls. Some left angry, especially among the religious leaders who heard their entire system challenged.

But none left unchanged. The words had been too penetrating, too authoritative. This wasn't a teacher offering opinions for debate. This was someone speaking with the authority of heaven itself.

One scribe, gathering his robes to leave, muttered to his companion, "He teaches as one who has authority, not as we do." There was both admiration and fear in his voice. Their teaching was derivative, quoting this rabbi and that, building careful arguments from precedent. Jesus spoke as if he were the source, not just an interpreter.

As the twelve apostles gathered around Jesus, they looked different than they had that morning. The calling had been formal, but the teaching had shown them what they were called to. This wasn't going to be about gaining power or prestige. It was going to be about becoming different kinds of people entirely—salt and light in a decaying, dark world.

"Master," Peter said, speaking for them all, "we have much to learn."

Jesus smiled, the first time he'd done so during the entire discourse. "Yes, Simon. But you have begun. That's what matters—beginning. The Father will complete what he has started in you."

"Will you explain more?" Thomas asked. "Some of the parables, the meanings..."

"Everything will be explained in time," Jesus assured them. "For now, understand this: the kingdom of God is not coming with signs to be observed. It's not a political revolution or a military conquest. The kingdom of God is within you, among you, changing hearts one at a time until the whole world is leavened."

They began the walk back down the mountain as the sun reached its zenith. Behind them, small groups continued discussing what they had heard. Arguments broke out between those who embraced the teaching and those who rejected it. But the words had been planted like seeds. Some would fall on hard ground, some among thorns, and some in shallow soil. But some would find good ground and produce a harvest beyond imagining.

Halfway down, Jesus paused and looked back at the mount where he had taught. In years to come, it would be called the Mount of Beatitudes, and pilgrims would come trying to recapture the power of this moment. But the power wasn't in the place. It was in the words, and more than the words, in the One who spoke them.

"Did we choose correctly, Lord?" James asked, voicing the question several were thinking. "The twelve of us—are we the right ones?"

Jesus looked at each of them in turn—these imperfect men who would carry his perfect message. "You did not choose me," he said gently. "I chose you. And I chose correctly. Not because you're strong or wise or righteous, but because you're willing. That's all I need—willingness. I can work with that."

As they continued down toward Capernaum, Jesus began to explain some of the harder teachings to the twelve. They had front-row seats to the kingdom and access to the king himself. They would need it. The sermon had laid out the constitution of the kingdom. Now would come the harder work of learning to live by it.

"The old way was external," Jesus explained as they walked. "Do this, don't do that. Follow the rules and you're righteous. But I'm after something deeper—transformation from the inside out. Not just avoiding murder but dealing with anger. Not just avoiding adultery but purifying desire. Not just keeping oaths but being so truthful that oaths become unnecessary."

"But Master," Judas Iscariot said, "how can we change what's inside? We can control our actions, but our hearts..."

Jesus looked at him with particular compassion, knowing the battles that would rage in that heart. "You can't change your own heart, Judas. But the Father can. That's why I told you to ask, seek, and knock. You're not meant to do this in your own strength."

They reached the edge of Capernaum as the afternoon heat peaked. Crowds were already gathering at Peter's house, bringing sick relatives, hoping for healing. The sermon was over, but the ministry continued. Theory had to become practice.

"What do we do now?" Matthew asked, overwhelmed by both the teaching and the crowds.

"Now," Jesus said, "we live it. Day by day, choice by choice. You've heard the words. Now watch how I embody them. Learn not just from my teaching but from my life. See how I treat enemies and friends. Watch how I handle possessions and power. Notice how I pray and serve and love."

A leper approached, falling on his face. "Lord, if you are willing, you can make me clean."

The crowd backed away in horror. Lepers were unclean and untouchable. But Jesus reached out his hand and touched the man—a living demonstration of the radical love he had just preached.

"I am willing. Be clean."

The leprosy vanished instantly. The crowd gasped. But the twelve were beginning to understand—every miracle was a parable, every healing a glimpse of the kingdom. This was what it looked like when God's will was done on earth as in heaven.

As they entered Peter's house, his wife had prepared a simple meal. They reclined around the table, exhausted from the emotional and spiritual intensity of the day. But the learning continued.

"In the kingdom," Jesus said, breaking bread and passing it around, "everything is shared. The first are last, the last first. The greatest serves all. Power is expressed through sacrifice, not domination."

"It's so different," Andrew said. "Everything we've been taught, everything the world values—you're turning it all upside down."

"Or right-side up," Jesus corrected gently. "The world is upside down, twisted by sin and selfishness. I'm showing you how things were meant to be from the beginning. How they will be again when the kingdom comes in fullness."

"When will that be?" John asked eagerly.

Jesus smiled. "The kingdom is already here, John, growing like a seed, spreading like leaven. But its fullness... that's for the Father to know. Your job—our job—is to live as kingdom citizens now, showing the world a different way is possible."

As the meal ended and evening approached, the twelve dispersed to their homes or sleeping quarters. But Peter lingered, struggling with everything he had heard.

"Master, I want to follow you. I want to live by your teachings. But I know myself. I'm weak and impulsive. I speak before I think. I act before I pray. How can someone like me ever be perfect as the heavenly Father is perfect?"

Jesus placed a hand on the fisherman's shoulder. "Simon, do you think I chose you because you were already perfect? I chose you because you know you're not. That's the beginning of wisdom. The proud think they can achieve righteousness on their own. But you know you need help. That humility is the good soil where kingdom life can grow."

"But what if I fail? What if I let you down?"

Jesus looked at him with eyes that seemed to see future betrayals and future victories all at once. "You will fail, Simon. All of you will. But failure isn't final unless you make it so. The kingdom is built on grace, not performance. Fall down seven times, get up eight. That's the way of discipleship."

Peter nodded, somewhat comforted but still overwhelmed. As he headed to his own room where his wife waited, Jesus called after him.

"Simon?"

"Yes, Lord?"

"Today you were named an apostle. Someday you'll understand what that means—to be sent out with my authority, to speak my words, to do my works. It's a heavy calling. But remember—I don't send you alone. Where I send, I go. Where I call, I enable."

With that promise echoing in his mind, Peter went to rest. But sleep was hard to come by for any of the twelve that night. The Sermon on the Mount played over and over in their minds. The Beatitudes challenged everything they thought they knew about blessing. The call to perfection seemed impossibly high. The narrow way looked dauntingly difficult.

But they had seen something in Jesus as he taught—an authority that came from living every word he spoke. He wasn't calling them to something he hadn't already embodied. When he said, "Love your enemies," they remembered how he had treated the Pharisees who opposed him. When he said, "Don't worry about tomorrow," they recalled his perfect peace in every storm.

This wasn't just a new teaching. It was a new way of being human. And somehow, despite their fears and failures, they had been chosen to learn it and live it and eventually teach it to the world.

The kingdom of God had come near. The teacher had spoken. The revolution had begun—not with swords and political upheaval, but with transformed hearts and radical love.

As Capernaum slept, heaven watched. Angels who had announced this king's birth now saw him gathering his kingdom community. The ancient promise was being fulfilled in ways no one had expected. God was dwelling with his people again, not in a temple made of stone but in the person of a carpenter's son who spoke with the authority of eternity.

The Sermon on the Mount would echo through history, challenging every generation to choose—the wide way or the narrow, sand or rock, hearing or doing. But for the twelve apostles sleeping fitfully in Capernaum that night, it was intensely personal. They had been chosen. They had heard. Now they had to learn to live it.

Tomorrow would bring new crowds, new challenges, and new opportunities to see the kingdom in action. But today had been the turning point. Today, twelve ordinary men had been called to an extraordinary purpose. Today, the manifesto of the kingdom had been proclaimed from a Galilean hillside.

Today, everything had changed.

And in the quiet darkness, Jesus prayed for them—these imperfect men who would carry his perfect message. He prayed for their faith to grow, their love to deepen, and their courage to strengthen. He prayed for the multitudes who had heard his words, that the seeds would find good soil. He prayed for the religious leaders who had been offended, that their hearts might soften. But mostly, he thanked the Father for this day—for the privilege of speaking truth, for the joy of calling disciples, and for the beginning of the community that would outlast empires.

The Sermon on the Mount was finished. But the kingdom it described was just beginning.

Chapter 8: Faith of a Soldier

Marcus Quintus Gallus stood on the flat roof of his quarters, watching the sun paint Capernaum's skyline in shades of amber and blood. The Sea of Galilee stretched before him like hammered bronze, its surface disturbed only by the occasional fishing boat returning with the day's catch. He could smell the fish market from here—that peculiar mixture of salt, scales, and slow decay that had become as familiar as his own sweat.

Five years. Five years since Rome had stationed him in this backwater of the Empire, commanding a century of men tasked with keeping peace among a people who wanted nothing more than to see every Roman throat slit. Five years of careful diplomacy, calculated kindness, and the constant weight of being hated for the eagle on his standard.

"Dominus." The voice came from the stairs—Gaius, his optio, second in command, and the closest thing to a friend a centurion could afford. "The evening report."

Marcus didn't turn. "Summarise."

"Two disputes in the market. That pottery merchant, Mordechai, claimed Thaddeus the Greek shortchanged him. Settled with a warning to both. One drunk—a local fisherman, not one of ours. And..." Gaius paused. "The Zealot graffiti appeared again. On the tax collector's house."

"Same message?"

"Death to Rome and all who serve her." Creative, aren't they?"

Marcus finally turned, studying his subordinate. Gaius was a good soldier—brutal when necessary, restrained when possible. Like Marcus, he'd learnt that ruling through fear alone was like building on sand. It might stand for a season, but eventually, the foundation would shift.

"Double the night watch around the tax office," Marcus ordered. "But use local auxiliaries, not our men. Let them see their own people protecting the tax collector."

"The Jews protecting a publican?" Gaius raised an eyebrow. "They hate tax collectors more than they hate us."

"They hate the idea of Roman soldiers in their streets even more. Trust me on this."

Gaius saluted and turned to go, then hesitated. "How is he?"

Marcus's jaw tightened. "The same."

"The physician—"

"Has done all he can. As have the others." Marcus gripped the parapet, knuckles white against the stone. "Go. See to the watch."

Alone again, Marcus let his shoulders sag. Below, Capernaum went about its evening routines—women drawing water from wells, men closing shop shutters, and children called in from play by worried mothers. A normal evening in an abnormal situation: Jews living under Roman rule, trying to maintain their lives despite the boot on their necks.

He understood their hatred. Had their positions been reversed, had Jewish soldiers occupied his homeland, treated his people as sources of revenue and potential rebellion... yes, he would hate too. But understanding didn't make his job easier. If anything, it made it harder.

A soft moan from below drew his attention. Marcus descended the stairs quickly, his hobnailed boots echoing against stone. The sound had come from the small room adjacent to his quarters—a space that should have held armor and weapons but had been converted into a sickroom.

Dimitri lay on the narrow bed, his dark skin ashen with approaching death. Sweat beaded on his forehead despite the evening cool, and his breath came in shallow, painful gasps. The Greek physician had diagnosed it as a paralysis of the organs, spreading from his limbs inward. Soon it would reach his heart or lungs, and that would be the end.

Marcus knelt beside the bed, taking the younger man's hand. Dimitri's eyes fluttered open, focusing with effort.

"Dominus," he whispered. Even that single word seemed to cost him.

"Save your strength," Marcus commanded gently. "The new physician arrives tomorrow. From Tiberias. He's treated the governor himself."

Dimitri's lips curved in what might have been a smile. They both knew the truth—no physician could cure what ailed him. This creeping death had no remedy in all the empire's medical knowledge.

"Water?"

Marcus lifted a cup to Dimitri's lips, supporting his head with practiced care. How many times had he performed this simple service? A Roman centurion, commander of a hundred men, playing nursemaid to a slave. His fellow officers would laugh themselves sick if they knew.

But Dimitri had never been just a slave to him. The boy—though he was twenty-five now, Marcus still thought of him as a boy—had been with him for eight years. Purchased from a Syrian trader who'd beaten him half to death for some minor infraction, Dimitri had expected more of the same from his new master. Instead, he'd found something neither of them had quite understood at first.

Respect. Friendship. Love, though Marcus would never speak that word aloud.

In Rome, such relationships between master and slave were common enough, though rarely acknowledged publicly. Here in Judea, among a people whose law forbade such things, it was even more dangerous. But Marcus had never touched the boy and never would. What existed between them transcended the physical—a meeting of minds, a harmony of souls that asked nothing more than presence and loyalty.

Now that presence was fading, that loyalty being tested by death itself.

"The rabbi," Dimitri managed, his Greek accented with the musical tones of his homeland. "The one they talk about. Jesus."

"What about him?" Marcus kept his voice neutral. He'd heard the stories, of course. All of Capernaum buzzed with tales of the Nazarene teacher who'd made their city his base of operations. Miracles, they claimed. Healings. Demons are cast out with a word. Marcus had dismissed it as typical Jewish mysticism, no different from their endless prophets and would-be messiahs.

"They say... he healed Simon's mother. The fever. Gone in an instant."

"Fever is not paralysis," Marcus replied. "And stories grow in the telling. By next week, they'll claim he raised her from the dead."

"Perhaps." Dimitri closed his eyes. "But what if...?"

He didn't finish. He didn't need to. Marcus understood the unspoken question: What if the stories were true? What if this rabbi could do what no physician could?

"Rest," Marcus ordered, though his tone was gentle. "Save your strength."

He stayed until Dimitri's breathing deepened into sleep, then stepped out into the courtyard. The stars were emerging, foreign constellations that still felt wrong after all these years. In Rome, he'd known every star, every story written in the night sky. Here, even the heavens were alien.

"Dominus." Another voice, this time Lucius, the youngest of his legionaries. Barely eighteen, with the downy beard of a boy playing at being a man. "There's a delegation to see you. Jews. They say it's urgent."

Marcus sighed. There was always a delegation. Always something urgent. "How many?"

"Five. Elders, by their dress. They're waiting at the gate."

Elders meant politics. Politics meant careful navigation between Roman law and Jewish custom. Marcus straightened his tunic and checked that his gladius hung properly at his side. The sword was ceremonial here—he hadn't drawn it in anger in two years—but it served as a reminder of what backed his authority.

The delegation waited in the torch-lit entrance, five men with greying beards and the particular dignity of those who'd found ways to maintain their authority under occupation. Marcus recognised three of them: Jabez, the wool merchant; Eleazar, who oversaw the synagogue's funds; and old Tobias, who seemed to have his fingers in every business deal in Capernaum.

"Honoured sirs," Marcus greeted them in Aramaic. He'd worked hard to learn their language, knowing that every properly pronounced word was a small victory against their hatred. "How may Rome serve you this evening?"

The elders exchanged glances. It was Jabez who spoke, his merchant's voice smooth as oil. "Centurion, we come on a matter of mutual concern. The teacher, Jesus of Nazareth."

Marcus kept his face neutral. "What about him?"

"He returned to the city today. Already the crowds gather. By tomorrow, the streets will be impassable."

"And you want me to disperse them? Arrest him?" Marcus had played this game before. The Jewish leaders, threatened by any popular movement, often tried to use Roman authority to eliminate their rivals. But it was a dangerous game—suppress the wrong prophet, and riots could follow.

"No!" Eleazar stepped forward, and Marcus was surprised to see genuine distress on the old man's face. "We come to ask... that is, we hope..." He faltered, looking to his companions for support.

Tobias, ancient and direct, cut through the hesitation. "Your servant. The Greek boy. We know he's dying."

Marcus stiffened. "That's no concern of yours."

"But it is," Jabez insisted. "You have been... kind to us. Fair. When the procurator wanted to place images of the emperor in our synagogue, you argued against it. When the auxiliary troops desecrated our cemetery, you punished them. You learnt our language and respect our customs. You are not like other Romans."

"Get to the point."

"The teacher—Jesus—he truly heals. We have seen it with our own eyes. Not tricks or temporary remedies, but genuine healing. If you were to ask him..."

"You want me to beg help from a Jewish rabbi?" Marcus couldn't keep the incredulity from his voice. "I am a centurion of Rome. I don't bow to wandering preachers."

"Not bow," Eleazar said quietly. "Simply ask. What harm could it do? Your physicians have failed. Your servant worsens. If there's even a chance..."

Marcus studied them, these Jews who should hate him, coming in darkness to offer hope. He searched for the trick, the hidden agenda. Found none. Just five old men who'd somehow found compassion for their oppressor.

"Why?" he asked finally. "Why do you care if my servant lives or dies?"

Tobias answered, his voice carrying the weight of years. "Because you built us a synagogue."

The words hung in the air between them. The synagogue—Marcus's most controversial act as garrison commander. When the old building had collapsed during an earthquake three years ago, the Jewish community had despaired. They lacked funds for rebuilding, and Roman law certainly didn't mandate helping them.

But Marcus had seen an opportunity. A synagogue built with Roman money, Roman engineering, and Roman goodwill—it would be a bridge between occupier and occupied. His superiors had called him mad. His fellow officers had laughed. But he'd paid for it from his own funds, supervised the construction personally, and ensured every detail met Jewish requirements.

"You didn't have to," Jabez added. "You gained nothing from it. But you gave us back our centre, our heart. Let us try to give something back."

Marcus turned away, staring into the darkness beyond the torches. To ask help from a Jewish teacher—it went against everything Roman pride demanded. He was the conqueror here, the representative of the greatest empire the world had ever known. To humble himself before a carpenter's son from Nazareth...

But Dimitri was dying. And pride was a cold comfort when weighed against a life.

"Where is he?" Marcus asked without turning. "This is Jesus."

"Simon Peter's house, by the shore. But Centurion—" Eleazar hesitated. "Perhaps it would be better if we went on your behalf. A Roman soldier approaching might cause... complications."

Marcus almost agreed. It would be easier and cleaner. Let these Jews negotiate with their rabbi while he maintained his dignity. But something in him rebelled against the cowardice of it. If he was going to seek help, he would do it directly.

"No," he decided. "If I'm to ask, I'll ask myself. But not tonight. Tomorrow, when he teaches publicly. I won't skulk in shadows like a thief."

The elders exchanged more glances, communicating in that wordless way of men who'd known each other for decades.

"As you wish," Jabez said finally. "We will... prepare the way. Let him know you come in peace."

They left, and Marcus remained in the courtyard, wrestling with thoughts that chased each other like dogs. A Jewish healer. Miracles and wonders. It was everything his Roman education had taught him to dismiss as superstition.

He'd grown up worshipping the traditional gods—Jupiter, Mars, and Minerva. But his years in the legions had worn away that faith like water on stone. He'd seen too much death to believe in divine intervention, too much suffering to trust in celestial justice. The gods, if they existed, cared nothing for individual human pain.

But what if the Jews were right? What if their singular, invisible God actually acted in the world? What if this Jesus was truly his prophet, armed with power beyond Roman understanding?

"Dominus?" Gaius had returned, looking concerned. "Is all well?"

"Double the guard tomorrow," Marcus ordered. "The Nazarene teacher returns. There will be crowds."

"The zealots might use it as cover for mischief."

"Perhaps. But use a light hand. No violence unless absolutely necessary. These people come to hear teaching, not start riots."

Gaius frowned. "Since when do we care about Jewish preachers?"

"Since this one draws crowds that could turn ugly if mishandled. Do as I command."

His tone brooked no argument. Gaius saluted and withdrew, leaving Marcus alone with his thoughts and the weight of tomorrow's humiliation.

He returned to Dimitri's room and found the young man awake and struggling to breathe. The paralysis was advancing faster now, crushing his chest with invisible hands. Marcus helped him sit up, propping him with cushions.

"Tomorrow," Dimitri whispered. "You'll go?"

Marcus started. "You heard?"

"Voices carry. The elders... they honour you."

"They pity me. There's a difference."

"Is there?" Dimitri managed a ghost of his old smile. "Pride, Dominus. Always your weakness."

"And compassion is yours," Marcus countered. "Look where it's brought you."

He referred to the moment of their meeting—Dimitri taking a beating meant for a younger slave, protecting a child he didn't even know. That selfless courage had caught Marcus's attention and led to the purchase that changed both their lives.

"No regrets," Dimitri said. "Never regrets. But promise me—if this Jesus refuses..."

"He won't refuse." Marcus spoke with more confidence than he felt. "I'll make him understand."

"No." Dimitri's hand found his, grip weak but insistent. "No force. No threats. If he refuses, accept it. Promise me."

Marcus wanted to argue. He commanded a century of Rome's finest soldiers. He could compel this rabbi to act and could threaten consequences if he refused. But looking into Dimitri's eyes, he saw the plea there. Even dying, the young Greek clung to his principles.

"I promise," Marcus said quietly. "No force."

"Good." Dimitri relaxed against the cushions. "Tell me about Rome. About the gardens of Lucullus in spring."

So Marcus talked, painting word pictures of a city neither of them might see again. He described the gardens terraced down the Pincian Hill, the roses that bloomed in impossible profusion, and the fountains that caught sunlight like scattered jewels. He talked until Dimitri slept, then continued talking to himself, to the night, to whatever gods might be listening.

When dawn came, filtering through the window slats in bars of gold, Marcus hadn't slept. He'd spent the night in the chair beside Dimitri's bed, watching each laboured breath, wondering if it would be the last. But the young man clung to life with the same stubborn courage that had first drawn Marcus's attention.

"Dominus." Gaius appeared in the doorway, fully armed. "The men are positioned. The crowds are already gathering at the shore."

Marcus rose, his joints protesting the night's vigil. "How many?"

"Hundreds. Maybe more coming. They say he'll teach from a boat, so all can hear."

"Any signs of trouble?"

"None yet. The mood seems... peaceful. Expectant. Like they're waiting for something wonderful."

197

Marcus washed his face and straightened his uniform. The red cloak of his rank felt heavier than usual as he fastened it. His gladius, his vine staff of office, his medals of service—all the symbols of Roman authority that meant nothing if they couldn't save one dying young man.

"I'm going to the shore," he told Gaius. "You have command until I return."

"Dominus—" Gaius hesitated. "You're going to see him, aren't you? The Jewish healer."

"Yes."

"The men won't understand. A Roman centurion seeking help from—"

"The men follow orders," Marcus cut him off. "As do you. Or would you prefer I report your questioning of a superior officer?"

Gaius paled. "No, Dominus. I simply... I worry for your reputation."

"My reputation." Marcus laughed, a sound devoid of humour. "I abandoned that when I built their synagogue. What's one more humiliation?"

He left before Gaius could respond, taking only two guards—enough to mark his status, not enough to seem threatening. The streets of Capernaum were indeed crowded, streams of people flowing toward the waterfront. Marcus noted the diversity—not just local Jews, but travellers from throughout Galilee and beyond. He heard Greek, Egyptian, and even Latin among the languages.

The crowd parted before his Roman uniform like water before a ship's prow. Some faces showed fear, others resentment, and a few the careful blankness of those who'd learnt to survive by being invisible. But Marcus caught other expressions too—curiosity, even anticipation. The elders had done their work. Word had spread that the Roman centurion sought the healer.

At the shore, the press of bodies became almost impenetrable. Marcus could see fishing boats drawn up on the beach, one pushed slightly into the shallows. A figure sat in it—just a man, from this distance. Nothing remarkable about him. Certainly nothing that suggested divine power.

"Make way!" One of his guards began pushing through the crowd, hand on sword hilt.

"No," Marcus commanded. "We wait. Like everyone else."

So they stood in the morning sun, three Romans surrounded by hundreds of Jews, waiting for a carpenter to speak. The irony wasn't lost on Marcus. Five years ago, he would have laughed at the very idea. Now, with Dimitri dying and all hope exhausted, he waited with something that might have been faith if he'd known how to name it.

The teacher began to speak. His voice carried clearly across the water, strong without shouting, somehow reaching even those farthest back. He spoke in Aramaic, but slowly enough that Marcus could follow most of it. Stories, mostly. Simple tales about farmers and seeds, merchants and pearls, wedding feasts and lost coins. Nothing that seemed revolutionary. Nothing that explained the rapt attention of the crowd.

Yet there was something... Marcus found himself leaning forward, straining to catch every word. The stories were simple, yes, but layered with meaning. When Jesus spoke of a tiny seed becoming a great tree, he wasn't really talking about agriculture. When he described a woman searching for a lost coin, the joy in finding it transcended mere economics.

"The kingdom of heaven," Jesus said, and his voice took on a different quality—authority mixed with invitation. "It's among you. Within you. Closer than your breath, more precious than all the gold in Caesar's treasury."

A murmur ran through the crowd at the mention of Caesar. Bold words, potentially seditious. Marcus tensed, but Jesus continued without pause. "You've heard it said, 'Love your neighbour and hate your enemy.' But I tell you, love your enemies. Pray for those who persecute you. If a Roman soldier demands you carry his pack one mile, carry it two. If someone strikes your right cheek, offer the left."

The words hit Marcus like physical blows. He knew the law Jesus referenced—Roman soldiers could compel Jews to carry their equipment for one mile, no more. It was a hated symbol of occupation. Yet here was this teacher, telling his people not just to comply but to exceed the requirement. To transform compulsion into choice, hatred into love.

Madness. Beautiful, impossible madness.

The teaching continued, but Marcus found his attention drawn to the teacher himself. Jesus looked younger than expected—early thirties, perhaps. His hands bore the calluses of manual labour, his skin the dark tan of one who worked outdoors. When he gestured, it was with the economy of movement that came from years of precise craft. A builder's hands, shaping invisible materials into structures of thought.

His face... Marcus had seen many faces in his years of service. Politicians with their calculated smiles, generals with their iron determination, and emperors with their assumption of divinity. But he'd never seen a face like this. It held authority without arrogance, compassion without weakness, and joy without naivety. When Jesus laughed at something someone called out, it was rich and genuine. When his expression turned serious, it carried the weight of mountains.

But it was the eyes that held Marcus. Even from this distance, they seemed to see everything, everyone. Several times, Marcus could have sworn Jesus looked directly at him, seeing past the uniform to the desperate man within. Impossible, of course. Trick of the light and angle. Yet the feeling persisted.

The sun climbed higher. The crowd showed no signs of dispersing. If anything, it grew as latecomers arrived. Marcus saw the elders from last night, positioned where Jesus could see them. They kept glancing back at him, clearly waiting for him to act.

But how did one approach a prophet? Marcus had negotiated with kings, dined with governors, and received commendations from the emperor himself. Yet none of that prepared him for this moment. To walk through this Jewish crowd, to publicly seek help from their teacher—it would be crossing a line that could never be uncrossed.

"Dominus." One of his guards, nervous. "The heat. Perhaps we should—"

"Quiet."

Jesus was speaking again, something about forgiveness. About debts cancelled, slates wiped clean. He told a story of a servant who owed an impossible sum, forgiven by his master, who then refused to forgive a fellow servant a tiny debt. The crowd murmured recognition—they knew about debt, about the crushing weight of owing what could never be repaid. "So my heavenly Father will do to you," Jesus concluded, "if you do not forgive your brother from your heart."

From the heart. Not just words, not just ritual, but genuine release of grievance. Marcus thought of every slight he'd catalogued, every offence he'd stored away. His mental ledger of debts owed stretched back years. To forgive from the heart—what would that even look like?

The teaching seemed to be winding down. Jesus spoke with those in the nearest boats, laughing at something Peter said. The big fisherman gestured wildly, nearly capsizing his vessel, which drew more laughter. Such ordinary men, these followers of his. Fishermen, tax collectors, zealots. Not the educated elite who usually surrounded religious teachers. Men who worked with their hands, who knew struggle and sweat.

Men not unlike the legionaries Marcus commanded.

Now. It had to be now, before courage failed entirely. Marcus stepped forward, and the crowd parted again. This time, though, the movement rippled outward, drawing attention. Heads turned. Voices fell silent. A Roman centurion approaching the teacher—this was unexpected drama.

Marcus kept his eyes fixed on Jesus, peripherally aware of the disciples tensing. Peter's hand moved to his belt, where fishermen kept their gutting knives. Another—one of the sons of thunder, James or John—half-rose from his seat. They saw a threat approaching their master.

But Jesus raised a hand slightly, and they stilled. He watched Marcus come with those penetrating eyes, expression unreadable. When Marcus stopped at the water's edge, perhaps twenty feet from the boat, silence had fallen over the entire gathering. Hundreds of people held their breath, waiting to see what would happen when Rome met Galilee.

Marcus had prepared words. Careful phrases that maintained dignity while requesting aid. All of them died in his throat. Standing there, his uniform marking him as the oppressor, he found only simple truth would serve.

"Teacher," he said in Aramaic, his voice carrying in the silence. "I have a servant who is dear to me. He lies at home paralysed, suffering terribly."

There. Said. The admission of need, of powerlessness. He waited for laughter, for rejection, for the scorn that was every conquered people's right toward their conquerors.

Instead, Jesus leaned forward slightly, interest sharpening his features. "I will come and heal him."

The simple statement hit Marcus like a cavalry charge. No negotiation, no extraction of promises or payment. Just immediate willingness to enter a Roman house to help a Roman soldier. The crowd stirred, surprised as Marcus at this ready acceptance.

"Lord—" The word came unbidden. Not a teacher now, but something more. "Lord, I do not deserve to have you under my roof."

The words poured out, shaped by sudden understanding. This wasn't just about ritual purity, about a Jew entering a Gentile home. This was about authority—real authority, not the kind that came from Rome's legions.

"But say the word, and my servant will be healed."

Marcus drew a breath, finding an analogy that might bridge their worlds. "For I myself am a man under authority, with soldiers under me. I tell this one, 'Go,' and he goes; and that one, 'Come,' and he comes. I say to my servant, 'Do this,' and he does it."

He gestured to his guards, who straightened automatically at the attention. "I understand command. I recognise it in you. You need not come to my house; you need not touch him. Speak your word here, and I know—I know—it will be done."

Silence stretched. Jesus stared at him, and Marcus saw something shift in those remarkable eyes. Surprise? Respect? Joy? All of those and something more, something that made Marcus want to kneel despite the hundreds watching.

Then Jesus turned to the crowd, voice carrying new energy. "Truly I tell you, I have not found such faith even in Israel!"

The words rang across the water. Such faith. A Roman centurion commended for faith by a Jewish prophet. The crowd buzzed with discussion, some pleased, others clearly disturbed by the praise given to their oppressor.

Jesus continued, his voice taking on prophetic weight. "I say to you that many will come from the east and the west and will take their places at the feast with Abraham, Isaac, and Jacob in the kingdom of heaven. But the subjects of the kingdom will be thrown outside, into the darkness, where there will be weeping and gnashing of teeth."

Hard words. Marcus heard the warning in them—privilege of birth meant nothing if it didn't produce faith. Being Abraham's descendant, being Roman, or being anything external counted less than the internal reality of trust.

Jesus looked back at him, and now the joy was unmistakable. "Go! Let it be done just as you believed it would."

That was all. No gestures, no incantations, no visible display of power. Just words spoken with quiet certainty. Yet Marcus felt something shift in the universe, as if a cosmic door had opened and closed in the space between heartbeats.

"Thank you," he managed, the words pathetically inadequate. "Thank you, Lord."

He turned to go, then stopped. The crowd watched, waiting. Marcus reached for his purse, heavy with silver. Payment for services rendered, the Roman way.

"No." Jesus's voice stopped him. "No payment. What God gives freely cannot be bought."

Marcus nodded, understanding. This wasn't a transaction. It was a gift, pure and unearned. He saluted—not the casual gesture given to civilians, but the crisp military honour offered to superior officers. Then he turned and walked back through the crowd, guards falling in behind.

The journey back to his quarters seemed both endless and instant. Marcus's mind raced, replaying every word, every moment. Had it worked? Could words spoken at a distance truly heal? Part of him wanted to run, to confirm or deny. Part feared what he might find.

The streets cleared before them, but Marcus caught expressions he hadn't seen before. Wonder. Speculation. A few smiles from those who'd witnessed the exchange. The Roman who'd built their synagogue had humbled himself before their teacher and been commended for faith. The implications would ripple through Capernaum for days.

At his quarters, Marcus barely acknowledged the salute of the gate guards. He took the stairs two at a time, hobnailed boots ringing against stone. The door to Dimitri's room stood open, and Marcus could hear voices within. He burst through—

And stopped so suddenly his guards nearly collided with him.

Dimitri sat upright in bed, colour returned to his cheeks, examining his own hands with wonder. The household servants clustered around, some weeping, others laughing. Old Sarah, who'd been with Marcus since his first posting, pressed her hands to her mouth in speechless joy.

"Dominus!" Dimitri's voice was strong, clear, and free of the laboured wheeze that had marked recent days. "I felt it happen. Like fire, but not burning. Like water, but from inside. Everything locked suddenly freed, everything dying suddenly alive. I tried to tell them you'd gone to the healer, but they wouldn't believe—"

Marcus crossed the room in three strides and pulled the younger man into an embrace that violated every social convention. He didn't care. Dimitri was alive, whole, and restored. The miracle he'd dared hope for had happened. "Stand up," he ordered, pulling back. "Let me see."

Dimitri swung his legs over the bed's edge and stood. No trembling, no weakness. He took a few experimental steps, then laughed—a bright, joyous sound that Marcus hadn't heard in months.

"I can feel everything," Dimitri marvelled. "Every toe, every finger. Look!" He bent, touched his toes, straightened, and stretched his arms overhead. Simple movements that would have been impossible an hour ago.

"What time?" Marcus demanded. "When exactly did this happen?"

Sarah answered, voice trembling. "Just now, Dominus. Perhaps a quarter of an hour passed. He gasped, arched like a bent bow, and then... then this."

A quarter of an hour. Precisely when Jesus had spoken. "Let it be done just as you believed it would." And it had been. Across distance, through walls, past every barrier of nation and custom and possibility.

"The rabbi," Dimitri said, understanding dawning. "You found him. You asked.

"I asked." Marcus sank into the chair he'd occupied all night, suddenly exhausted. "And he... spoke. That's all. Spoke words, and you were healed."

"Tell me everything."

So Marcus did, while the servants dispersed to spread the news and his guards stood bewildered in the doorway. He described the teaching, the approach, and the exchange of words. When he mentioned commending him for faith, Dimitri smiled.

"Faith," he repeated. "You, who mock every god and prophet."

"I didn't mock him." Marcus rubbed his face. "I couldn't. There's something about him, Dimitri. Authority, yes, but more. Like he sees into the heart of things, past all pretence. When he looked at me, I felt..."

"What?"

"Known. Completely known, and not found wanting despite everything." Marcus laughed shakily. "I'm not making sense."

"You're making perfect sense." Dimitri sat on the bed's edge, facing him. "You encountered the divine. It changes a man."

"He's just a teacher. A healer."

"Is he?" Dimitri tilted his head. "A teacher whose words carry across distance? A healer who cures with command alone? What if he's more?"

"The Jews claim he's their Messiah."

"And what do you claim?"

Marcus had no answer. His world, ordered and rational, built on Roman discipline and Greek philosophy, had cracked like an egg. Through the cracks, light poured in—terrible, wonderful light that illuminated everything differently.

"I need to think," he said finally. "And you need to eat. Build back strength. Sarah! Bring food. Real food, not invalid's gruel."

The household erupted into motion, joy spreading like contagion. Within minutes, Dimitri was surrounded by offerings—bread, oil, olives, cheese, and watered wine. He ate with an appetite that brought tears to old Sarah's eyes.

Marcus stepped onto the roof, seeking air and clarity. Below, Capernaum went about its business, but he caught signs of disturbance. People gathered in small groups, gesturing excitedly. The news was spreading—the Roman's servant healed, the centurion's faith commended.

What had he set in motion?

"Dominus." Gaius appeared, looking troubled. "I heard... that is, the men are saying..."

"It's true. All of it. The teacher healed Dimitri with words alone."

Gaius stared. "That's not possible."

"I would have agreed this morning. Now..." Marcus shrugged. "Now I know different."

"The men won't understand. Rome doesn't bow to provincial magic workers."

"Not magic." The certainty in Marcus's voice surprised him. "Something else. Something real as steel, just... different."

"Different." Gaius spat over the parapet. "This will cause problems, Dominus. The governor won't appreciate Roman officers seeking help from Jewish prophets. And the priests in Jerusalem—they already view this Jesus with suspicion. If they think he has Roman support..."

Politics. Always politics. Marcus had navigated those waters for years, balancing interests and managing perceptions. But today, faced with a miracle, such concerns seemed as petty as children's squabbles.

"Let me worry about the governor," he said. "Your concern is the garrison. Any man who speaks against what happened today will answer to me personally."

"And if they ask, what did happen? How do I explain the impossible?"

Marcus turned to face his second in command. "Tell them a Jewish teacher showed more power than all our physicians. Tell them words spoken in faith accomplished what Roman medicine couldn't. Tell them whatever you like, Gaius. But don't tell them it didn't happen. I won't have truth buried for convenience."

Gaius saluted stiffly and withdrew. Marcus knew he'd created a problem and knew there would be consequences. Roman officers weren't supposed to acknowledge power outside the Empire's structure. But denying Dimitri's healing would be like denying the sun—foolish and futile.

Evening came, painting shadows long across Capernaum. Marcus ate with Dimitri for the first time in weeks, watching the younger man's enthusiasm for simple food. They talked of inconsequential things—garrison gossip, local politics, anything but the miracle that sat between them like a third presence.

Finally, as lamps were lit against gathering darkness, Dimitri set down his cup. "What will you do?"

"About what?"

"About him. The teacher. You can't pretend today didn't happen."

"I'm not pretending anything." Marcus pushed food around his plate. "I'm grateful. Profoundly grateful. But that doesn't mean..."

"Doesn't mean what? That you'll follow him? Listen to his teaching? Consider that maybe, just maybe, he's exactly what he claims to be."

"And what does he claim to be?"

Dimitri smiled. "That's what you need to find out, isn't it?"

Later, alone in his chamber, Marcus stood at the window watching stars emerge. The same stars that had witnessed his desperate vigil now looked down on joy he couldn't quite process. Dimitri lived. The impossible had become possible through words Marcus barely understood.

"For I myself am a man under authority..."

His own words echoed back. He'd recognised command in Jesus and had gambled everything on that recognition. And he'd been right. But what kind of authority commanded disease itself? What kind of power flowed through simple speech to heal across distance?

Not Roman authority, based on force and law. Not Greek philosophy, based on reason and argument. Something older, deeper, more fundamental. Authority that spoke and expected reality itself to conform.

In the beginning, the Jewish texts said, God spoke and worlds came to be. "Let there be light," and there was light. Marcus had always dismissed such stories as primitive metaphor. But what if they pointed to truth? What if that same creative power walked the shores of Galilee, taught from fishing boats, and healed Roman servants?

The thought should have terrified him. Instead, he felt something like peace. The universe was larger than Rome's understanding and contained mysteries Caesar couldn't conquer. And somehow, impossibly, a Jewish teacher had looked at a Roman soldier and found faith worth commending.

Tomorrow would bring complications. Word would spread to Tiberias, to Jerusalem, and eventually to Rome itself. The delicate balance Marcus maintained would shift. But tonight, with Dimitri sleeping peacefully in the next room, such worries seemed as distant as the stars.

Marcus had asked for a miracle and received it. More than that—he'd been invited into something larger than healing. "Many will come from east and west," Jesus had said. A kingdom that transcended birthright, that welcomed Romans alongside Jews, that valued faith over ethnicity.

Madness to consider. Treason, possibly. But Marcus had felt the power in those words and had seen their effect in Dimitri's restoration. Whatever this kingdom was, wherever this authority originated, it was as real as Roman steel and more enduring.

He'd been a man under authority his entire adult life. Tomorrow, he would still command his century, still serve Rome's interests in this corner of the Empire. But something fundamental had shifted. He'd encountered an authority that made Rome look small, a kingdom that made the Empire seem temporary.

And strangest of all, that authority had looked at him—foreign oppressor, symbol of everything Jews hated—and found something worth praising. Faith. Simple trust that power could flow through words, that compassion could cross every human boundary.

Marcus, Centurion of Rome, had met something greater than Caesar. And in meeting it, he had discovered he was more than uniform and rank. He was a man who could recognise truth when it stood before him, who could ask and receive, and who could believe despite every rational argument against belief.

The stars wheeled overhead, indifferent and eternal. But Marcus no longer felt alone beneath them. Somewhere in Capernaum, a teacher slept who carried heaven's authority in his voice. Somewhere, disciples pondered their master's praise of an enemy. Somewhere, the kingdom of heaven advanced one healing, one heart at a time.

Tomorrow would bring what it brought. But tonight, Marcus Quintus Gallus, soldier of Rome, slept at peace. He'd witnessed the impossible. He'd been commended for faith. And in his quarters, living proof of a miracle breathed easily, deeply, and fully alive.

It was enough. More than enough.

It was everything.

Chapter 9: Death Has No Victory

The funeral procession wound its way down from Nain like a river of grief, black-clad mourners flowing between the white limestone houses toward the tombs carved into the hillside below. The afternoon sun beat down mercilessly, drawing the scent of myrrh and aloes from the wrapped body carried on its wooden bier, mixing with the dust kicked up by hundreds of shuffling feet.

Miriam bat Samuel walked behind her son's body like a woman already dead.

She had no tears left. They had all been spent in the three days since Yonah's fever had broken, not in healing but in death, taking with it her last anchor to this world. First her husband, Micah, taken by the Romans' building accident two winters past. Now Yonah, her only child, her laughing boy who had grown into a man she'd been so proud of—gone at nineteen, leaving her with nothing but memories and the terrible weight of tomorrow.

The professional mourners wailed around her, their practiced keening rising and falling in ancient rhythms. She envied them their artifice. Their grief would end when the last coin was placed in their palms. Hers would end only when the earth finally claimed her too, and perhaps—if the Almighty was more merciful than He had thus far proven—she would find her men waiting in Abraham's bosom.

"The Lord gives and the Lord takes away," Rabbi Eleazar intoned from somewhere ahead, his voice carrying over the lamentations. "Blessed be the name of the Lord."

The words scraped against Miriam's heart like broken pottery. What had the Lord given her that He had not snatched back with interest? A husband to love—taken. A son to cherish—taken. Even the humble carpentry shop that had been their livelihood would now pass to Micah's brother, leaving her to subsist on charity, that bitter bread of the destitute widow.

"Steady, Miriam." Her sister Rachel's arm tightened around her waist. "Just a little further."

A little further to what? To watch them seal Yonah into the same tomb where Micah lay? To return to an empty house that would echo with the absence of his voice, his footsteps, and his gentle teasing? To face the years ahead alone, dependent on the grudging kindness of relatives who had their own mouths to feed?

The path curved, and the tombs came into view—a row of caves sealed with rolling stones, the resting places of Nain's dead for generations uncounted. The one at the end stood open, waiting. Micah's tomb. Soon to be Yonah's tomb. Eventually, if God showed that much mercy, her tomb as well.

The bearers slowed as they approached the final turn, adjusting their grip on the bier's poles. Miriam forced herself to look at the wrapped form of her son one last time. So still. Yonah had never been still in life, always moving, always working, his hands shaping wood as his father had taught him. Those hands were bound now, pressed against his sides beneath the linen strips.

"Mother?"

For a moment, her heart seized, thinking she'd heard—but no. It was just the wind, or her mind finally breaking under the weight of loss. Yonah would never call her mother again. Never bring her the first figs from the tree behind their house. Never marry the baker's daughter; he'd been too shy to court properly. Never give her grandchildren to brighten her declining years.

The procession had stopped. Miriam looked up, confused. They hadn't reached the tombs yet. Why were they—

A group of travellers blocked the path ahead. No, not blocked—they had simply been walking up as the funeral procession walked down, and now the two groups met where the path narrowed between two large sycamore trees. The travellers should have stepped aside and allowed the dead to pass. It was custom, it was respect, it was—

The man at the front of the travelling group wasn't moving aside.

Miriam blinked, trying to focus through her exhaustion. He was young, perhaps thirty years old, with the sun-darkened skin of one who lived beneath open skies. His clothes marked him as neither rich nor destitute—a simple tunic and cloak, dust-covered from the road. But it was his eyes that held her. Dark eyes that looked at her—not at the crowd, not at the spectacle of grief, but at *her*—with such profound compassion that she felt her knees threaten to buckle.

"Who dares impede the dead?" Rabbi Eleazar demanded, pushing forward through the crowd. "Stand aside! Have you no respect?"

217

But the stranger wasn't looking at the rabbi. He was still looking at Miriam, and in his gaze she saw something that made no sense. Understanding. As though he knew the exact shape and weight of her loss. As though he felt it too.

He moved then, not aside but forward, toward the bier where Yonah lay. The bearers looked at each other uncertainly. The mourners' wailing faltered, dying into confused murmurs.

"Don't weep," the stranger said, and his voice carried despite its gentleness, reaching her across the crowd as clearly as if he stood beside her.

Don't weep? The words were so absurd she almost laughed. Or would have, if she remembered how. Don't weep for her only son? Don't weep for the end of her family line, her security, her purpose? Don't weep for the empty chair, the unused tools, and the silence where laughter should be.

But the stranger had reached the bier now, and he did something that stopped every voice, every movement, and every breath.

He touched it.

The gasp that ran through the crowd was like wind through grain. To touch the dead was to become unclean, to separate oneself from the community for seven days. No observant Jew would willingly—

"Young man," the stranger said, his hand resting on the wrapped form, "I say to you, arise."

The words fell into the silence like stones into still water, sending ripples of shock through the crowd. What was he doing? What kind of cruel mockery—

The body on the bier moved.

A convulsion ran through the wrapped form, the linen strips straining. Then, as the crowd watched in stunned disbelief, Yonah sat up.

His movements were awkward, constrained by the burial wrappings, but unmistakably, impossibly alive. His head turned, wrapped as it was, seeming to seek something. Then his voice, muffled by the cloth but undeniably *his* voice:

"Mother?"

The same word Miriam had imagined on the wind, but real now, present, impossible, and true.

Hands flew to help him—the stranger's companions moving with practiced efficiency to unwrap the cloths from his face and arms. As the linen fell away, revealing Yonah's confused but living face, Miriam's legs finally gave out. But she didn't hit the ground. The stranger caught her, supported her, and guided her to her son, who was even now being helped down from the bier, his legs unsteady but growing stronger with each moment.

"Yonah?" Her voice was a whisper, a prayer, and a question all at once.

"Mother, I..." Her son looked around, blinking in the afternoon sunlight. "I was... there was darkness, and then... warmth. Like someone calling me back from very far away." His eyes found the stranger. "You called me back."

The stranger smiled—a smile that held joy and sorrow in equal measure—and gently took Yonah's hand, placing it in Miriam's. "He is yours," he said simply. "As he always was."

Miriam clutched her son's warm, living hand and felt the frozen places in her heart crack open. The tears came then—not the bitter tears of grief but something else entirely. Tears of wonder. Of gratitude too large for words. Of joy so sharp it was almost pain.

Around them, chaos had erupted. Some people had fallen to their knees. Others pressed forward, trying to touch Yonah, to confirm with their own hands that he was truly alive. The professional mourners stood silent, their wails forgotten, their purpose suddenly obsolete.

"A prophet!" someone shouted. "A great prophet has risen among us!"

"God has visited His people!" another voice cried.

But Miriam barely heard them. She was touching her son's face, feeling the warmth of his skin and the pulse at his throat. He was thinner than he'd been—three days of death had left their mark—but he was *here*. The eyes that looked back at her were confused but clear, alive with questions and wonder.

"I remember being sick," Yonah said slowly. "The fever... I remember you singing to me the lullabies from when I was small. And then... nothing. Until his voice. He looked again at the stranger, who was now being pressed by the crowd, everyone wanting to touch him, to speak to him, to understand what they had witnessed.

"Who is he?" Miriam asked one of the stranger's companions, a weathered fisherman by his look.

"Jesus of Nazareth," the man replied, his own eyes wide with awe despite clearly having seen wonders before. "My master. He... he does things like this. Though never..." He shook his head. "Three days dead. The boy was three days dead."

Jesus. The name meant 'The Lord saves.' Miriam looked at the man who had given her back her son, who had touched death and commanded it to retreat. He was speaking to the crowd now, his words carrying despite the tumult:

"Do not be amazed at this. The hour is coming when all who are in the tombs will hear the voice of the Son of Man and come out. Those who have done good to the resurrection of life, and those who have done evil to the resurrection of judgement."

The words should have sounded like madness. A man claiming authority over death itself? Claiming that all the dead would one day rise at his command? But Miriam had just watched him prove that authority. Her son stood beside her, solid and real and alive, because this Jesus had spoken and death had fled like darkness before dawn.

Rabbi Eleazar pushed through to them, his face a battlefield of emotions—awe warring with scepticism, joy with theological concern. He reached out tentatively to touch Yonah's arm, jerking back as if burnt when he felt living flesh.

"How?" he whispered. "The boy was dead. I myself confirmed it. No breath, no heartbeat, the colour of death upon him. We wrapped him according to the law. How?"

"Does it matter how?" Miriam asked, surprising herself with the strength in her voice. "My son was dead, and now he lives. Is this not the work of the Almighty?"

"But through this man?" The rabbi's eyes found Jesus, who was now healing others in the crowd—a blind beggar's eyes opening, a lame woman's legs straightening. "Who is he to wield such power? By what authority?"

"By the authority of the One who sent me," Jesus said, apparently having heard despite the distance and noise. "I do nothing on my own, but only what I see the Father doing. For the Father loves the Son and shows him all that he himself is doing."

The crowd had swelled as word spread with impossible speed through Nain. The funeral procession had become something else entirely—a celebration, a marvel, a gathering of the bewildered and amazed. Some ran to spread the news. Others stood rooted, unable to process what their eyes had seen.

Yonah swayed slightly, and Miriam immediately supported him. "You need food," she said, maternal instincts overriding wonder. "And rest. Real rest, not..." She couldn't finish the sentence. Not death-sleep. Not the rest of the grave from which he'd been called back.

"Come," Rachel said, finally finding her voice. "Both of you. Let's get him home."

But Yonah pulled back gently. "Wait. Please. I need..." He moved toward Jesus, who turned as if expecting him.

The crowd quieted as the young man who had been dead approached the one who had raised him. Yonah stood there for a moment, seeming to search for words. Then, with the simple directness that had always been his nature, he knelt.

"I was dead," he said, loud enough for all to hear. "I know it as surely as I know I now live. There was darkness, and silence, and a sense of waiting. And then your voice, calling me back. Calling me by name, though we've never met." He looked up at Jesus. "Why? Why me? Why did you call me back?"

Jesus reached down and raised him to his feet with gentle hands. "Because your mother's tears moved my heart," he said. "Because death is an enemy that will one day be destroyed entirely. Because the Kingdom of God is breaking into this world, pushing back darkness, reclaiming what was lost." He paused, his eyes moving from Yonah to Miriam. "And because it is not yet your time. You have work still to do, life still to live, and love still to give and receive."

"What work?" Yonah asked eagerly. "Tell me and I'll do it. My life is yours—you gave it back to me."

But Jesus smiled and shook his head. "Your life is your own, to live in the light of what you've experienced. Love your mother. Serve your community. When you marry and have children, tell them that death is not the final word. That is work enough for any man."

He turned to address the crowd, his voice carrying to the farthest edges. "You have seen a sign today, but do not seek after signs. Seek after the God who gives them. The same power that called this young man from the tomb is available to call you from other kinds of death—death of spirit, death of hope, death of purpose. The Kingdom of God is near. Repent and believe the good news."

Some in the crowd pressed forward with questions, with requests for healing, and with declarations of faith. But Jesus's companions—disciples, Miriam heard someone call them—began to create a path through the crowd. Their master had other places to go, other lives to touch, and other deaths to defy.

As they prepared to leave, Jesus paused once more before Miriam. This time, she was the one who knelt.

"Lord," she said, the title coming unbidden but feeling right, "I had nothing left. No hope, no future, no reason to draw another breath. You've given me back my son, but more than that. You've given me back faith that the Almighty sees, that He cares, that our tears are not ignored in heaven."

"Your faith is beautiful," Jesus said softly, helping her rise. "But know this—even if I had not come today, even if Yonah had remained in the tomb until the final day, God's love for you would be unchanged. He treasures every tear, knows every sorrow, and holds every broken heart. What you've seen today is just a glimpse of the restoration that is coming."

He looked around at the crowd, at the abandoned funeral bier, and at the professional mourners who had begun to sing—not dirges now but psalms of praise.

"Tell them what you have seen," he said to all within hearing. "Tell them that the prophet Isaiah spoke truly: 'He will swallow up death forever, and the Lord God will wipe away tears from all faces.' That day is coming. But it begins now, wherever faith makes room for it."

And then he was walking away, his disciples flanking him, moving on down the road that led away from Nain. The crowd parted to let them pass, many calling out blessings, some following, others standing stunned and silent. Miriam watched until they disappeared around a bend in the road, this strange rabbi and his unlikely followers who had transformed the worst day of her life into something beyond comprehension. Then she turned to her son—her living, breathing, impossible son—and took his face in her hands.

"Are you truly here?" she whispered. "Tell me I'm not dreaming."

"You're not dreaming," Yonah assured her, covering her hands with his own. "Though I feel as if I might be. Mother, I was dead. I know it sounds mad, but I remember... not darkness exactly, but absence. Like sleeping without dreams. And then warmth, and light, and a voice calling me back. His voice."

"The neighbours will think we've all gone mad," Rachel said, but she was smiling through her tears. "The whole town saw him laid out for burial. They brought funeral gifts. They—" She stopped, laughing suddenly. "We'll have to return the funeral gifts!"

The absurdity of it broke through the otherworldly atmosphere, and suddenly they were all laughing—Miriam, Yonah, Rachel, the cousins, and friends who had gathered to mourn and now didn't know whether to dance or flee. The professional mourners had given up entirely and were asking anyone who would listen what exactly they were supposed to do now. Did one get paid for a funeral that became a resurrection?

"Home," Miriam said finally, wiping tears of mirth from her eyes. "Let's go home. Yonah needs food and rest, and I..." She paused, trying to find words for what she needed. "I need to hold my son and know this is real."

They made their way back up the path to Nain, but it was a very different procession than the one that had descended. Where before there had been wails, now there was wonder. Where grief had weighted every step, now joy gave them wings. The news had already reached the town, and people poured from their houses to see for themselves.

"Yonah! It's really him!"

"Miriam, your son! Your son lives!"

"The prophet from Nazareth—he touched the bier and spoke, and the dead boy sat up!"

"God has visited His people! Blessed be the name of the Lord!"

The words Rabbi Eleazar had spoken over Yonah's body—words that had seemed like mockery then—now rang with truth. The Lord had given. The Lord had taken away. And then, impossibly, the Lord had given again. Blessed be His name indeed.

Their small house looked exactly as Miriam had left it that morning, when she'd forced herself to wash and dress for her son's burial. Yonah's tools still lay on his workbench, a half-finished cabinet waiting for hands that should never have touched wood again. His cloak hung on its peg. His cup sat on the table.

Yonah walked through the space like a man relearning the world. He touched everything—walls, furniture, tools—as if confirming their solidity. When he reached his workbench, he picked up a piece of olive wood he'd been carving, turning it over in his hands with wonder.

"I thought I'd never..." He set it down carefully, then turned to his mother. "How long was I gone?"

"Three days," Miriam said softly. "Three days that felt like three years."

"The fever," he said, sitting heavily on a bench. "I remember the fever. It came on so fast. One moment I was working, the next I could barely stand. And you were there, weren't you? Cooling my face with water, singing the old songs."

"I never left your side," Miriam confirmed, sitting beside him. "I prayed every prayer I knew. Made every bargain I could think of. Promised God anything if He would just let you stay." Her voice broke. "But the fever took you anyway. Just after dawn, three days ago. You spoke my name, and then... nothing."

"I'm sorry," Yonah said, taking her hand. "I'm so sorry you had to endure that."

"Sorry?" Miriam laughed through fresh tears. "My son, you have nothing to apologise for. If anyone should be sorry, it's me. I lost faith. When you died, I thought God had abandoned us entirely. First your father, then you. I was ready to curse His name."

"But you didn't?"

"I couldn't. Even in my anger, even in my despair, something held me back. And now..." She squeezed his hand. "Now I understand. This Jesus, whoever he is, whatever he is—God sent him at just the right moment. Not a moment before you died, but after. So we would know."

"Know what?"

"That death isn't stronger than love. That God hears our weeping. That miracles still happen, even in little towns like Nain that the world barely knows exist."

Rachel bustled in with food—bread and cheese and dried figs and a cup of well-watered wine. "Eat," she commanded Yonah. "You've been fasting for three days, after all."

The mundane act of eating seemed to ground them all. Yonah ate slowly at first, then with increasing appetite, while Miriam watched every bite, every swallow, every sign of returning strength. The afternoon light slanted through the window, painting ordinary walls with golden warmth.

A knock at the door interrupted the quiet meal. Rabbi Eleazar stood outside, and behind him was what seemed like half the town. The rabbi's face still wore that expression of confused wonder, as if his orderly world had been shaken and he wasn't sure how to set it right again.

"Forgive the intrusion," he said. "But the people... we all... that is to say..." He stopped, took a breath, and started again. "Yonah, may we come in? There are questions. So many questions."

Miriam looked at her son, who nodded. "Let them come," he said. "I have little enough to tell, but what I know, I'll share."

They crowded in—neighbours, friends, curiosity seekers, sceptics, and believers. The small house filled with the warmth of bodies and the buzz of amazed conversation. Everyone wanted to touch Yonah, to hear his story, and to understand what had happened on the road below Nain.

"Tell us about being dead," someone called out. "What did you see?"

"Was there light? Angels? Abraham and the patriarchs?"

"Did it hurt to come back?"

"How did you know it was time to return?"

Yonah held up his hands for quiet. "I wish I had grand visions to report," he said. "But the truth is simpler. There was... absence. Like the deepest sleep without dreams. No pain, no fear, but also no joy or awareness. Just... waiting, though I didn't know I was waiting until I heard the voice calling me back."

"The Nazarene's voice?"

"Yes. Though I'd never heard it before, I knew it immediately. It had authority unlike anything I've ever experienced. Not harsh or commanding, but... inevitable. Like when God spoke creation into being—that kind of voice. It said, 'Arise,' and I had no choice but to obey. More than that, I *wanted* to obey. The voice was life itself calling to whatever spark remained in me."

"And you just... woke up?"

Yonah smiled ruefully. "If you can call it that. I woke up wrapped like a package, lying on a board, surrounded by people wailing. For a moment I thought I'd been buried alive—that was more terrifying than being dead, I can tell you. But then hands were unwrapping me, and I saw the sky, and my mother's face, and the face of the one who called me back."

"What did he look like, this Jesus?" a woman asked.

"Ordinary," Yonah said, then shook his head. "No, that's not right. His appearance was ordinary—travel-worn clothes, dusty feet, and a face that wouldn't stand out in a crowd. But his eyes..." He paused, searching for words. "Have you ever met someone and felt they could see right through to your soul? Not in judgement, but in complete understanding? That's what his eyes were like. Compassionate and powerful and somehow ancient, though he couldn't be more than thirty years old."

"They say he's been performing miracles all over Galilee," another neighbour added. "Healing the sick, casting out demons, even calming storms. My cousin in Capernaum swears he saw him heal a paralysed man."

"Those are tricks compared to this," Rabbi Eleazar said quietly. "Healing the sick is one thing. Even the prophets of old did such works. But raising the dead? Only Elijah and Elisha are recorded to have done so, and those were immediately after death. This..." He gestured at Yonah. "Three days dead. The spirit long departed. The body beginning to..." He stopped, unwilling to speak of corruption in front of Miriam.

"Perhaps he is Elijah," someone suggested. "Returned to prepare the way for the Messiah."

"He denied being Elijah when asked," another countered. "I heard it from a merchant who was in Capernaum. He claims to be something else entirely."

"What does he claim?"

The room fell silent, everyone leaning in for the answer.

"He speaks of himself as the Son of Man," the merchant's friend said slowly. "And sometimes... sometimes he speaks as if he and God the Father are..." He paused, clearly uncomfortable. "As if they are especially close. Closer than any prophet has claimed."

The implications hung in the air like incense, too powerful to name directly. The Messiah? The Anointed One promised by the prophets? But the Messiah was supposed to be a warrior king who would free Israel from Rome's iron grip. Not a wandering teacher who raised widows' sons in backwater towns.

"Does it matter what he claims?" Miriam asked suddenly, her voice cutting through the theological speculation. "I know what he did. My son was dead, and now he lives. If that's not the finger of God at work, then what is?"

"But we must be careful," Rabbi Eleazar cautioned. "There are false prophets and false messiahs. We must test everything against the scriptures, against the law..."

"Test this then," Yonah said, standing. "I was dead. You yourself confirmed it, Rabbi. You helped wash my body according to the law. You saw them wrap me in grave clothes. You led the prayers at my bier. Was I dead or not?"

The rabbi's face flushed. "You were dead," he admitted. "Beyond any doubt."

"And now I live. By the word of Jesus of Nazareth, I live. What does your law say about that?"

The question hung unanswered because there was no precedent, no careful rabbinical ruling on what to do when the dead walked out of their funeral processions. The law spoke of uncleanness from touching the dead, of proper burial procedures, and of mourning periods. It did not address resurrection.

The gathering continued long into the evening, neighbours coming and going, questions asked and reasked, and the same wonder expressed a hundred different ways. Food appeared as if by magic—the community's response to crisis had always been to feed it. Soon Miriam's table groaned under the weight of bread and stews and honeyed cakes.

"It's like a wedding feast," Rachel marvelled. "This morning we were heading to a tomb, and tonight we feast like a bridegroom has come home."

The comparison struck Miriam as particularly apt. There was something matrimonial about the joy that filled her house—the sense of new beginnings, of futures restored, of love triumphant over separation.

As the evening wore on, Yonah grew quieter, though he answered every question with patience. Miriam watched him carefully, noting the moments when his eyes went distant, as if he were seeing something beyond the crowded room.

"You're tired," she said finally, using her maternal authority to begin ushering people toward the door. "My son needs rest. "Real rest," she added with a touch of dark humour that made several people laugh nervously. "Come back tomorrow if you must, but for tonight, let us be."

The crowd dispersed reluctantly, each person wanting one last word, one last touch to confirm the miracle's reality. Rabbi Eleazar lingered at the door.

"I need to think," he said, more to himself than to them. "To pray. To search the scriptures. What happened today changes... everything. If the dead can be raised by a word, if this Jesus truly has such authority, then we are living in days the prophets could only dream of."

After he left, the house felt startlingly quiet. Rachel made her own farewells, promising to return in the morning to help with what would undoubtedly be another day of visitors. And then it was just Miriam and Yonah, mother and son, alone with the miracle of each other's presence.

"I'll sleep in the workshop tonight," Yonah said. "I know it sounds strange, but I'm almost afraid to close my eyes. What if I don't wake up again?"

"Then I'll go to Nazareth and drag that prophet back by his ears," Miriam said fiercely, which surprised a laugh out of her son.

"I believe you would." He grew serious again. "Mother, what do you think he meant? About having work still to do?"

Miriam considered. "I think he meant exactly what he said. Live your life. Love deeply. Bear witness to what you've experienced. Not everyone gets a second chance at life, my son. Don't waste yours looking for some grand destiny. The ordinary life of a good man is miracle enough."

"Is it?" Yonah moved to the window, looking out at the night sky. "I've touched death, Mother. Been beyond the veil and back. How do I return to shaping wood and discussing the weather and pretending that any of it matters the way it used to?"

"It matters more," Miriam said softly, joining him at the window. "Every sunrise you see is one you shouldn't have had. Every meal, every laugh, every tear—they're all gifts. Bonus rounds in the great game. Live them fully, not because they lead to something greater, but because they themselves are the greatness."

"When did you become so wise?"

"About three hours ago, when a stranger gave me back my son." She turned from the window, suddenly exhausted. "Sleep in your own bed, Yonah. I'll sit with you if you're afraid. I've had three nights of practice watching over your sleep."

They settled into a quiet routine—Yonah in his bed, Miriam in a chair beside him, a single oil lamp casting dancing shadows on the walls. For a while, neither spoke, both lost in the enormity of the day.

"Tell me about the funeral," Yonah said suddenly. "I know it's morbid, but I need to know. Who came? What did they say?"

So Miriam told him. About the whole town turning out, about the professional mourners Rachel had hired despite the cost, about the gifts of food and the tears of his friends. She told him about old Hannah, who had praised his kindness to her when her roof leaked. About the Roman centurion who had commissioned work from him sending unexpected condolences. About the children who had left wildflowers on his bier.

"You were loved," she said simply. "More than you knew."

"And yet he called me back." Yonah's voice was wondering. "Not a priest, not a scholar, not anyone important. Just a carpenter from Nain who hadn't even taken a wife yet. Why?"

"Because your mother wept," Miriam quoted Jesus's words. "Because he had compassion. Because in the Kingdom he speaks of, every life matters. Even ours."

"Especially ours, perhaps," Yonah said thoughtfully. "The overlooked ones. The ordinary ones. The ones in power pass by without seeing." He yawned suddenly, hugely. "I think I can sleep now. Will you stay?"

"Always," Miriam promised.

She watched as his breathing deepened, as sleep claimed him naturally this time. Watched the rise and fall of his chest and the flutter of his eyelids as dreams took him. Ordinary things that would never be ordinary to her again.

Outside, Nain slept, but Miriam knew the town would never be the same. By tomorrow, word will have spread to the surrounding villages. Within a week, all of Galilee would know. The prophet from Nazareth had raised the dead. God was moving in Israel again.

But for now, in this quiet room, a mother kept vigil over her living son and pondered all these things in her heart. The oil lamp flickered, casting its small circle of light against the darkness. It was enough. More than enough. It was everything.

The first light of dawn was painting the eastern sky when Miriam finally dozed in her chair. She woke to find Yonah already up, standing at his workbench, running his hands over his tools with the air of a man greeting old friends.

"I thought I'd finish this," he said, indicating the half-completed cabinet.

"Mr. Mordechai commissioned it for his daughter's wedding. I suppose I should tell him there'll be no delay after all."

The normalcy of it—her son planning his work day—made Miriam's throat tight with emotion. "Eat first," she managed. "I'll make breakfast."

They fell into their usual morning routine, but everything carried weight it hadn't before. The simple act of sharing bread. The sound of Yonah humming as he worked. The way sunlight fell across the floor, they'd walked together for years.

A knock at the door interrupted their peace. Miriam opened it to find a young man she didn't recognise, travel-stained and breathing hard.

"Is this the house of Yonah the carpenter?" he asked. "The one who was... who died and..."

"Yes," Miriam said warily. "What do you want?"

"I've come from Capernaum," the young man said. "My master is dying. We heard what happened here, about the prophet Jesus, about your son. Please, where did he go? Which direction? My master is wealthy—he'll pay anything if the prophet will only come and heal him."

"We don't know where he went," Yonah said, joining them at the door. "He left yesterday, heading east on the main road. But he could have turned off anywhere."

The young man's face fell. "Then I'll follow the road and ask at every village. Someone must have seen him." He looked at Yonah with desperate eyes. "Is it true? Were you really dead?"

236

"For three days," Yonah confirmed gently. "And now I live. If you find Jesus of Nazareth, your master will be healed. I'm certain of it."

"What does he look like? How will I know him?"

Yonah thought for a moment. "Look for the crowds," he said finally. "Where people gather in hope, where the sick and desperate press close, where you hear teaching that makes your heart burn within you—there you'll find him. But more than that, look for compassion walking on two feet. You'll know him by his eyes—they hold the kind of love that raises the dead."

The messenger left with renewed hope, and Miriam closed the door on what she suspected would be the first of many such seekers. Word of resurrection wouldn't stay contained in Nain.

"Should we have gone with him?" she asked. "Helped him search?"

But Yonah shook his head. "I think we're meant to be here. To live the life that was given back. To tell our story to those who come seeking. To be proof that death isn't the end."

Over the following days, that's exactly what they became. Pilgrims came to Nain specifically to see the young man who'd been raised. Some came sceptical, others desperate, and many simply curious. Yonah received them all with patience, showing them his grave clothes (which his mother had inexplicably saved), telling his story, and pointing them toward the travelling teacher who had authority over death itself.

The baker's daughter, Naomi, came often, ostensibly to bring fresh bread but really to stare at Yonah with wonder-struck eyes. The third time she came, he finally found the courage to ask her to stay and share the meal.

"I thought you were lost to me," she admitted, blushing. "I never got to tell you..."

"Tell me now," Yonah encouraged. "I've learnt not to waste time."

Miriam, watching from the doorway, smiled and found somewhere else to be. Life was reasserting itself in all its ordinary glory. There would be a wedding after all, and grandchildren, and the continuation of life that death had tried to steal.

Rabbi Eleazar became a frequent visitor, bringing scripture scrolls and engaging Yonah in long discussions about the theological implications of his experience.

"There's precedent," he said one evening, unrolling a scroll of Kings. "Elijah raised the widow's son. Elisha raised the Shunammite's child. But those were immediately after death, when perhaps the soul hadn't fully departed. Your case..." He shook his head. "Three days. It challenges everything we thought we knew about the boundaries between life and death."

"Maybe that's the point," Yonah suggested. "Maybe this Jesus came to show us that the boundaries we think are fixed—between life and death, between clean and unclean, between who's in and who's out—maybe they're not as solid as we believed."

The rabbi tugged his beard thoughtfully. "You sound like him. The reports I'm getting from those who've heard him teach—he speaks of God's kingdom as if the rules are different there. As if the last become first and the dead become living and the impossible becomes everyday reality."

"Because I've been there," Yonah said simply. "To the boundary. And I've seen someone with authority to move it."

Weeks passed. The steady stream of visitors slowed but never stopped entirely. Yonah finished the cabinet and delivered it to a stunned Mr. Mordechai, who tried to refuse payment on the grounds that one shouldn't charge for work completed in the afterlife. They compromised on half price and a promise of more commissions.

Life in Nain found a new rhythm, one that accommodated the miracle in their midst while still attending to daily needs. The harvest came in. Children were born. Couples married. The Romans collected taxes. And through it all, Yonah worked wood and told his story and lived with a gratitude that transformed everything it touched.

One day, about two months after the resurrection, another visitor came. But this one didn't ask to hear the story. He already knew it.

"Simon," Yonah said, recognising one of Jesus's disciples who had been there that day. "Welcome. What brings you back to Nain?"

The fisherman's face was grave. "I bring word from the master. He wanted you to know... things are becoming more dangerous. The religious authorities are watching him. Some seek to trap him in his words. Others speak openly of silencing him." He paused. "He said to tell you that what he did for you, he did as a sign of what's coming. But before the ultimate victory, there must be suffering."

"Is he safe?" Miriam asked, concerned for the man who'd given her back her son.

"For now. He continues teaching, healing, and proclaiming the kingdom. But he speaks often of Jerusalem, of a confrontation that must come."

Simon looked directly at Yonah. "He said to tell you specifically: 'Live fully. Love deeply. When the dark day comes, remember that you are proof it's not the end.'"

"What dark day?" Yonah asked, but Simon was already turning to go.

"I don't know," the disciple admitted. "But the master does. And he faces it without fear. Says it's why he came." He gripped Yonah's shoulder briefly. "Be well, friend. You carry a piece of the kingdom's future in your very breath. Don't forget that."

After he left, Yonah and Miriam stood in troubled silence. The idea that harm might come to Jesus seemed impossible. Who could successfully oppose someone with power over death itself?

"Perhaps we should go to him," Yonah suggested. "Warn him. Protect him somehow."

But Miriam shook her head. "He knew what he was doing when he touched your bier. A man with that kind of authority doesn't need our protection. But perhaps..." She paused, working through the thought. "Perhaps he needs our witness. Our living proof that whatever comes, death isn't stronger than the power he carries."

That night, Yonah carved while Miriam spun thread, both finding comfort in familiar tasks. The oil lamp flickered between them, creating a circle of light in the darkness. Outside, Nain slept peacefully, unaware that forces were gathering that would shake the foundations of everything they thought they knew about God and power and the nature of victory.

"I've been thinking," Yonah said suddenly, his hands still working the wood. "About what Jesus said—that I had work still to do, life still to live. I thought he meant carpentry, marriage, and ordinary things. And he did. But I think he also meant this—being ready to testify. When whatever's coming comes, people will need to know that death isn't the end. That there's power available that can reach beyond the grave."

"My wise son," Miriam said softly. "Raised from death and raised to wisdom too."

"I just keep thinking about others like us. Other mothers weeping for their children. Other children grieving their parents. Other families broken by loss. What if they could know what we know? Not just as a story, but as a living reality?"

"Then tell them," Miriam said simply. "Every chance you get. It's not just about your resurrection but about the one who performed it. About the kingdom he says is coming where tears are wiped away and death has no dominion."

Yonah nodded, returning to his carving with renewed purpose. He was working on something special—a gift for the teacher if their paths ever crossed again. It was a simple piece of olive wood, but he was carving it with all the skill his father had taught him, all the patience his mother had instilled, and all the gratitude his second life had given him.

The design was taking shape slowly—a tree. Not the tree of death that had claimed the first Adam, but a tree of life, its branches reaching toward heaven, its roots deep in earth. Where the trunk split, he carved an empty tomb, its stone rolled away. It was his testimony in wood, his understanding of what had happened on the road below Nain.

Death had come to collect what it thought it owned. But Life himself had been walking by, and Death's claim had proven negotiable. The kingdom of God looked like a young teacher touching an unclean bier. It sounded like a voice calling the dead to rise. It felt like the impossible joy of a mother receiving back her son.

As Yonah carved and Miriam spun, as Nain slept and the world turned toward whatever confrontation awaited in Jerusalem, the miracle lived on in ordinary acts performed with extraordinary gratitude. A carpenter worked wood with hands that had been still. A mother prepared meals for a son who had been beyond all nourishment. Life continued, precious and precarious and shot through with wonder.

And in the quiet spaces between heartbeats, between breaths, between the falling of one wood shaving and the next, the echo of that commanding voice remained: "Young man, I say to you, arise."

He had arisen. They all had, in ways they were only beginning to understand. Death had been put on notice. The kingdom was breaking in. And in a carpenter's shop in Nain, the proof lived and worked and wondered at the mystery of second chances.

The lamp burnt low as the night deepened, but neither mother nor son moved to replenish the oil. They worked on in the dying light, comfortable with darkness now that they knew it wasn't final. Somewhere beyond Nain's walls, Jesus of Nazareth continued his inexorable journey toward Jerusalem and whatever awaited him there.

But here, now, in this moment, death had no victory. Love had won. A mother had her son. A son had his life. And both had a story that would outlive them all—the story of the day heaven touched earth on a dusty road, and a funeral became a resurrection, and the world tilted toward hope.

The last flame flickered and died, leaving them in darkness. But it was a different darkness now—pregnant with possibility, temporary as sleep, and unable to overcome the light that had been kindled in their hearts.

"Rest well, my son," Miriam said into the quiet.

"Rest well, Mother," Yonah replied. "Tomorrow we tell the story again."

And they would. As long as breath remained, as long as hearts beat with borrowed time, as long as people needed to know that death's reign was ending. They would tell of the teacher from Nazareth who had compassion on a widow's tears. They would speak of authority that made tombs give up their dead. They would bear witness to the kingdom coming near in the form of a hand touching an unclean bier and a voice calling life out of death.

The miracle of Nain would not be forgotten. It lived on in every sunrise Yonah saw, every meal Miriam prepared, every wedding celebrated, every child born, and every story told of the day death lost its grip and life won a victory that would echo into eternity.

And somewhere in the Galilean night, walking roads that led inevitably to a cross, Jesus of Nazareth carried the tears of a widow and the joy of resurrection, knowing that both would meet again in Jerusalem, where the ultimate funeral would become the ultimate rising, and death itself would die.

But that was still to come. For now, there was sleep, and dreams, and the promise of tomorrow. In Nain, the dead lived. The widow had her son. And the kingdom of God had left its calling card in the form of an empty bier and a grave that couldn't keep its hold.

Glory to God in the highest. And on earth, peace to those on whom his favour rests—even widows, even orphans, even the dead who hear his voice and rise.

Chapter 10: The Forerunner's Doubt

The fortress of Machaerus rose from the barren hills east of the Dead Sea like a clenched fist raised against heaven. Built by Herod the Great as a bulwark against his enemies, it now served his son Antipas as both palace and prison. In its bowels, where daylight never penetrated and the air tasted of despair, John the Baptist sat in chains, counting the days by the changing of guards and the arrival of his meagre meals.

Six months. Six months since Herod's soldiers had dragged him from the Jordan's banks, his camel-hair garment still dripping with baptismal water. Six months of stone and iron, of darkness and doubt. The voice that had thundered across the wilderness, calling Israel to repentance, was now reduced to a hoarse whisper echoing off indifferent walls.

John shifted on the mouldy straw, trying to find a position where the shackles didn't bite into his wrists. His body, once hard as leather from years of desert living, had grown soft and pale in captivity. But it wasn't the physical deterioration that tormented him most—it was the silence from heaven.

Where was the voice that had driven him from his father's comfortable priest's quarters into the wilderness? Where was the Spirit that had blazed through him like fire, compelling him to preach repentance to tax collectors and soldiers, Pharisees and prostitutes alike? Most troubling of all—where was Jesus?

The heavy door groaned open, and John squinted against the torchlight. Two figures entered—his disciples, Andrew and Simon, their faces gaunt with worry. They came when they could, bribing the guards with what little money the movement had left, bringing news from the outside world that seemed increasingly distant and unreal.

"Master," Andrew knelt beside him, trying not to show his shock at John's deteriorated condition. The wild prophet who had made kings tremble now looked like any other prisoner—hollow-eyed, beard matted, skin stretched tight over prominent bones.

"Don't call me master," John rasped. "I'm no one's master. I'm not even sure I'm a prophet anymore." He attempted a laugh that turned into a cough. "Perhaps I never was. Perhaps the voice I heard was just the desert wind playing tricks on a zealot's mind."

Simon—not the fisherman who followed Jesus, but another disciple—pulled bread and dried figs from his pouch. "You mustn't speak so, Teacher. All Israel knows you're a prophet. Even Herod fears to kill you because the people—"

"The people!" John's chains rattled as he gestured dismissively. "The people came to see a spectacle—the wild man eating locusts, baptising in the Jordan. They came for entertainment, not transformation. Where are they now? Do they storm the fortress demanding my release? Do they refuse to pay taxes until justice is done?"

The disciples exchanged troubled glances. This bitterness was new, more disturbing than the physical decline. The John they knew had been fierce but never bitter, confrontational but never cynical.

"Tell me of Jesus," John said after a moment, his voice softer. "What news from Galilee?"

Andrew's face lit up. "Master, the things we've heard! He teaches with such authority that even the scribes are amazed. He heals the sick—lepers, paralytics, and even those possessed by demons flee at his word. The crowds follow him everywhere. Some say he's establishing the kingdom, that soon—"

"Soon what?" John interrupted. "Soon he'll march on Jerusalem? Soon he'll overthrow Herod and Caesar? Soon he'll establish justice and righteousness with a rod of iron?" He shook his head slowly. "I've been waiting for 'soon' for six months, Andrew. Tell me—does he speak of me? Does he say anything about the one who prepared his way now rotting in Herod's dungeon?"

Simon leaned forward. "He speaks of you with honour, calling you the greatest born of women. Just last week in Capernaum—"

"While I sit here in chains." The bitterness crept back into John's voice. "The greatest born of women, imprisoned for speaking truth about an illegal marriage. Tell me, friends—what kind of Messiah leaves his herald to waste away in darkness? What kind of kingdom begins with its prophet in prison?"

The questions hung in the foetid air like accusations. These were the doubts that gnawed at John in the endless nights, more painful than hunger, more tormenting than the guards' casual cruelty. He had been so certain that day at the Jordan when Jesus came to be baptized. The heavens had opened, the Spirit had descended like a dove, and the Voice had spoken: "This is my beloved Son."

But now, in the darkness, even that miraculous moment seemed distant and doubtful. Perhaps he had imagined it. Perhaps the carpenter from Nazareth was just another false hope in Israel's long history of disappointed messianic expectations.

"Master," Andrew said carefully, "perhaps you should send us to him. Let us ask directly—"

"Ask what?" John's laugh was bitter. "Ask if he's really the one, or should we look for another? Ask why he heals strangers but leaves his own cousin to rot. Ask why the kingdom we proclaimed seems no closer than when I first cried out in the wilderness."

But even as he spoke, John felt something shift within him. Pride, perhaps—the last luxury of a condemned man—finally cracking under the weight of need. He had to know. The uncertainty was more unbearable than the chains.

"Yes," he said finally. "Go to him. Find him wherever he teaches and ask him plainly, 'Are you the one who is to come, or should we wait for another?'"

Simon looked shocked. "Master, surely you don't doubt—"

"I doubt everything," John said simply. "In this darkness, I've had time to examine every certainty I ever held and found them all wanting. I need to hear from him. I need..." He paused, searching for words. "I need to know that my life hasn't been wasted on a beautiful delusion."

Andrew gripped John's manacled hands. "We'll go immediately. We'll find him and bring back his answer."

"And if he confirms what you believe?" John asked. "If he declares himself the Messiah? What then? Will he speak a word and these walls crumble? Will he command, and Herod's heart will soften?" He shook his head. "No, I think not. I think I'm learning that God's kingdom comes in ways we don't expect, through paths we wouldn't choose. Go. Ask him. But prepare yourselves for an answer that may puzzle more than it clarifies."

After they left, John slumped against the wall, exhausted by the effort of conversation. The guards would bring his evening meal soon—thin gruel and stale bread, sometimes crawling with maggots. He'd learnt to eat it anyway. Pride was a luxury he could no longer afford.

In the upper palace, far above the dungeons, Herod Antipas reclined on silk cushions, wine cup in hand, trying to ignore the voice of conscience that sounded disturbingly like the prisoner below. Herodias lounged beside him, her beautiful face marred by the perpetual sneer she wore whenever John's name arose.

"You should kill him," she said for the thousandth time. "Every day he lives is an insult to our marriage, to our authority."

"The people consider him a prophet," Herod replied, also for the thousandth time. "To kill him would risk uprising."

"The people!" Herodias spat. "Since when does the tetrarch of Galilee fear fishermen and farmers? Your father would have—"

"My father killed infants in Bethlehem and died mad, eaten by worms," Herod snapped. "I won't follow his path."

But it went deeper than political calculation. There was something about John that both fascinated and terrified Herod. He would sometimes have the prophet brought up from the dungeon, ostensibly to mock him but really to hear him speak. Even in chains, even weakened by imprisonment, John's words carried a weight that made Herod's soul tremble.

"Repent," John would say, his eyes boring into Herod's. "The kingdom of heaven is at hand. Every tree that doesn't bear good fruit will be cut down and thrown into the fire."

And Herod would send him back to the dungeon, disturbed and strangely moved, while Herodias raged about the insult to her dignity.

"There's news from Galilee," Herodias said, changing tactics. "About that other preacher—Jesus of Nazareth. They say he performs miracles and that crowds follow him everywhere. Some even whisper he might be the Messiah."

Herod's hand tightened on his wine cup. Another prophet. Another voice calling for repentance and transformation. How many would God send before Herod either submitted or silenced them all?

"Perhaps," Herodias continued silkily, "you should investigate this Jesus. If he proves troublesome, you could arrest him too. The dungeon is large enough for two prophets."

"Enough!" Herod stood abruptly, wine sloshing from his cup. "I won't discuss this tonight. Tomorrow is my birthday feast—let's speak of pleasanter things."

Herodias smiled, a cold expression that never reached her eyes. "Of course, my lord. Tomorrow will be a day of celebration. I've arranged entertainment that will delight you—my daughter Salome has prepared a special dance."

Herod nodded absently, his thoughts still on the prophet in his dungeon and the other one wandering free in Galilee. He didn't notice the calculating gleam in his wife's eyes or the way her fingers drummed against her couch—the gesture of a patient spider who has finally finished spinning her web.

Meanwhile, Andrew and Simon made their way north, travelling by night to avoid the worst of the late summer heat. The journey from Machaerus to Galilee took three days of hard travel, following trade routes that skirted the Dead Sea before turning north through the Jordan Valley.

As they walked, they debated how to approach Jesus with John's question. It seemed almost blasphemous—the Baptist doubting the one he had proclaimed. How would Jesus react? Would he be disappointed? Angry? Would he send thunder from heaven to shatter John's prison, proving his identity beyond doubt?

"Remember the day John baptised him?" Andrew said as they rested in the shade of a tamarisk tree. "I was standing close enough to see John's face. He was trembling—the man who feared no one, who called Pharisees a brood of vipers to their faces, trembling as he lowered Jesus into the water.

"And the voice from heaven," Simon added. "We all heard it. 'This is my beloved Son, in whom I am well pleased.' How can John doubt after that?"

"Six months in darkness can make anyone doubt," Andrew replied soberly. "Even the strongest faith can crack under enough pressure. John is human, Simon. Perhaps that's the lesson—that God uses human vessels, with all our weaknesses and doubts."

They found Jesus in Capernaum, teaching in the synagogue to a crowd that overflowed into the courtyard. His voice carried clearly, speaking of a kingdom where the last would be first, where mercy triumphed over judgement, and where God's reign broke into the world not through military might but through transformed hearts.

Andrew and Simon waited at the edge of the crowd, watching the man John had proclaimed. Jesus looked ordinary enough—a craftsman's build, work-roughened hands, and features more weathered than handsome. But when he spoke, something electric filled the air. Authority radiated from him, not the borrowed authority of scribes quoting other scribes, but something original, primordial, as if the Word that spoke creation into being was speaking still.

When the teaching ended, people pressed forward with requests—heal my daughter, bless my business, settle this dispute with my neighbour. Jesus dealt with each patiently, touching the sick with compassion, speaking words of wisdom to the troubled. Andrew noticed how tired he looked, how the constant demands drained him even as he gave freely of himself.

Finally, as evening approached, the disciples of Jesus formed a protective barrier, allowing their master space to breathe. It was then that Andrew and Simon approached.

Peter—Simon the fisherman—recognised them first. "Andrew! Simon! Brothers, what brings you from the wilderness?" His face fell as he remembered. "John—how is he?"

"Alive," Andrew said simply. "But troubled. We need to speak with the master."

Peter led them to where Jesus sat with his inner circle. Up close, Andrew could see the toll the ministry was taking—the lines of exhaustion around his eyes, the weight he carried that had nothing to do with physical burden.

"Master," Peter said, "these are disciples of John the Baptist. They've come from Machaerus."

Jesus looked up, and Andrew felt those eyes see straight through him—not in judgement but in complete understanding. "John," Jesus said softly. "My cousin. My friend. The voice crying in the wilderness. How does he fare in Herod's cage?"

"His body weakens," Simon said, "but it's his spirit we fear for most. Master, he sent us with a question."

Jesus nodded, unsurprised. "Ask."

Andrew took a breath. "He wants to know: Are you the one who is to come, or should we wait for another?"

The words fell into silence. Several of Jesus's disciples looked shocked—John doubting? The Baptist questioning the one he had proclaimed? But Jesus showed no surprise, no offence. Instead, a deep sadness crossed his features, the sorrow of understanding the weight of doubt that could drive such a question.

"Sit," Jesus said. "Rest from your journey. Stay with us for the day. Watch and listen. Then return to John and tell him what you see and hear."

It wasn't the direct answer they'd expected. No thunderous declaration, no miraculous sign specifically for John. But Andrew sensed wisdom in it—Jesus would let his works speak louder than any words.

The next morning began before dawn with a leper approaching the house where Jesus stayed. The man's approach caused panic—"Unclean! Unclean!" people shouted, backing away. But Jesus walked straight toward him and, in full view of everyone, touched the diseased flesh.

"Be clean," Jesus said simply.

Andrew watched in amazement as the corruption fled the man's skin like shadows before sunrise. Pink, healthy flesh emerged where moments before there had been rotting sores. The man fell to his knees, sobbing—not from pain but from the overwhelming realisation that he could return to his family, to human touch, to life.

"Go, show yourself to the priest," Jesus instructed. "Offer the gift Moses commanded as a testimony to them."

As the morning progressed, more came. A centurion seeking healing for his servant, showing faith that amazed even Jesus. A widow whose only son lay near death, restored with a word. Demons cast out with authority that made them shriek in recognition before fleeing.

But it wasn't just the miracles that struck Andrew. It was how Jesus performed them—not as displays of power but as acts of compassion. He touched the untouchable, spoke to the ignored, and brought dignity to the despised. This was power in service of love, might bent toward mercy.

At midday, they encountered a funeral procession leaving the city gates. A widow walked behind her son's bier, her wails piercing the air. Andrew knew that grief—a mother burying her only child, her sole support in a world that had little use for widows.

Jesus stopped the procession. The mourners looked at him in confusion—who was this stranger interrupting their grief? But Jesus approached the bier, and something in his bearing made even the professional mourners fall silent.

"Young man," Jesus said, touching the funeral platform, "I say to you, arise."

For a moment, nothing. Then the wrapped figure stirred, sat up, and began unwinding the burial cloths with living hands. The crowd's shocked silence exploded into chaos—shouts of joy, cries of fear, and prayers of thanksgiving. The widow collapsed, not in grief now but in overwhelming relief as her son embraced her.

"A great prophet has risen among us!" someone shouted. "God has visited His people!"

Andrew and Simon exchanged glances. This was more than healing—this was resurrection, the power of life conquering death itself. If John could see this...

But as the day wore on, Andrew noticed something else. For all his power, Jesus seemed constrained by something—the very humanity he had taken on, perhaps. He grew tired and needed rest. He felt hunger and required food. When crowds pressed too close, he sought solitude to pray. This was divinity choosing limitation, power accepting weakness.

That evening, as they prepared to return to John, Jesus called them aside. They walked to a quiet spot overlooking the Sea of Galilee, the setting sun painting the water in shades of gold and crimson.

"Tell John what you have seen and heard," Jesus said. "The blind receive sight, the lame walk, lepers are cleansed, the deaf hear, the dead are raised, and good news is preached to the poor." He paused, looking out over the water. "And blessed is the one who is not offended by me."

Andrew heard the layers in those words. The miracles echoed Isaiah's prophecies about the Messiah, answering John's question indirectly but clearly. But the final phrase carried a gentle rebuke and a deeper challenge. Would John accept a Messiah who didn't match his expectations? Who came not as a political liberator but as a healer of bodies and souls?

"Master," Simon ventured, "John prepared your way. He proclaimed your coming. Why do you leave him in prison? A word from you could free him."

Jesus turned to them, and Andrew saw pain in his eyes—the pain of omnipotence choosing restraint. "John has his role to play, as I have mine. The kingdom of God doesn't come through force but through faithful witness, even unto death. John lit a torch in the darkness. That light will not be extinguished, even when the torchbearer falls."

"Then he will die?" Andrew asked, though his heart already knew the answer.

"All who speak truth to power risk death," Jesus said. "But death is not the final word. Tell John that his work is not in vain, that the axe he laid at the root of the trees is still cutting, and that the wheat he began to gather will fill barns he'll never see. Tell him..." Jesus's voice caught slightly. "Tell him I have not forgotten him. Tell him he is loved."

They left that night, carrying more questions than answers but also carrying something else—a glimpse of a kingdom that operated by different rules than any earthly realm. As they travelled south, they discussed what they had seen, trying to find words for their report to John.

"He didn't directly answer the question," Simon observed.

"Didn't he?" Andrew countered. "What more direct answer than raising the dead? Who but the Messiah could do such things?"

"But why leave John imprisoned? Why not establish the kingdom now, with such power at his command?"

Andrew remembered Jesus's tired eyes, his very human need for food and rest. "Perhaps because he's showing us a different kind of power. Not the power to dominate but to serve. Not the power to force change but to inspire it."

They reached Machaerus on the evening of the third day, bribing their way past guards who had grown accustomed to their visits. The fortress was unusually active—servants scurrying about, musicians tuning instruments, and the smell of roasting meat wafting from the kitchens.

"The tetrarch's birthday feast," one guard explained with a leer. "There'll be wine flowing like water tonight, and entertainment to make a saint blush."

Andrew felt a chill of premonition. Something dark was stirring in the fortress, something that boded ill for their master. They hurried to the dungeon, finding John barely conscious on his filthy straw.

"Master," Andrew knelt beside him, lifting his head gently. "We've returned from Jesus."

John's eyes flickered open, focusing with effort. "Tell me."

They poured out their report—the healings, the resurrections, and the teaching with authority. John listened without interrupting, his expression unreadable in the dim light. When they finished with Jesus's final message, silence stretched between them.

"The blind see, the lame walk," John murmured finally. "Isaiah's words. He claims the prophet's mantle but not the warrior's sword." A ghost of a smile touched his cracked lips. "I wanted fire from heaven, judgement on the wicked, the proud brought low, and the humble exalted by force. Instead, he brings sight to blind beggars and hope to widows."

"Are you disappointed?" Simon asked.

"Disappointed?" John considered the word. "No. Confused, perhaps. Humbled, certainly. I thought I understood God's ways, but I was like a child drawing pictures of the ocean who then sees the actual sea. His kingdom is vaster and stranger than I imagined."

From somewhere above, music drifted down—flutes and lyres, the sound of celebration beginning. John's face tightened.

"My time is short," he said with sudden certainty. "I feel it in my bones. Herod's wife has hated me too long to let me live much longer." He gripped Andrew's hand with surprising strength. "Listen to me. When I'm gone, follow Jesus. Take everyone who'll listen and follow him. He is the One—I know that now, not with the certainty of sight but with the deeper certainty of faith tested by doubt."

"Master, don't speak of death—"

"Why not? I've proclaimed it often enough. Every tree that doesn't bear fruit will be cut down. I pray I've borne fruit, that my work prepared soil for the seed he's planting." John's voice grew stronger, more like the prophet of old. "Tell the others—tell them the Baptist's final message. The Lamb of God has come to take away the sins of the world. I saw him and bore witness. Let my witness stand, even when I fall."

The music above grew louder and wilder. They could hear the rhythm of dancing feet and the drunken laughter of nobles. In the dungeon, three men prayed together—not for deliverance but for faithfulness, not for rescue but for courage to face whatever came.

When Andrew and Simon finally left, they both knew it was for the last time. John knew it too. He watched them go with peaceful eyes, the doubt that had tormented him replaced by a quiet certainty. Not certainty about outcomes—he still didn't know if he'd die tomorrow or linger for months. But certainty about the One he had proclaimed, the cousin whose way he had prepared, the Messiah who came not as expected but as needed.

Alone again in the darkness, John found himself thinking of his mother, Elizabeth, dead these many years. She had known, even before his birth, that her son was destined for an unusual path. "He will go before the Lord," she had sung while he kicked in her womb, "in the spirit and power of Elijah."

Elijah. The prophet who had confronted wicked kings and queens, who had called down fire from heaven, who had been taken up in a whirlwind without tasting death. John had always imagined his story would echo Elijah's—dramatic confrontation, divine vindication, miraculous deliverance.

Instead, he would die in a dungeon, his head likely decorating a platter at a drunken feast. No chariot of fire for the Baptist. No whirlwind to carry him to glory. Just the axe of an executioner and the satisfaction of a vengeful woman.

Yet strangely, the bitterness was gone. In its place was something harder to define—not quite peace, for his flesh still recoiled from what was coming. Not quite joy, for he grieved the work left undone. But a deep settledness, a sense of completion. He had been a voice crying in the wilderness. He had prepared the way. He had pointed to the Lamb. His work was finished.

Above, the feast reached its crescendo. Salome danced, her young body moving in ways that inflamed the drunken king. Herodias watched with satisfaction as her daughter's sensuality wove a trap around Herod's wine-soaked judgement.

"Ask anything," Herod slurred when the dance ended, "up to half my kingdom!"

Salome glanced at her mother, who nodded toward the dungeons below. The girl's request, when it came, cut through the drunken revelry like a blade: "Give me the head of John the Baptist on a platter."

Even drunk, Herod felt the world tilt. He looked at the expectant faces of his nobles, at Herodias's triumphant smile, and at the girl standing before him with outstretched hands. To refuse would be to break a public oath, to lose face before his court. To agree would be to murder a prophet, to bring blood guilt on his reign.

In the end, cowardice won. The order was given. The executioner was summoned.

In his cell, John heard the approaching footsteps and knew. No reprieve would come. No earthquake would shake the prison. No angel would break his chains. He would die as mortals die, his blood soaking into indifferent stone.

He thought of Jesus, somewhere in Galilee, healing the sick and preaching good news to the poor. Would he feel it when John died? Would he pause in mid-sentence, touched by the knowledge that his herald had fallen? Or would he continue his work, the kingdom advancing even as its prophet perished?

The door opened. The executioner entered—a professional, not unkind, embarrassed by his task. "It'll be quick," he promised.

John nodded. There were no last words for history to record, no final proclamation to echo through the ages. He had said all he needed to say. The Word had become flesh, and John had borne witness. What more was there?

He knelt on the stone floor, neck extended. For a moment, fear clutched at him—the basic human terror of extinction. Then, like a father's hand on a frightened child's shoulder, he felt a presence. Not visible, not audible, but absolutely real. The same presence that had driven him into the wilderness, that had burnt in him as he preached, that had recognised itself in Jesus at the Jordan.

Well done, good and faithful servant.

The blade fell.

In Herod's feast hall, the music had stopped. Nobles averted their eyes as the grotesque trophy was presented to Salome, who carried it to her mother with trembling hands. Herodias's moment of triumph turned to ash as she looked into the dead prophet's face. What had she expected to feel? Satisfaction? Victory? Instead, there was only emptiness and a creeping fear that she had won a battle but awakened something far more dangerous than a desert preacher.

Herod fled to his chambers but found no escape from the accusing voice that now seemed to come from within. He would hear it for the rest of his life—in quiet moments, in the darkness before dawn, whenever his conscience stirred. "Repent, for the kingdom of heaven is at hand."

Andrew and Simon, camping outside the fortress, saw the torches flare and heard the wailing begin. They knew without being told. As dawn broke, other disciples of John arrived, and together they approached the fortress. To their surprise, the guards let them pass. Herod, desperate to rid himself of the evidence of his crime, had ordered the body released.

They found their master's remains and carried them away for burial, wrapping him in clean linen and washing away the dungeon's filth. As they worked, they wept—for the voice silenced, for the prophet fallen, for their own confusion about what came next.

But Andrew remembered John's final charge: "Follow Jesus." So after they had laid the Baptist in his tomb, after they had mourned and prayed and sung the psalms of lamentation, they set out for Galilee. The voice in the wilderness was silent, but the Word he had proclaimed still spoke. The herald had fallen, but the king remained.

They found Jesus by the Sea of Galilee, and as they approached, they saw his shoulders bow as if under a great weight. He knew. Before they could speak, he knew. He dismissed the crowds and withdrew to a desolate place, and they understood he needed to mourn alone—the cousin who had leaped in the womb at his presence, the prophet who had recognised him at the Jordan, and the friend who had decreased so he might increase.

The disciples of John watched from a distance as Jesus prayed, sometimes in words they could hear—anguished words about the cost of truth, the price of prophecy, and the mystery of his Father's will that included such suffering. When he finally returned, his eyes were red with weeping, but there was steel in them too.

"John was a burning and shining lamp," he told them, "and you were willing to rejoice for a while in his light. But the testimony I have is greater than John's. The works that the Father has given me to accomplish—the very works I am doing—bear witness about me that the Father has sent me." Some of John's disciples struggled with this. They had followed the Baptist, not the carpenter. They had been drawn to the austere prophet, not the teacher who ate with tax collectors. But Andrew remembered John's words—"He must increase, but I must decrease"—and understood this was what their master had prepared them for.

In the days that followed, as word of John's death spread through Galilee and Judea, Jesus spoke often of his cousin. To the crowds, he proclaimed John as more than a prophet—the very Elijah who was to come. To his close disciples, he spoke more soberly of a baptism he must undergo and a cup he must drink, intimating that the Baptist's fate foreshadowed his own.

And in the fortress of Machaerus, Herod Antipas found no peace. When reports reached him of Jesus's miracles, his guilty conscience conjured a terrible possibility: "John, whom I beheaded, has been raised from the dead!" The prophet's voice, which he had thought to silence with an executioner's sword, now haunted him more persistently than ever.

The kingdom John had proclaimed continued to advance, but not as he had envisioned. No axe fell on the corrupt tree of Herod's rule—at least, not visibly. No divine fire consumed the palace of adultery and murder. Instead, the kingdom grew quietly, like a seed in soil, like yeast in dough. It grew in transformed lives, in healed bodies, and in hearts that turned from sin to grace.

John would have been puzzled by this patient kingdom, this realm that advanced through suffering rather than around it. He had expected judgement; Jesus brought mercy. He had proclaimed wrath; Jesus offered forgiveness. He had envisioned revolution; Jesus embodied a longer, deeper transformation.

But perhaps, in those final moments in the dungeon, John had glimpsed this truth. Perhaps that's why he could face death with peace—knowing that God's ways, though mysterious, were perfect. The voice in the wilderness had fallen silent, but the Word he proclaimed would echo through eternity. The forerunner's race was run. He had doubted, but through doubt found a faith refined by fire. He had questioned but received an answer that transcended his questions. He had prepared the way, and now that way stretched forward into a future he couldn't see but had learnt to trust.

In death, as in life, John the Baptist pointed beyond himself to the One who was to come—who had come—who would come again. His doubt had been answered not with thunderous certainty but with quiet demonstration. His faith had been validated not by his deliverance but by his Lord's continuation of the work they had begun together at the Jordan.

The greatest born of women lay in a tomb, his voice stilled, his work complete. But the kingdom he had announced rolled on like a river that had broken through a dam, flooding the world with grace, judgement, and hope. The herald was dead. Long live the King, he had proclaimed.

Chapter 11: Anointed for Burial

The invitation had arrived that morning, delivered by a servant whose pressed linen tunic and carefully groomed beard spoke of a wealthy household. Simon bar Jonah—not to be confused with Simon Peter—stood in the doorway of his substantial home in Capernaum's upper district, watching the messenger depart with measured satisfaction.

Jesus of Nazareth had accepted his invitation to dine.

Simon allowed himself a small smile as he turned back into his courtyard. The other Pharisees would be impressed. Where they had failed to draw the controversial rabbi into their scholarly debates, Simon had succeeded with a simple dinner invitation. Tonight, he would take the measure of this man who claimed to speak for God yet ate with tax collectors and sinners.

"Hannah," he called to his wife, who emerged from the kitchen area with flour dusting her hands. "The teacher has accepted. We'll need to prepare for additional guests—I suspect his inner circle will accompany him."

Hannah's expression tightened almost imperceptibly. "How many should I prepare for?"

"Twenty, perhaps twenty-five. I've invited several colleagues from the synagogue. This could be an important evening for establishing our position regarding the Nazarene."

His wife nodded, already calculating quantities in her mind. "I'll need to send Miriam to the market for more lamb."

"Spare no expense," Simon instructed, straightening his prayer shawl.

"Everything must be perfect. The teacher may dress like a common labourer, but he'll find no fault with our hospitality."

As Hannah disappeared back into the kitchen, calling for servants, Simon moved to his private study. He had preparations of his own to make—not for food, but for the careful theological examination he planned to conduct. The reports about Jesus were contradictory and troubling. Some claimed he was a prophet; others whispered about demonic power. The man's teachings often aligned with scripture, yet his associations and practices violated numerous traditions.

Simon pulled a scroll from its designated shelf, unrolling it to a familiar passage. The words of Isaiah stared back at him: "The Spirit of the Lord is upon me, because he has anointed me to proclaim good news to the poor." According to witnesses, Jesus had read these very words in the Nazareth synagogue, claiming their fulfilment in himself. The audacity of it still made Simon's jaw clench.

Yet the miracles were harder to dismiss. Just last week, a Roman centurion's servant had been healed—Simon had spoken with the synagogue elders who witnessed it. The centurion himself, a man named Gaius Cornelius who had funded their synagogue's construction, swore the healing occurred the moment Jesus spoke the word, without even visiting the sick man.

Simon rolled the scroll carefully, returning it to its place. Tonight, he would observe this Jesus firsthand. He would test the man's knowledge of the law, probe his understanding of the prophets, and determine once and for all whether they dealt with a misguided zealot or something more dangerous.

The afternoon sun slanted through the narrow window, reminding him of the time. He had arrangements to make with his fellow Pharisees, ensuring they understood the evening's purpose. This was not merely a social gathering—it was an examination and possibly a trial.

The market square of Capernaum bustled with its usual late afternoon energy. Merchants hawked their wares with practiced enthusiasm while customers haggled with equal vigour. The smell of fresh bread competed with the salt tang from the nearby harbour, where fishermen were beginning to prepare their nets for the night's work.

Miriam, daughter of Joanna, moved through the crowd with practiced efficiency, her servant's tunic marking her as a member of Simon's household. She had served the Pharisee's family for three years now, ever since her father's fishing business had failed. It was respectable work, and Simon was known as a fair employer, if somewhat demanding in his religious observances.

She paused at the butcher's stall, examining the lamb with a critical eye. Simon had been specific—only the best would do for tonight's gathering. As she negotiated with the merchant, she became aware of whispers rippling through the market.

"She's here again," an elderly woman muttered to her companion. "Bold as brass, as if she has any right to walk among decent people."

Miriam didn't need to look to know who they meant. Mary of Magdala—though most simply called her "the sinful woman"—had that effect wherever she went. The whispers followed her like shadows, though what precisely constituted her sins varied depending on who told the tale.

Some said she had been a prostitute; others claimed she was merely a woman who had lived outside the strict bounds of propriety. What everyone agreed on was that she was unclean, unworthy, and unwelcome in polite society.

Against her better judgement, Miriam glanced toward the disturbance. Mary stood at a perfume merchant's stall, her face partially hidden by a dark head covering. Even so, Miriam could see the tension in her shoulders, the way her hands trembled slightly as she examined an alabaster jar.

"That's worth more than she could earn in a year," the elderly woman continued, loud enough for Mary to hear. "Unless she's returned to her old ways."

The perfume merchant, a Syrian named Demetrius, seemed torn between the prospect of a sale and the social implications of serving such a customer. "Perhaps the lady would prefer something more... modest?" he suggested, reaching for a smaller clay vessel.

"No," Mary's voice was quiet but firm. "This one. How much?"

Demetrius named a price that made Miriam gasp. It was indeed a year's wages—she knew because it was more than she earned serving in Simon's household. The alabaster jar contained pure nard, imported from the distant mountains of India, reserved for the most sacred occasions or the wealthiest patrons.

To everyone's surprise, Mary produced a leather purse and began counting out silver coins. The crowd's whispers turned to outright speculation. Where had she gotten such money? Had she returned to her former life? Or had she perhaps stolen it?

Miriam completed her own purchase quickly, eager to distance herself from the brewing scandal. As she turned to leave, laden with packages, she nearly collided with Mary, who was clutching the alabaster jar as if it were more precious than life itself.

For a moment, their eyes met. Miriam expected to see defiance or shame but instead found something else entirely—a profound sadness mixed with an even deeper determination. Mary's eyes were red-rimmed, as if she'd been crying, but there was a light in them that Miriam couldn't quite define.

"Pardon me," Mary whispered, stepping aside.

Miriam nodded stiffly and hurried past, but something made her glance back. Mary stood in the midst of the hostile crowd, seemingly oblivious to their stares and whispers, cradling the precious jar against her chest. There was something in her posture that reminded Miriam of a woman preparing for battle—or perhaps for sacrifice.

Shaking off the strange thought, Miriam quickened her pace toward Simon's house. She had work to do, and the master would not tolerate delays. Still, she couldn't quite forget the look in Mary's eyes or the way she held that alabaster jar as if it contained her very soul.

The sun was beginning its descent toward the western hills as Jesus and his disciples made their way through Capernaum's winding streets. Peter walked beside his master, unable to shake a feeling of unease about the evening's invitation.

"I still don't trust him, Rabbi," Peter muttered, keeping his voice low. "Simon's been one of your most vocal critics in the synagogue. Why accept his invitation now?"

Jesus glanced at his disciple with that knowing look that always made Peter feel like a child stating the obvious. "Tell me, Simon Peter, who needs a physician more—the healthy or the sick?"

"The sick, of course, but—"

"And who needs light more—those who can see or those who are blind?"

Peter sighed. He'd walked into that one. "The blind, Master. But Simon doesn't think he's blind. He thinks you're the one who needs correcting."

"Precisely," Jesus said, a slight smile playing at the corners of his mouth. "And that, my friend, is exactly why we're going."

John, walking on Jesus's other side, spoke up. "The others are worried it might be a trap. The Pharisees have been gathering, planning something. We've heard rumours..."

"There are always rumours," Jesus replied calmly. "But Simon has offered hospitality, and we will receive it in good faith. Besides," he added, his eyes taking on that distant look that meant he saw something beyond the present moment, "tonight's dinner will offer teaching opportunities that Simon hasn't anticipated."

The disciples exchanged glances over their master's head. They'd learnt to recognise that tone—it usually preceded events that turned their understanding upside down.

As they climbed the stone steps leading to Capernaum's upper district, the houses grew larger and more elaborate. Simon's residence stood near the crest of the hill, its whitewashed walls gleaming in the late afternoon light. The courtyard gate stood open, with servants already positioned to receive guests.

"Welcome, Teacher," a servant bowed low, though Peter noticed he didn't offer the customary foot washing. The slight was subtle but deliberate—guests of honor were always offered water for their feet upon arrival. "My master awaits you in the dining hall."

Jesus simply nodded, showing no sign that he'd noticed the discourtesy. But Peter saw it, and his jaw clenched. So it was to be that kind of evening—hospitality offered with one hand while honor was withheld with the other.

They were led through a beautifully appointed courtyard where a fountain tinkled softly and jasmine perfumed the air. Other guests had already arrived, Peter noticed—several Pharisees in their distinctive robes, a few scribes, and surprisingly, some of the more prominent merchants of Capernaum. Whatever Simon's purpose, he'd assembled an audience of influence.

The dining hall was arranged in the formal Roman style, with low couches arranged in a U-shape around low tables. Simon stood at the centre of the arrangement, resplendent in his finest robes, phylacteries prominently displayed on his forehead and arm.

"Teacher," Simon greeted, inclining his head precisely as much as courtesy demanded and no more. "You honour my house with your presence."

"The honour is mine, Simon," Jesus replied warmly, as if greeting an old friend rather than a suspicious critic. "I thank you for your invitation."

Peter watched Simon's eyes narrow slightly, perhaps thrown off by the genuine warmth in Jesus's response. The Pharisee had probably expected defensiveness or perhaps an attempt to curry favour. Simple graciousness seemed to puzzle him.

"Please, recline here." Simon gestured to a couch that was respectable but not the place of highest honour. Another calculated slight. "Your... companions may take the lower places."

The disciples filed in, taking their positions with varying degrees of grace. Matthew, the former tax collector, seemed comfortable with the formal setting, while James and John looked ready to bolt at the first opportunity. Peter positioned himself where he could watch both his master and their host.

As the other guests took their places, Peter observed the careful choreography of social positioning. The Pharisees clustered near Simon, while the merchants and scribes arranged themselves according to some invisible hierarchy. The atmosphere was thick with unspoken agendas.

Simon raised his hand for silence. "Before we begin, perhaps the teacher would offer a blessing?"

It was another test, Peter realised. The exact words of the blessing, the scriptural references chosen, even the pronunciation would be scrutinised. But Jesus simply smiled and lifted his hands.

"Blessed are you, Lord our God, King of the universe, who brings forth bread from the earth," he began, using the traditional words. But then he continued, his voice taking on that quality that made even simple words seem to resonate with deeper meaning. "Blessed are you who feed the hungry and give drink to the thirsty. Blessed are you who welcomes the stranger and clothes the naked. For in serving the least of these, we serve you."

A ripple of reaction ran through the room. The blessing was orthodox enough, but the addition—while scripturally sound—carried implications that made several of the Pharisees shift uncomfortably.

Simon's smile tightened. "Indeed. Let us eat."

Servants appeared with the first course—fresh bread, olives, and honey. The meal began with polite conversation, but Peter could feel the undercurrents of tension. This was not a celebration but an inquisition dressed in the clothes of hospitality.

As plates were filled and wine was poured, Simon leaned toward Jesus with studied casualness. "Tell me, Teacher, I'm curious about your interpretation of the prophet Isaiah's words regarding the acceptable year of the Lord. Some say you claimed these scriptures were fulfilled in Nazareth. Surely this was misunderstood?"

And so it begins, Peter thought, watching his master's face. But Jesus merely reached for a piece of bread, his movements unhurried.

"Tell me, Simon," Jesus said, "when you read the prophets, do you see promises for a distant future, or do you look for God's kingdom breaking into the present?"

It was a masterful response, turning the question back on the questioner. Simon's eyes glinted with something that might have been respect or irritation.

"The prophets speak of God's ultimate plan," Simon replied carefully. "We must be cautious not to presume upon divine timing."

"And yet," Jesus said, breaking the bread with deliberate care, "when a farmer sees green shoots breaking through the soil, does he not know the harvest is coming? When a woman feels the child quicken within her, does she not know that new life is on its way?"

One of the other Pharisees, a man named Nathanael, leaned forward. "But surely you're not suggesting that you yourself are the fulfilment of messianic prophecy? The scriptures speak of one who will restore the kingdom to Israel, who will break the yoke of Roman oppression."

"The scriptures speak of many things," Jesus replied. "A suffering servant. A prince of peace. A stone the builders rejected. Tell me, Nathanael, must the kingdom of God come with swords and armies? Or might it arrive as quietly as a seed falling on good soil?"

The room had grown quiet, all pretence of casual conversation abandoned. This was what they'd come for—to see the controversial teacher defend his claims, to find the heresy they were certain lurked beneath his words.

But before Nathanael could respond, a disturbance at the entrance drew everyone's attention. A servant stood there, clearly agitated, trying to block someone from entering.

"You cannot come in here," the servant hissed. "This is a private gathering. The master has important guests."

"Please," a woman's voice replied, thick with emotion. "I must... I need to..."

Simon's face darkened with annoyance. "What is the meaning of this interruption?"

The servant turned, his face flushed. "Master, forgive me. This... woman insists on entering. I've told her it's not permitted, but she won't leave."

That's when Peter saw her—Mary of Magdala, the woman whose reputation preceded her wherever she went. She stood in the doorway, clutching something against her chest, her eyes wide and desperate. Her gaze swept the room until it found Jesus, and something in her face changed—a mixture of relief, determination, and profound sorrow.

"I know who she is," Simon said coldly. "How dare she defile my house with her presence? Remove her at once."

But Mary had already moved, slipping past the servant with surprising agility. She crossed the room with quick, purposeful steps, her eyes never leaving Jesus. The guests recoiled as she passed, as if her very presence might contaminate them.

Peter tensed, ready to intervene if needed, but something in his master's expression stopped him. Jesus was watching Mary approach with a look of infinite compassion, as if he'd been expecting her all along.

She fell to her knees at his feet, and that's when Peter saw what she carried—an alabaster jar that caught the lamplight like captured moonbeams. Her hands shook as she held it, and tears were already streaming down her face.

"Master," Simon's voice cut through the shocked silence like a blade. "Surely you know what manner of woman this is who dares to touch you. She is a sinner, unclean, unfit for the company of righteous men."

But Jesus didn't move, didn't pull away. He simply watched as Mary's tears fell on his feet, her shoulders shaking with silent sobs.

What happened next would be debated in Capernaum for months to come. Mary broke the seal on the alabaster jar, and immediately the room filled with the rich, overwhelming scent of pure nard. The perfume was worth a fortune—everyone knew it—and she poured it over Jesus's feet with trembling hands.

The waste of it scandalised the room. Judas Iscariot was the first to voice what many were thinking. "Why this waste? This perfume could have been sold for a year's wages and given to the poor!"

But Mary seemed oblivious to the criticism. She let down her hair—another shocking breach of propriety—and began to wipe Jesus's feet with it, her tears mixing with the precious oil. She kissed his feet repeatedly, her actions speaking of a gratitude too deep for words.

Simon's face had turned to stone. He didn't need to speak; his thoughts were written clearly in his expression. If this man were truly a prophet, he would know what kind of woman was touching him. He would recoil from her uncleanness, demand she be removed. The fact that he sat there, allowing this display, proved everything Simon had suspected.

But Jesus, who had been silent throughout Mary's actions, finally spoke. "Simon, I have something to say to you."

The Pharisee straightened, perhaps glad to move past the uncomfortable scene. "Tell me, Teacher."

Jesus's voice was gentle, but it carried to every corner of the room. "A certain moneylender had two debtors. One owed five hundred denarii, and the other fifty. When they could not pay, he cancelled both debts. Now which of them will love him more?"

Simon's eyes narrowed, sensing a trap but unable to see it clearly. "I suppose the one who had the larger debt cancelled."

"You have judged correctly," Jesus said. Then he turned and looked directly at Mary for the first time, though his words were still addressed to Simon. "Do you see this woman?"

The question hung in the air like a challenge. Of course Simon saw her—how could anyone not see her, making such a spectacle of herself? But Jesus continued, his voice taking on an edge that Peter had rarely heard. "I entered your house; you gave me no water for my feet, but she has wet my feet with her tears and wiped them with her hair. You gave me no kiss of greeting, but from the time I came in, she has not ceased to kiss my feet. You did not anoint my head with oil, but she has anointed my feet with perfume."

Each comparison was like a hammer blow to Simon's carefully constructed facade of righteousness. The cultural implications were devastating—Simon had failed in the basic courtesies due to an honoured guest, while this "sinful woman" had exceeded them all.

"Therefore I tell you," Jesus said, his voice now ringing with authority, "her sins, which are many, are forgiven—for she loved much. But he who is forgiven little, loves little."

The room erupted in shocked whispers. Who was this man who claimed to forgive sins? That was God's prerogative alone! The theological implications were staggering, blasphemous even.

But Jesus wasn't finished. He looked down at Mary, who was gazing up at him with wonder and disbelief. "Your sins are forgiven," he said directly to her.

The whispers grew louder. "Who is this who even forgives sins?"

Jesus helped Mary to her feet with gentle hands. "Your faith has saved you," he told her, his voice meant for her alone though all could hear. "Go in peace."

Mary stood there for a moment, swaying slightly as if the weight she'd carried for so long had suddenly been lifted. Her tear-stained face was radiant with a joy that seemed to light her from within. She looked around the room as if seeing it for the first time—all these important men in their fine robes, all these judges who had condemned her without knowing her story.

Then she straightened her shoulders, wiped her eyes, and walked out with a dignity that her entrance had lacked. The empty alabaster jar lay on its side where she'd left it, a mute testimony to an act of love that had cost everything and gained even more.

The silence that followed her departure was deafening. Simon sat rigid on his couch, his face a mask of conflicting emotions. The careful trap he'd laid had somehow entangled him instead. His failure as a host had been exposed before all his peers, while a sinful woman had been elevated as an example of true love and worship.

One of the Pharisees, bolder than the rest, finally spoke. "Teacher, surely you don't mean to say that this woman's emotional display somehow earns her forgiveness? What of the law? What of justice?"

Jesus reached for his cup, taking a slow sip before answering. "Tell me, Eli, if your child fell into a well on the Sabbath, would you wait until the next day to pull them out?"

"Of course not," Eli replied, frowning. "The law permits the saving of life."

"Then why," Jesus asked, "do you object when a daughter of Abraham is pulled from the well of sin and death? Is her soul worth less than a body?"

"But the manner of it," another Pharisee interjected. "Such unseemly emotion, such... excess. Surely repentance should be more dignified, more ordered."

Jesus's eyes swept the room, taking in each face. "When you find a lost sheep, do you criticise it for bleating too loudly? When a father receives back a son he thought was dead, do you tell him his joy is excessive?"

He stood then, and Peter recognized the signs—his master was about to deliver one of those teachings that would be repeated and debated for generations.

"You sit here in your fine robes, measuring out your righteousness in careful portions, afraid to give too much lest you have none left for yourselves. You tithe your mint and dill and cumin, but you have neglected the weightier matters of the law—justice, mercy, and faithfulness."

Several of the Pharisees shifted uncomfortably. The reference to tithing herbs was particularly pointed—it was exactly the sort of meticulous religious observance they prided themselves on.

"That woman," Jesus continued, "understood something you have missed. She knew the depth of her need, so she could appreciate the height of mercy. She knew the weight of her chains, so she could celebrate the joy of freedom. You, who believe yourselves already righteous, have no room in your hearts for the overwhelming gratitude that leads to such love."

Simon found his voice at last. "So you're saying that sin is actually an advantage? That those who have fallen furthest have gained the most?"

"I'm saying," Jesus replied, turning to face his host directly, "that those who know they are sick seek a physician. Those who know they are lost look for a shepherd. Those who know they are in darkness yearn for light. But those who believe they already have all these things... what can be offered to them?"

He moved toward the door, his disciples rising to follow. But at the threshold, he turned back one more time.

"Simon, you invited me here tonight to examine me, to test my teaching against your understanding of righteousness. But I tell you truly—that woman you despised has shown more understanding of God's kingdom than all your careful theology. She gave everything she had, holding nothing back, because she understood the value of what she was receiving. Can you say the same?"

With that, he was gone, leaving behind a room full of educated, important men struggling to process what they'd witnessed. The lingering scent of nard seemed to mock their confusion—such waste, such extravagance, such inappropriate excess.

But Simon sat in silence, staring at the empty alabaster jar. Something in the teacher's words had found its mark, piercing through layers of self-righteousness he'd built up over years of careful religious observance. The woman's tears, her complete abandon in worship, the transformation in her face when forgiveness was pronounced—it all spoke of a reality he'd never experienced despite all his prayers and fasting and study.

One by one, his guests made their excuses and departed, the evening's purpose derailed by an uninvited woman and her alabaster jar. Soon only

Simon remained, alone with his thoughts and the lingering fragrance of pure nard.

Hannah appeared in the doorway, surveying the abandoned feast with dismay. "Shall I have the servants clear away the food?"

Simon nodded absently, his mind elsewhere. "Hannah," he said suddenly, "what would you do if you discovered that everything you'd built your life on was... incomplete? Not wrong exactly, but missing something essential?"

His wife studied him with concern. "I don't understand. Did the teacher say something to upset you?"

"Yes," Simon admitted. "No. Both." He rubbed his face wearily. "He held up a mirror, and I didn't like what I saw."

Hannah moved closer, sitting beside him with uncharacteristic informality. "Tell me."

So Simon told her about the woman, about the parable of the two debtors, and about his own failures as a host. As he spoke, he began to see the evening's events in a new light. His invitation had been calculated, his hospitality minimal, and his intentions judgemental. He'd offered the bare minimum required by custom while planning to dissect and discredit his guest.

And that woman—that sinful, broken, desperate woman—had shown him what true worship looked like.

"Perhaps," Hannah said softly when he'd finished, "the teacher's mirror showed you not who you are, but who you could become."

283

Simon looked at his wife in surprise. In all their years of marriage, focused on maintaining their position in the community, he'd rarely heard her speak of spiritual matters with such insight.

"The woman knew she needed forgiveness," Hannah continued. "She came ready to pour out everything for it. You came ready to judge whether the teacher was worthy of your approval. Which one of you was truly seeking God?"

The question hung between them like an accusation and an invitation combined. Simon thought of the woman's tears, of the teacher's compassion, and of the forgiveness proclaimed with such authority. He thought of his own carefully measured religion, doled out in acceptable portions, never excessive, never embarrassing, never transformative.

"I need to find him," Simon said suddenly, standing. "The teacher—I need to speak with him again."

Hannah smiled, the first genuine smile he'd seen from her in years. "Then go. But Simon?" She reached for the abandoned alabaster jar, holding it up to the lamplight. "Perhaps consider what you're willing to pour out. Half-measures won't suffice for what you're seeking."

Simon stared at the jar—empty now, its precious contents spilt in an act of worship that had scandalised the religious and transformed the sinner. Was he willing to be equally extravagant with his own carefully guarded righteousness? To pour out his pride and position in exchange for... what? For the kind of forgiveness that had lit that woman's face with joy? For the kind of relationship with God that prompted such overwhelming gratitude?

He didn't know. But for the first time in his life as a Pharisee, Simon bar Jonah wanted to find out.

The streets of Capernaum were quiet as he made his way down the hill, following the path the teacher had taken. The moon was rising over the Sea of Galilee, painting the water silver. Somewhere in this town, Jesus was probably teaching his disciples about what had happened, drawing lessons from the evening's strange turn.

And somewhere else, a woman who had entered his house as a sinner walked free, forgiven, transformed by an encounter with excessive grace.

Simon quickened his pace. He had much to learn about the kingdom of God, and he suspected his education had only just begun.

In a modest home near the harbour, Mary sat in darkness, still trying to comprehend what had happened. Her sister Martha busied herself with a lamp, bringing light to chase away the shadows.

"You're back," Martha said simply, but her voice carried volumes of relief and question.

Mary nodded, unable to speak past the emotion still thick in her throat. The house felt different somehow—or perhaps she was the one who had changed. The weight that had pressed on her chest for so long, the shame that had colored every interaction, the guilt that had whispered condemnation with every breath—it was gone.

"I did it," she finally managed. "I found him at Simon's house, just as we heard. I... I anointed his feet."

Martha's eyes widened. "You went to Simon the Pharisee's house? Mary, how could you? The risk—"

"I had to," Mary interrupted. "Don't you understand? After everything, after all the darkness, when I heard he was here, that he accepts people like me... I had to try."

She thought of the market square and of the whispers and stares as she'd purchased the nard. Every piece of silver had represented months of saving, planning for a future that might redeem her past. Some had thought she was saving for a dowry; others suspected less honourable intentions. None had guessed the truth—that she'd been waiting for this moment, for this chance.

"Tell me everything," Martha urged, settling beside her sister.

So Mary told her about the terror of walking into that room full of righteous men who knew her reputation, about falling at Jesus's feet and finding herself unable to do anything but weep. She described the breaking of the alabaster jar, the scent of nard filling the room, and the shocking moment when she'd let down her hair to wipe his feet.

"I couldn't speak," she admitted. "I had words planned, a confession, a plea for mercy. But when I saw him, when I was actually there... all I could do was cry. All those years of shame, all the choices I wished I could take back, all the nights I've lain awake knowing that I was beyond redemption—it all just poured out with the tears."

Martha reached for her sister's hand. "What did he say?"

Mary's voice dropped to a whisper. "He defended me. Can you imagine? Simon was thinking terrible things—I could see it in his face—and Jesus told him a story about two debtors. He said..." She paused, still struggling to believe it. "He said my sins were forgiven. All of them. Because I loved much."

"He forgave your sins?" Martha leaned forward, intense. "Just like that?"

"Just like that." Mary laughed, a sound mixed with tears. "The others were scandalised. Who is this who forgives sins? But I knew. I've known since the first time I heard him teach. This is no ordinary rabbi, Martha. When he speaks, heaven listens. When he forgives, chains break."

She stood and moved to the window, looking out at the moonlit water. "He told me to go in peace. Peace, Martha. When was the last time I felt peace? When was the last time I walked through town without shame dogging my steps?"

"And the perfume?" Martha asked. "It cost everything you had saved."

Mary turned back, her face serene. "It cost everything, and it was barely enough. If I had ten thousand alabaster jars, I would break them all at his feet. What is perfume compared to forgiveness? What is money compared to being made clean?"

A knock at the door interrupted them. The sisters exchanged worried glances—visitors at this hour rarely brought good news. Martha went to answer it, returning with a surprised expression.

"There's a Pharisee asking for you," she told Mary. "He says his name is Simon bar Jonah."

Mary's heart skipped. Had he come to berate her further? To demand recompense for disrupting his dinner? But when Simon entered, she saw something unexpected in his face—uncertainty, even humility.

"Forgive the intrusion," he began formally, then stopped, seeming to struggle with his words. "I... that is... what happened tonight at my house..."

"I'm sorry for interrupting your dinner," Mary said quickly. "I know it was inappropriate—"

"No," Simon interrupted, surprising them both. "No, that's not why I'm here." He took a breath, visibly gathering courage. "I came to ask... how did you know?"

Mary frowned, not understanding. "Know what?"

"That he would forgive you. That it would be... real. Complete." Simon's carefully controlled composure cracked slightly. "I've studied the law all my life. I've followed every commandment, observed every feast, and maintained ritual purity. But tonight, watching you, seeing the transformation when he spoke forgiveness... I've never experienced anything like that."

Mary studied the Pharisee who had looked at her with such disdain just hours ago. Now she saw not arrogance but hunger—a spiritual starvation that all his religious observance hadn't satisfied.

"I knew," she said slowly, "because I had nowhere else to turn. When you reach the end of yourself, when you know that no amount of good deeds can balance the scales, when you accept that you're drowning and cannot save yourself—that's when you're ready to receive grace."

Simon flinched. "But I've tried to live righteously—"

"And I tried to live without regard for righteousness," Mary countered gently. "Both paths led to the same place—a need for mercy we couldn't earn. The only difference is that I knew my need. You're just discovering yours."

The Pharisee sank onto a bench, his fine robes pooling around him. "The teacher said something about those who are forgiven little love little. I thought I needed little forgiveness because I'd sinned little. But now..."

"Now you're beginning to see that self-righteousness might be the greatest sin of all?" Mary suggested.

Simon's head snapped up, but instead of anger, she saw recognition in his eyes. "Yes," he whispered. "Yes, that's exactly it. I've been so proud of my clean hands that I never noticed my filthy heart."

Martha, who had been silent throughout this exchange, suddenly spoke. "Then perhaps you understand why my sister did what she did. When you truly see your need for forgiveness, no response seems adequate except complete abandonment."

Simon looked between the two women—these common folk he would have dismissed as unlearned just hours ago—and saw teachers where he'd expected students. "What must I do?" he asked, echoing a question asked by many who encountered Jesus.

Mary smiled, remembering her own journey to this moment. "Go to him. Take whatever you've been holding back—pride, position, the approval of your peers—and pour it out at his feet. He won't turn you away."

"But I'm a Pharisee. My colleagues will—"

"I was a sinful woman," Mary interrupted. "My reputation was destroyed. Which of us has more to lose? And which of us has more to gain?"

Simon stood slowly, understanding dawning in his eyes. The careful structure of his life—the social position, the religious authority, the respect of his peers—suddenly seemed as fragile as an alabaster jar, and perhaps just as meant to be broken.

"Thank you," he said simply, including both sisters in his gaze. "I came here thinking to question you further about the teacher. Instead, you've taught me what I should have learnt years ago in all my study."

He moved toward the door, then paused. "The perfume," he said. "It must have cost everything you had."

Mary nodded. "Everything."

"And yet you poured it all out. Not a drop saved back."

"How could I?" Mary asked. "When you've been forgiven a debt you could never pay, how can you measure your gratitude? How can you calculate your love?"

Simon had no answer. Or rather, he had too many answers—all the careful calculations of his religious life, all the measured responses, all the acceptable limits. None of them adequate for what he'd witnessed tonight.

He left the sisters' house and walked slowly through the empty streets. The moon had risen higher, flooding Capernaum with silver light. Somewhere, Jesus was probably still teaching, still transforming lives with his radical message of grace.

Simon thought of the empty alabaster jar on his dining room floor. Such waste, his guests had said. Such excess. But now he understood—when you've glimpsed the kingdom of God, no response is excessive. When you've encountered true forgiveness, no gratitude is too much.

Tomorrow, his fellow Pharisees would want to discuss the evening's events. They would analyse the teacher's words, debate the theological implications, and plan their next move. But Simon would not be there. He had an alabaster jar of his own to break—a lifetime of self-righteousness to pour out in exchange for the forgiveness he'd never known he needed.

The scent of nard still clung to his robes, a reminder of worship that held nothing back. Simon breathed it in deeply, then quickened his steps. The night was still young, and he had much to learn about loving much.

The next morning brought a different Capernaum than the one that had existed the day before. News of the dinner at Simon's house had spread through the night like spilt perfume, seeping into every corner of the town. The story grew with each telling—the sinful woman who had dared to enter a Pharisee's home, the fortune in perfume poured out like water, the shocking pronouncement of forgiveness, and perhaps most surprising of all, Simon bar Jonah seen walking the streets at dawn, seeking the controversial teacher.

In the synagogue, a cluster of Pharisees and scribes gathered in heated discussion. Eli, who had been at the dinner, held court with his version of events.

"Blasphemy," he declared. "Pure and simple. No man can forgive sins—that is God's prerogative alone. And to pronounce such forgiveness on that woman, of all people, without any sign of proper repentance, without restitution, without even a sacrifice at the temple..."

"But what of Simon?" another asked. "Is it true he went to the woman's house afterward?"

Eli's face darkened. "A moment of weakness. The teacher has a way of confusing people with his stories and emotional appeals. Simon will come to his senses when he realises what associating with this man will cost him."

But Nathanael, who had also been present, was less certain. "Did you not see her face when she left? The transformation was... remarkable. And the teacher's words about the two debtors—can you really find fault with the logic?"

"Logic?" Eli sputtered. "Since when is logic determined by the tears of fallen women? We have the law, given by God himself through Moses. We don't need new interpretations from Galilean carpenters who consort with tax collectors and sinners."

Yet even as he spoke, doubt niggled at the edges of his certainty. He too had seen Mary's transformed countenance and had felt the power in Jesus's words. The comfortable boundaries of his faith—clean divisions between righteous and sinner, acceptable and outcast—had blurred in that room filled with the scent of nard.

Meanwhile, in the harbour district where the common people lived and worked, the story took on a different tone. Mary of Magdala, whom most had written off as beyond redemption, walked with her head high for the first time in years. Those who had whispered behind their hands now watched in amazement as she moved with the quiet dignity of one set free. At the well where women gathered to draw water and exchange news, the conversation buzzed with speculation and wonder.

"She looks different," one woman observed, watching Mary fill her water jar. "Younger somehow. As if years have fallen away."

"It's hope," another said quietly. "I haven't seen hope in her eyes since... well, since before everything went wrong."

An elderly woman named Tabitha, respected for her wisdom, spoke thoughtfully. "If the teacher can forgive her sins—really forgive them, not just speak empty words—then perhaps there's hope for all of us."

"But we're not like her," a younger woman protested. "We haven't... that is, we don't need..."

"Don't we?" Tabitha challenged gently. "Are your hands so clean? Is your heart so pure? I've lived long enough to know that we all carry secret shames, hidden sins we think disqualify us from grace. Perhaps Mary's only crime was that her sins were more visible than ours."

The women fell silent, each examining their own hearts. How many of them harboured bitterness, nursed grudges, whispered gossip, and envied their neighbours? How many small sins accumulated to equal one large one? And if forgiveness was available—real, transformative forgiveness—did the size of the debt really matter?

Peter, James, and John sat by the shore, mending nets while they discussed the previous evening's events. The mundane task of checking for tears and retying knots provided a familiar rhythm for processing the extraordinary.

"I've never seen the Master handle the Pharisees quite like that," James said, working a particularly stubborn knot. "Usually he answers their challenges with questions. Last night, he told them exactly what he thought.

"Because they weren't really challenging him," Peter replied. "They were attacking her. And the Master never stands by when someone attacks the vulnerable."

John, the youngest and often the most perceptive, added, "Did you notice how he looked at her? Not with pity or disgust, but with... recognition. As if he saw who she really was beneath all the shame."

"And now Simon's seeking him out." Peter shook his head in amazement. "Simon the Pharisee, who invited us to dinner just to trap the Master. The kingdom of God turns everything upside down."

"Or right-side up," John suggested. "Maybe we've been looking at everything backwards. We think the religious leaders are close to God and the sinners are far away. But what if it's the opposite? What if knowing your need brings you closer than thinking you have no need?"

They worked in silence for a while, each lost in thought. The events of the previous evening had challenged their assumptions about righteousness, forgiveness, and the nature of God's kingdom. They'd left everything to follow Jesus, thinking they understood his mission. But nights like last night reminded them how much they still had to learn.

In her small workshop, a tentmaker named Priscilla found herself unable to concentrate on her work. She had not been at the dinner, but her husband had brought home the story, and it wouldn't leave her alone.

All her life, she'd been taught that God's favor was earned through careful obedience to the law. Blessings came to the righteous; judgement fell on sinners. The system was clear, predictable, and safe. But this teacher from Nazareth was overturning everything with his radical forgiveness, his welcoming of outcasts, and his criticism of the very religious leaders she'd been taught to revere.

"What troubles you, my love?" her husband, Aquila, asked, entering with supplies.

"That woman—Mary. I've avoided her for years, crossing the street rather than encountering her. We all have. And now..."

"Now she's been forgiven," Aquila finished. "Publicly. Completely. It challenges everything, doesn't it?"

Priscilla nodded. "If she can be forgiven so easily, what was the point of all our careful living? All our observances, all our efforts to maintain purity?"

Aquila set down his bundles and took his wife's hands. "Perhaps the point wasn't to earn God's love but to respond to it. Perhaps we've been so focused on being good enough that we've missed being loved."

"But then anyone could be forgiven," Priscilla protested. "Any sin could be washed away. There would be no justice, no consequences."

"Or perhaps," Aquila suggested gently, "there would be a different kind of justice. One that transforms sinners rather than destroying them. One that offers hope instead of condemnation."

Priscilla thought of Mary's tear-stained face, of the alabaster jar poured out without reservation. "She gave everything she had," she murmured.

"Because she understood what she was receiving," Aquila replied. "Maybe that's the difference. We who think we have much to offer God give little. Those who know they have nothing to offer but their need give everything."

The workshop fell quiet as they returned to their tasks, but both carried the weight of reconsidered faith. Around them, throughout Capernaum, similar conversations unfolded as the scandal of grace rippled outward like waves on the sea.

By midday, Simon bar Jonah had found Jesus teaching by the lakeside. The crowd was smaller than usual—perhaps word of the previous night's controversy had made some wary. But those who remained listened with unusual intensity as Jesus spoke of God's kingdom using simple stories of seeds and soil, wheat and weeds.

Simon stood at the edge of the gathering, his fine Pharisee robes marking him as distinctly out of place among the fishermen and labourers. Several recognised him and whispered among themselves. What was he doing here? When Jesus finished speaking and the crowd began to disperse, Simon approached. Peter moved to intercept him—was this another confrontation?—but Jesus waved his disciple back.

"Simon," Jesus greeted him warmly, as if they were old friends meeting by chance. "Welcome."

The Pharisee cleared his throat, acutely aware of the disciples watching him with suspicion. "Teacher, I... after last night... I have questions."

"Walk with me," Jesus invited, and they strolled along the shore, leaving the others behind. For a while, they walked in silence, the only sounds the lapping of waves and the cries of gulls.

Finally, Simon spoke. "All my life, I've followed the law. Every commandment, every statute, every tradition passed down from our fathers. I thought that made me righteous."

"And now?" Jesus prompted gently.

"Now I see that I was like a man polishing the outside of a cup while the inside remained filthy. That woman—her sins were obvious, external. Mine were hidden, internal, but perhaps worse for being denied."

Jesus nodded, encouraging him to continue.

"Pride," Simon confessed, the word bitter on his tongue. "Self-righteousness. Contempt for those I deemed lesser. A heart that measured out God's mercy in careful portions while claiming unlimited amounts for myself." He stopped walking, turning to face Jesus directly. "Can such sins be forgiven? Can a heart so twisted be made straight?"

Jesus smiled, and in that smile, Simon saw the same compassion that had transformed Mary the night before. "Simon, what did I tell you about the two debtors?"

"That the one forgiven much loves much."

"Then the question is not whether you can be forgiven, but whether you can accept that you need forgiveness. Can you, a teacher of Israel, become like a child? Can you, who have built your life on being right, admit you have been wrong?"

Simon thought of his position, his reputation, and the respect of his peers—all balanced against the freedom he'd seen in Mary's eyes. "I want to," he admitted. "But I'm afraid. Afraid of what I'll lose, afraid of what others will say, afraid that I don't know how to live without my carefully constructed righteousness."

"Perfect love casts out fear," Jesus said. "And you've already taken the first step by coming here. The kingdom of God is not for those who have everything figured out, but for those willing to admit they don't."

They resumed walking, and Jesus began to teach him—not in parables as he did with the crowds, but directly, personally. He spoke of God not as a distant judge tallying infractions but as a father watching for his children's return. He talked about righteousness not as a ladder to climb but as a gift to receive. He painted a picture of the kingdom where the last would be first, the lost would be found, and the broken would be made whole.

As the sun reached its zenith, they circled back to where the disciples waited. Peter watched suspiciously as Simon approached, but his expression changed when he saw the Pharisee's face. Gone was the cold superiority of the previous night. In its place was something Peter recognised—the wonder of one who had encountered grace.

"Thank you," Simon said simply to Jesus. Then, gathering his courage, he turned to the disciples. "I owe you an apology. Last night, I offered hospitality with one hand while planning judgement with the other. I see now that I was the one being tested, and I failed." He paused, swallowing his pride. "But perhaps failure is the beginning of wisdom."

The transformation of Simon bar Jonah would become another thread in the tapestry of testimonies growing around Jesus. A Pharisee humbled, a sinner exalted, the religious framework of centuries challenged by acts of radical grace—the kingdom of God was indeed at hand, and it looked nothing like what anyone had expected.

As word spread of Simon's visit to Jesus, the religious establishment of Capernaum found itself in crisis. If one of their own could be so swayed, what did that mean for their authority? Emergency meetings were called, strategies debated, lines drawn between those who saw Jesus as a dangerous revolutionary and those beginning to wonder if he might be something more.

But in the harbour district, among the common people, hope spread like sunrise. If Mary could be forgiven, if Simon could be transformed, then perhaps the kingdom of God had room for all of them—tax collectors and fishermen, prostitutes and Pharisees, the desperate and the doubting.

The alabaster jar remained in Simon's house, empty but somehow still fragrant, a reminder of worship that held nothing back. Hannah would sometimes find her husband holding it, lost in thought, learning the hardest lesson of his religious life—that sometimes you had to pour out everything you thought you knew to receive what you never knew you needed.

And Mary? She continued to live in Capernaum, but she was no longer defined by her past. The woman who had entered Simon's house weeping left it walking in peace. The one who had been known only for her sins became known for her worship. She would follow Jesus throughout his ministry, one of the women who supported him, who stood at the cross when others fled, and who came to the tomb expecting to anoint a body and instead became the first to announce the resurrection.

But that was still to come. For now, in the days following that transformative dinner, Capernaum buzzed with the scandal of grace. Religious leaders debated, common people hoped, and somewhere between the two, hearts began to understand that the kingdom of God was not about earning God's love but about receiving it, not about measuring out righteousness but about pouring out gratitude.

The empty alabaster jar had become a symbol, though different people saw different meanings in it. For some, it represented waste—a fortune spent in a moment of emotion. For others, it spoke of judgement on a religious system that had forgotten mercy. But for those who had witnessed the transformation it brought, the alabaster jar told a simpler story: when you've been forgiven everything, nothing is too much to give in return.

And so the kingdom of God advanced in Capernaum, not through force or argumentation, but through tears and perfume, through broken pride and mended hearts, through a teacher who saw sinners as children of God and religious leaders as needing the very grace they thought to judge.

The revolution had come to dinner, and nothing would ever be the same.

Chapter 12: Following the Teacher

The morning mist still clung to the shores of Galilee when Mary Magdalene first saw the procession. She stood at the edge of the market square in Magdala, her fingers absently rubbing the smooth stones in her pocket—a habit from darker days when she needed something solid to anchor her to reality. The crowd moving through the streets was unlike any she'd seen before: fishermen and tax collectors, zealots and farmers, all following a single figure whose presence seemed to bend the very air around him.
"There," whispered Joanna, touching Mary's elbow. "That's him. The teacher from Nazareth."
Mary had heard the stories, of course. Everyone in Galilee had. A carpenter's son who spoke with authority that made rabbis falter. A healer whose touch drove out fevers and straightened twisted limbs. Some whispered he was a prophet. Others claimed he was dangerous, a threat to the careful balance between Rome and the Temple.
But as Mary watched him pause to speak with a leper the crowd had parted to avoid, she saw something else entirely. The way he looked at the man—not through him or past him, but truly at him, as if seeing every moment of pain and rejection the disease had brought. When Jesus touched the leper's shoulder, the crowd gasped. Mary found herself holding her breath.
"He's not afraid," she murmured.
"Of leprosy?" Joanna asked.

"Of anything," Mary replied, though she couldn't have explained how she knew.

The healing, when it came, was almost anticlimactic. No theatrical gestures, no lengthy incantations. Jesus simply spoke a few quiet words, and the white patches on the man's skin faded like frost before the sun. The former leper fell to his knees, weeping, trying to kiss Jesus's feet. But the teacher lifted him up, whispered something that made the man laugh through his tears, and sent him on his way.

That's when Jesus looked up and saw Mary watching from across the square. Their eyes met for a moment that stretched like honey from a spoon, and Mary felt exposed in a way that had nothing to do with her carefully modest clothing or the veil covering her hair. It was as if he could see through all her carefully constructed walls to the broken places she'd spent years trying to hide.

Seven demons. That's what they'd called her affliction. Seven distinct voices that had once raged in her mind, each with its own flavour of torment. The religious leaders had tried exorcisms that left her bruised and exhausted. The physicians had prescribed treatments that drained her family's money and her body's strength. In the end, she'd been left to manage her madness alone, finding ways to function despite the chaos in her head.

But in that moment, under the teacher's gaze, the old familiar pressure began building behind her eyes. Not again, she thought desperately. Not here, not in front of everyone. She turned to flee, but Joanna caught her arm.

"Mary, what's wrong?"

"I need to go. I can't—" The words tangled in her throat as the first voice began its familiar litany of accusations. *Unclean, unworthy, unwanted...*

"Peace."

The word cut through the rising chorus like a blade through silk. Jesus stood before her, though she hadn't seen him cross the square. Up close, she could see the dust of travel on his robes and the calluses on his hands from years of working wood. Human details that somehow made his presence more, not less, overwhelming.

"Mary of Magdala," he said, and hearing her name in his voice was like hearing it for the first time. "You've carried these burdens long enough."

"You don't know what I—" she began, but the words died as he placed his hand on her forehead. Heat and cold, light and darkness, a sensation like being turned inside out and right-side up all at once. The voices rose to a shriek, then scattered like birds before a storm.

The silence that followed was so profound that Mary gasped, her knees buckling. Strong hands caught her—not Jesus's, but those of the men who travelled with him. A burly fisherman with kind eyes and work-roughened hands helped her to a bench.

"Easy now," he said. "It takes a moment to adjust. I'm Peter, by the way. This here's my brother Andrew."

Mary barely heard him. Her mind was her own for the first time in seven years. No competing voices, no constant battle for control. Just... quiet. She began to laugh, then cry, then both at once.

"Is she all right?" That was Joanna, hovering anxiously nearby.

"She's free," Jesus said simply. "And freedom can be overwhelming at first."

He knelt before Mary, bringing himself to her eye level. "The demons will try to return. They'll whisper that this peace is temporary, that you don't deserve it. When they do, remember this moment. Remember that you are seen, known, and loved exactly as you are."

"I don't understand," Mary managed through her tears. "Why would you—I'm nobody. I'm nothing."

"You're a daughter of Abraham," Jesus replied. "Made in God's image, precious beyond measure. The world may have told you otherwise, but the world is often wrong about what matters most."

He stood, addressing Joanna as well. "The harvest is plentiful, but the workers are few. We have need of those who understand brokenness and healing, who can minister to the wounds that run deeper than flesh."

Mary saw Joanna's face transform as understanding dawned. Joanna carried her own hidden wounds—a marriage to Herod's steward that had brought wealth but little warmth, a childlessness that marked her as cursed in many eyes, and a keen mind trapped in a society that valued women primarily as vessels for sons.

"You're asking us to join you," Joanna said slowly. "To travel with you like your male disciples do."

Peter made a sound of surprise. "Master, surely that's not—women travelling with us? What would people say?"

Jesus turned to him with a smile that held both affection and gentle reproof. "The same things they say now, Peter. That I eat with tax collectors and sinners. That I touch lepers and speak to Samaritans. Since when has the kingdom of heaven been bound by what people might say?"

"But the practical matters," another disciple interjected—a younger man with the careful speech of education. "Where would they sleep? How would it look? The scandal—"

"Judas raises valid concerns," Jesus acknowledged. "Which is why wisdom is needed. These women will not share our camps but will secure their own lodgings in the towns we visit. They'll contribute to our mission through their own gifts and resources."

Mary found her voice. "I have money. Not much, but... my family's fishing business has done well. I could help with provisions."

"And I have connections throughout Herod's territory," Joanna added, her chin lifting with sudden purpose. "Chuza's position opens doors that might otherwise remain closed."

Jesus nodded. "You see? The Father provides for his work in unexpected ways. Who better to support a mission of healing than those who have themselves been healed?"

Over the following days, Mary discovered that she and Joanna were not the only women drawn to follow the teacher. Susanna of Caesarea arrived with a retinue of servants she promptly dismissed, keeping only one elderly maid for propriety's sake. Her story tumbled out over shared meals: a wealthy widow whose only son had been dying of fever until Jesus spoke a word of healing from a distance.

"I tried to give him gold," Susanna explained, her aristocratic features animated with emotion. "He wouldn't take it. Said the gift of God couldn't be purchased. But surely I can use that gold to ensure he and his disciples don't go hungry while they spread this gift to others?"

Then came Salome, mother to James and John, drawn by her sons' transformation from ambitious fishermen to devoted disciples. "I need to see for myself," she declared, "what manner of man could change my boys so completely."

Rachel of Bethsaida, whose daughter had been freed from seizures. Martha and Mary of Bethany, who opened their home as a regular stopping place. Tabitha of Joppa, whose skill with needle and thread kept their robes mended and presentable.

Each woman brought her own story of encounter, her own reasons for leaving behind conventional life to follow this unconventional rabbi. They formed a parallel community to the male disciples, managing practical matters with an efficiency that surprised even them.

"We need a system," Joanna announced one evening as they gathered in the courtyard of an inn in Capernaum. "I'll handle negotiations with innkeepers and local officials. Susanna, you manage the common purse. Mary, you coordinate with the disciples about travel plans and teaching locations."

Mary had discovered an unexpected gift for organisation. Her mind, freed from its torment, proved sharp and capable. She found herself serving as liaison between the women's group and the twelve, navigating personalities and priorities with growing confidence.

Not that it was always smooth. The male disciples struggled to adjust to the women's presence. Some, like Peter and John, welcomed them warmly. Others, particularly Judas, maintained a careful distance marked by formal politeness and subtle disapproval.

"It's not proper," Mary overheard him complaining to Simon the Zealot one evening. "What will the Pharisees say when they hear women are funding our mission? They'll claim we're no better than Greek mystery cults with their temple prostitutes."

"Let them say what they will," Simon replied. Mary was surprised by the defence from the fierce nationalist. "I've seen these women's dedication. They ask nothing but to serve. How is that improper?"

The real test came in Nain, a small city nestled in the hills south of Nazareth. They'd arrived to find the town in mourning, a funeral procession winding its way toward the cemetery. The wails of professional mourners pierced the air, but beneath them, Mary heard something that made her heart clench—the broken sobs of a mother who had lost everything.

"Her only son," a townsperson explained. "And she's a widow. She'll have to beg now, or worse."

Mary watched Jesus's face change as he took in the scene. Without a word, he moved toward the procession. The disciples scrambled to follow, and Mary found herself swept along with them.

"Don't touch the bier!" Judas hissed. "You'll be ceremonially unclean—"

But Jesus was already reaching out, his hand on the wooden platform where the wrapped body lay. The procession stuttered to a halt. The mourners' wails cut off in confusion.

"Young man," Jesus said, his voice carrying despite its gentleness. "I say to you, arise."

For a heartbeat, nothing. Then the wrapped figure convulsed. Gasps rippled through the crowd as the grave clothes began to move. The young man sat up, clawing at the bindings around his face, very much alive and extremely confused.

"Mother?" he called out, and the widow's scream of joy could have raised the dead all by itself.

As the crowd erupted in amazement and praise, Mary noticed something others missed. Jesus had quietly stepped back, but not before she saw him sway slightly. Peter steadied him with a discreet hand.

"It costs him," she murmured to Joanna. "These miracles. They take something from him."

Joanna nodded. "I've seen it too. Especially when he heals many at once. He grows pale, tired."

"Then we make sure he eats," Mary said firmly. "And rests when he can. If he won't care for himself, we'll have to do it for him."

This became their unspoken mission within the mission. While the male disciples focused on crowd control and teaching opportunities, the women made sure Jesus actually ate the bread they provided and actually slept in the lodgings they arranged. They learnt his preferences—fresh fish over preserved, honey in his wine when his voice grew hoarse from teaching, and the way he relaxed when someone sang the old psalms his mother had taught him.

"You're mothering him," Peter accused one day, though his tone was more amused than annoyed.

"Someone has to," Mary shot back. "You men are so caught up in the grand vision, you forget he's human. He needs food and rest like anyone else."

Peter's expression grew thoughtful. "You're right. We do forget sometimes. When you see him command storms and raise the dead, it's easy to forget he gets tired and hungry."

The incident that truly cemented the women's place in the group came in Chorazin. Jesus had been teaching in the synagogue when a group of Pharisees from Jerusalem arrived, their intentions clearly hostile. They'd peppered him with trick questions, trying to trap him in blasphemy or sedition.

Mary watched from the women's section as Jesus deflected each attack with scripture and wisdom. But she also saw what others missed—the tremor in his hands, the way he shifted his weight to ease some hidden pain. He'd been travelling and teaching without a break for weeks.

When the Pharisees finally departed in frustration, Jesus emerged from the synagogue to find the usual crowd of sick and desperate people waiting. Mary saw him take a breath, squaring his shoulders to meet their needs despite his exhaustion.

"No," she said, stepping forward. "Not today."

The crowd turned to her in surprise. Even the disciples looked shocked at her audacity.

"The teacher needs rest," Mary continued, meeting their stares steadily. "He's given everything he has. Come back tomorrow."

"Who are you to speak for him?" demanded a man carrying a paralysed child.

Before Mary could answer, Jesus placed a hand on her shoulder. "She is my friend," he said simply. "And she speaks wisdom. I will heal your child, but then I must rest. The spirit is willing, but the flesh has limits."

After healing the child and a few urgent cases, Jesus allowed the women to guide him to the house they'd prepared. For once, he ate without prompting and fell asleep almost immediately on the simple pallet.

"Thank you," Peter said quietly, finding Mary keeping watch in the courtyard. "We should have seen it. Should have protected him better."

"We all serve in different ways," Mary replied. "You cast out demons in his name. We make sure he has strength to continue. Both are necessary."

As the ministry expanded, so did the women's roles. They became bridges to other women who might fear approaching the male-dominated group. Mary lost count of the quiet conversations in market corners, the gentle introductions that led to healing and transformation.

There was the prostitute in Bethsaida who wept when Mary told her she too had been freed from demons. "He would speak to me? Touch me? Even knowing what I am?"

"He knows what you could be," Mary assured her. "That's all that matters to him."

There was the Roman centurion's wife in Capernaum, desperate for help but afraid to approach a Jewish teacher. Joanna's connections and diplomatic skills smoothed the way, resulting in the healing of the centurion's servant and a powerful testimony that rippled through the occupying forces.

There was the Syrophoenician woman whose sick daughter became a lesson in persistent faith, largely because Susanna had coached her on how to approach Jesus in a way that would capture his attention.

Not every interaction was successful. In one village, the women were accused of being cult prostitutes, forced to flee under cover of darkness. In another, relatives of the women tried to drag them home, claiming they'd been bewitched.

"My own sister," Rachel said bitterly after her brother's attempt to forcibly remove her from the group. "She says I'm bringing shame on the family, following a man who's not my husband."

"Mine say worse," Mary admitted. "That the demons have returned, that this is just another form of madness."

"Let them say what they will," Joanna interjected. "We know the truth. We've seen what others only hear about. How could we go back to our old lives knowing what we know?"

The teacher himself seemed both grateful for and protective of the women who followed him. He included them in teachings when culture would have excluded them, defended their presence when religious leaders objected, and used their faith as examples in his parables.

"Why do you waste time teaching women?" a scribe challenged him one day. "They cannot be witnesses in court or students of Torah."

"The kingdom of heaven recognises witnesses that earthly courts reject," Jesus replied. "And the Torah was given to all God's children, not just half of them."

Mary treasured these moments, storing them in her heart like provisions for a coming famine. Something in the teacher's eyes when he looked toward Jerusalem told her that darker days lay ahead.

The shadow fell during a feast at a Pharisee's house. The women weren't invited, of course, but they waited nearby, ready to assist when the meal ended. Mary noticed the commotion first—raised voices, someone shouting about blasphemy.

Then she saw her: a woman she recognised from Magdala's darker streets, carrying an alabaster jar that must have cost a year's wages. Before anyone could stop her, the woman had pushed into the house.

"We have to help her," Mary said, starting forward, but Joanna held her back. "Wait. Look at the teacher's face."

Through the doorway, they could see Jesus watching the woman with an expression of profound compassion. She'd thrown herself at his feet, weeping so hard her tears washed the dust from his skin. Then she broke the alabaster jar, and the scent of pure nard filled the air.

The Pharisees recoiled in disgust. Even some of the disciples muttered about waste and impropriety. But Jesus lifted the woman's chin, speaking words too quiet for those outside to hear. Whatever he said transformed her face from despair to wonder.

"He knew," Mary breathed. "He knew she would come and what she would do."

"Just as he knew we would come," Susanna added softly. "Each of us, at just the right moment."

Later, walking back to their lodgings, the women reflected on what they'd witnessed.

"Did you notice how he defended her?" Joanna asked. "He said she'd anointed him for burial. What do you think he meant?"

Mary shivered despite the warm evening. "I've been having dreams. Dark ones. I think... I think something terrible is coming."

"Don't say that," Rachel protested. "He's the Messiah. He's going to restore the kingdom to Israel."

"Is he?" Mary challenged gently. "Is that really what he's been teaching? Or have we been hearing what we want to hear?"

The question hung between them like incense, sweet but somehow troubling. They'd all come to the teacher with expectations—healing, purpose, revolution, and restoration. But his kingdom seemed to operate by different rules than any earthly realm.

"Remember what he said in Capernaum?" Susanna offered. "His kingdom is not of this world. Maybe we need to stop thinking in earthly terms."

"Easier said than done," Joanna sighed. "Especially when my husband keeps asking when this teacher is going to make his move against Rome. Chuza's patience has limits."

Mary understood. They all faced pressure from families, friends, and society itself. Following an itinerant teacher who challenged every social norm wasn't just countercultural—it was dangerous. Yet none of them spoke of leaving.

The next morning brought news that John the Baptist had been arrested. The atmosphere around Jesus changed, becoming charged with an urgency that set everyone on edge. He spent more time in prayer, often slipping away before dawn to commune with his Father in solitude.

"He's preparing for something," Peter confided to Mary one evening. "I've asked what, but he only speaks in parables about seeds dying to bring forth fruit."

Mary thought of the woman with the alabaster jar, anointing him for burial while he still lived. "Maybe he's trying to prepare us, and we're not ready to hear."

Peter's face darkened. "Don't you start with the death talk. Thomas is bad enough with his pessimism. The Master is going to restore Israel. He has to. Why else would God send the Messiah?"

But Mary had learnt to read the teacher's moods, the weight that seemed to settle on him more heavily with each passing day. Whatever lay ahead, she sensed it would shatter all their expectations.

The turning point came in Caesarea Philippi. The women had secured lodgings in the predominantly Gentile city while Jesus took the twelve aside for private teaching. When the men returned, something had fundamentally changed.

Peter's face glowed with fervour, but the other disciples looked shaken. James and John huddled with their mother, Salome, speaking in urgent whispers. Judas stood apart, his expression unreadable.

"What happened?" Mary asked Andrew, who seemed less agitated than the others.

"Peter declared him the Christ," Andrew said slowly. "And the Master confirmed it. But then..." He shook his head. "He started talking about suffering and death. Peter tried to correct him, and the Master... I've never seen him so harsh. Called Peter 'Satan,' told him he was thinking like men, not God."

Mary's heart sank. The dreams, the forebodings, the veiled references—they were all converging on a truth none of them wanted to face.

"He's trying to prepare us," she said quietly. "Whatever's coming, he wants us ready."

"Ready for what?" Andrew demanded. "If he's the Messiah but he dies, what hope is there?"

Mary didn't have an answer. But that night, as she lay awake wrestling with the implications, she remembered something Jesus had said weeks ago: "Unless a grain of wheat falls into the earth and dies, it remains alone; but if it dies, it bears much fruit."

Perhaps the kingdom they sought wouldn't come through earthly triumph but through something far more costly and profound. Perhaps following the teacher meant walking a path none of them had imagined when they first left everything to follow him.

The next morning, she gathered the women. "We need to talk about what's coming. I think the teacher is heading toward something terrible and necessary. We need to decide if we're willing to follow him there."

"Where else would we go?" Joanna asked simply. "He has the words of eternal life."

One by one, the others nodded. They'd come too far to turn back now. Whatever lay ahead—triumph or tragedy, glory or grief—they would face it together.

"Then we prepare," Mary said firmly. "We save what money we can. We strengthen our connections in Jerusalem. And we pray for courage, because I think we're going to need it."

As if in confirmation, Jesus chose that day to begin teaching more openly about his coming suffering. The male disciples argued and resisted, but the women listened with heavy hearts and clear eyes. They'd learnt to trust the teacher's wisdom even when they didn't understand it.

"You're not trying to talk him out of it," Peter accused Mary after one particularly difficult teaching about taking up crosses.

"Would it do any good if I did?" Mary replied. "He knows something we don't, sees something we can't. All we can do is trust and follow."

"Even to death?" Peter's voice cracked on the word.

Mary thought of her seven demons, of the life she'd been given back. "He gave me life when I was as good as dead. If he asks for that life back, it's his to take."

Peter stared at her, then walked away shaking his head. But Mary saw him later, praying with a desperation that suggested her words had hit their mark.

The women's ministry continued, but now with an undercurrent of preparation for an unknown crisis. They stockpiled resources, strengthened networks, and most importantly, they documented. Mary began keeping detailed accounts of Jesus's teachings, knowing that memory alone might not be enough for what lay ahead.

"Why are you writing these things?" Judas asked one day, finding her scratching notes on parchment.

"Because truth has a way of getting twisted," Mary replied. "If something happens to him, people will tell the story their own way. Someone needs to remember what really happened."

Judas's expression was unreadable. "You really think something will happen to him?"

"Don't you?" Mary challenged. "You manage the money. You see how the authorities watch us, how the crowds grow more demanding. This can't continue indefinitely."

"No," Judas agreed quietly. "It can't."

There was something in his tone that made Mary uneasy, but before she could pursue it, Susanna called her away to deal with a lodging problem.

The final phase of their journey began with the teacher setting his face toward Jerusalem. The celebration of Tabernacles was approaching, and despite the disciples' protests about the danger, Jesus was determined to attend.

"It's a trap," Thomas insisted. "The authorities are waiting for any excuse to arrest you."

"Let them wait," Jesus replied calmly. "My hour has not yet come."

The women exchanged glances. His hour. He spoke of it often now, some appointed time known only to him and his Father. Mary suspected that when it arrived, all their preparation would prove inadequate.

Still, they did what they could. Joanna used her connections to secure safe houses in Jerusalem. Susanna distributed funds among them in case they were separated. Mary coordinated with sympathisers in the city, building a network of support for whatever lay ahead.

"You're planning for a siege," one of the disciples observed—Nathanael, the one they called the guileless.

"I'm planning for reality," Mary corrected. "He's walking into the heart of opposition. We'd be fools not to prepare."

Nathanael studied her with those penetrating eyes. "You've changed since Magdala. The demons truly left you, didn't they?"

"Seven of them," Mary confirmed. "But they left room for something else to enter. Faith. Purpose. Love." She paused. "Fear too, if I'm honest. Fear of losing him."

"But not enough fear to leave?"

"Never enough for that," Mary said firmly. "Whatever comes, I'll face it at his side. We all will."

The journey to Jerusalem took on the quality of a funeral procession and a victory march combined. Crowds gathered at each village, drawn by the teacher's reputation. He healed and taught with undiminished power, but Mary noticed how his eyes kept turning south, toward the city that killed its prophets.

One evening, camped outside Jericho, she found him sitting alone, gazing at the stars. The disciples had given him space, recognising one of his contemplative moods. But Mary approached with a cup of the honeyed wine he favoured when his throat was raw from speaking.

"Thank you," he said, accepting the cup. "Sit with me?"

She settled beside him, comfortable with the silence that fell between them. She'd learnt that the teacher's silences often said more than his words.

"You see it, don't you?" he finally asked. "What's coming?"

"I see shadows," Mary admitted. "Dark dreams. But not clearly."

"That's mercy," he said softly. "Clear sight would break your heart."

"It's already breaking," Mary confessed. "Every time you speak of leaving, of suffering. We've found life with you. How can we face death?"

He turned to her then, and in the starlight, she saw tears on his cheeks. "Oh, Mary. Always so direct. That's what I've treasured about you—no pretence, no hiding behind propriety."

"The demons took my ability to pretend," she said. "When you've been stripped of everything, including your own mind, social niceties seem pointless."

"And that's why you understand," he said. "The others follow me hoping for glory, for restoration, for a kingdom like David's. But you follow because you've already died and been reborn. You know that sometimes destruction precedes creation."

"Is that what's coming? Destruction?"

"And creation," he assured her. "A new covenant written in blood. A kingdom not of this world. A family not bound by flesh but by spirit." He paused. "But first, yes, destruction. Of everything they think they know about God and power and love."

Mary felt tears slip down her own cheeks. "Will we be strong enough?"

"No," he said simply. "You'll fail. Flee. Deny. But that's not the end of the story. My Father specialises in resurrection, in bringing life from death and hope from despair. Trust in that, when everything else fails."

He stood, offering her his hand. "Come. The others will worry if we stay out here too long. And tomorrow we enter Jericho, where a certain tax collector needs to meet his salvation."

Mary took his hand, feeling the calluses from years of carpentry, the strength that could calm storms and raise the dead. Human and divine, wrapped in mystery she'd never fully understand but would always trust.

"I'll follow you," she said. "Wherever this path leads."

"I know," he replied. "And that gift humbles me more than you can imagine."

They walked back to camp together, master and disciple, saviour and saved. Around them, the night sounds of Palestine continued—jackals calling in the distance, wind through ancient olive trees, and the eternal rhythms of a world that had no idea it was about to change forever.

The women's camp was still active, everyone preparing for tomorrow's journey. Mary moved among them, checking supplies, offering encouragement, and maintaining the practical ministry that kept the larger mission moving. But her mind kept returning to the teacher's words: destruction and creation, death and resurrection.

"You look troubled," Joanna observed, falling into step beside her.

"He confirmed it," Mary said quietly. "What we've feared. Something terrible is coming."

Joanna was silent for a moment. "Then we face it as we've faced everything else. Together. With faith."

"He said we'll fail," Mary admitted. "That we won't be strong enough."

"Then we'll fail," Joanna said with surprising calm. "And then we'll find out what comes after failure. If he says it's not the end, I believe him."

Mary squeezed her friend's hand, drawing strength from her steady faith. Around them, the camp settled for the night. Tomorrow would bring new crowds, new teachings, and new steps toward whatever destiny awaited in Jerusalem.

But tonight, they had this—friendship forged in service, purpose born from healing, and hope that transcended understanding. The women who followed Jesus had found more than they'd ever dared seek. Now they would learn if they had the courage to lose it all and trust in promises of resurrection.

The stars wheeled overhead, ancient witnesses to the drama unfolding below. And in a dozen hearts, faith wrestled with fear as the teacher's words echoed: "My Father specialises in resurrection."

They would need to remember that. In the dark days coming, when hope seemed as dead as a body in a tomb, they would need to remember that the God they served could bring life from death, joy from mourning, and from a small band of broken people, a kingdom that would never end.

Mary lay down that night with prayers on her lips and steel in her spine. Whatever came, she would not abandon the one who had refused to abandon her. The seven demons had taken much from her, but they had also taught her to fight. Now she would fight for hope, for faith, for the teacher who had given her back her life.

Tomorrow, the road to Jerusalem. Tonight, the quiet courage of women who had learnt that following the Messiah meant walking into mystery with open hands and willing hearts. They would stumble, doubt, and perhaps even despair. But they would not let go.

In the darkness before dawn, Mary rose to help prepare breakfast. The mundane task grounded her—bread to break, fish to distribute, water to draw. The teacher needed to eat. The disciples needed strength for the journey. Life continued its demands even as cosmic drama unfolded.

"Couldn't sleep either?" Susanna appeared beside her, already working dough for the bread.

"Too much to think about," Mary admitted.

"I've been thinking about my son," Susanna said quietly. "How close he came to death before the teacher healed him. I promised God that day that if he spared my boy, I'd serve him however he asked." She paused. "I never imagined it would lead here."

"Regrets?" Mary asked.

"No," Susanna said firmly. "Questions, fears, uncertainty—yes. But no regrets. How could I regret being part of this?"

As the camp stirred to life, Mary watched the teacher emerge from his tent, immediately surrounded by disciples with questions and plans. But he caught her eye across the busy space and nodded—a simple acknowledgement that carried weight beyond words.

They were in this together, all of them. The boastful fisherman and the doubting tax collector, the zealot and the scholar, and the women who served and supported and saw what others missed. An unlikely family bound by something stronger than blood—the call of a carpenter from Nazareth who spoke of kingdoms and crosses with equal authority.

"Ready?" Joanna appeared with the morning's logistics, the endless details that kept their movement functioning.

"As ready as anyone can be for the unknown," Mary replied.

And with that simple truth, they faced the new day. The road to Jerusalem stretched before them, leading to triumph and tragedy intertwined. But they would walk it as they had begun—following the teacher who had transformed their lives, trusting in purposes they couldn't fully see, carrying hope like a light in gathering darkness.

The women who followed Jesus had found their place, their purpose, and their voice. Now they would discover if their faith was strong enough to survive what lay ahead. And if it wasn't—if they failed as he predicted—they would learn what grace looked like on the other side of failure.

The sun rose over Galilee, painting the landscape in shades of gold and promise. Another day in the company of the teacher. Another step toward destiny. Another opportunity to serve, to love, to bear witness to the kingdom breaking into the world through the most unexpected channels.

Mary of Magdala, once tormented by seven demons, now freed to serve the Holy One of Israel, shouldered her pack and joined the procession. Behind her, the other women fell into line—each with their own story, their own reasons, and their own unshakeable commitment to follow wherever he led. The road to Jerusalem beckoned. They walked it together, these unlikely disciples, these women who dared to believe that God's kingdom had room for them too. And with each step, they moved closer to the hour when everything would change, when their faith would be tested by fire, and when they would discover that sometimes the greatest victory comes disguised as defeat.

But that was still ahead. For now, there was only the road, the teaching, the healing, and the presence of the one who had called them from darkness into light. It was enough. It had always been enough. And it would sustain them through whatever lay ahead.

Chapter 13: Stories of the Kingdom

The morning sun painted the Sea of Galilee in strokes of gold and sapphire as Jesus stood at the water's edge near Capernaum. The familiar scent of fish and brine mixed with the earthier aromas of the crowd gathering behind him—sweat, road dust, and the lingering fragrance of breakfast bread. Peter's fishing boat bobbed gently at anchor, twenty feet from shore, waiting.

"Master," Andrew called from the vessel, "we're ready when you are."

Jesus turned to survey the growing multitude. They came from everywhere now—farmers abandoning their fields at crucial growing seasons, merchants closing shops in the middle of profitable market days, and mothers carrying infants through the morning heat. Their faces bore the universal expression of the spiritually famished: hope mixed with desperation, scepticism wrestling with need.

Among them, Jesus spotted familiar faces. There was Joanna, wife of Herod's steward, her fine linen incongruous among the homespun robes of fishermen's wives. Mary of Magdala stood near the front, her eyes clear and focused where once seven demons had clouded them with madness. Susanna the merchant counted heads with practiced efficiency, already calculating how many loaves would be needed if the teaching extended past midday.

But it was the unfamiliar faces that drew his attention most. A Roman centurion lingered at the crowd's edge, helmet tucked under his arm, curiosity overcoming proprietary concern. A group of Pharisees from Jerusalem huddled together, their phylacteries broad and tassels long, whispering behind raised hands. Children darted between adults' legs, their laughter a bright counterpoint to the serious expressions of their elders.
"So many," Matthew murmured, moving to Jesus's side. The former tax collector's fingers twitched as if yearning for his old counting tablets. "Master, perhaps we should move to the hillside? There's more room—"
"No," Jesus said gently. "The water will carry my voice. And there are things to be said today that require the right setting." He glanced at the lake, its surface mirror-smooth in the windless morning. "Seeds need proper soil, Matthew. Even the seeds of words."
Thomas approached from the other direction, doubt etched in the furrows of his brow. "Teacher, the Pharisees from Jerusalem—they're not here to learn. I overheard them speaking of traps, of catching you in blasphemy."
"Let them listen," Jesus replied. "The kingdom of heaven plays no favourites. It comes to the religious and the outcast alike. Though," a smile tugged at his lips, "some find it harder to enter than others."

He waded into the shallows, the cool water a relief against the already-warming day. Peter and Andrew steadied the boat as he climbed aboard, his robe dripping lake water onto the weathered planks. The vessel had seen better days—nets patched and re-patched, oarlocks worn smooth by countless journeys, and the smell of fish permanently embedded in the wood. Yet for today's purpose, it would serve as perfectly as Solomon's throne.

"Push off," Jesus instructed. "But not too far. Let them see my face as well as hear my words."

The brothers obeyed, using long poles to position the boat perhaps thirty feet from shore. Close enough for expression to be visible, far enough for the water to create a natural amphitheatre. The crowd pressed forward until the first rank stood ankle-deep in the lake, children hoisted onto shoulders, the elderly given positions on borrowed stools.

Jesus sat in the boat's stern, letting silence settle over the assembly like morning mist. In that quiet, he saw their needs written plainly—the farmer worried about failing crops, the widow wondering how to feed her children, the sick hoping for healing, and the sinner aching for forgiveness. So many hungers. So many thirsts. And he had come to satisfy them all, though not in ways they expected.

"Listen," he began, his voice carrying clearly across the water. "A farmer went out to sow his seed."

The crowd leaned forward. Everyone here knew farming, whether they practiced it themselves or simply depended on its fruits. This was language they could grasp, images rooted in their daily reality.

"As he was scattering the seed, some fell along the path, and the birds came and ate it up."

Nods of recognition rippled through the gathering. How many times had they seen that very thing—precious seed devoured before it could even think about sprouting? In the boat, Peter shifted restlessly. He was a fisherman, not a farmer, but even he knew the frustration of wasted effort.

"Some fell on rocky places, where it did not have much soil. It sprang up quickly because the soil was shallow. But when the sun came up, the plants were scorched, and they withered because they had no root."

Miriam, the potter's widow, touched the pouch at her belt where she kept her few remaining denarii. She knew about shallow soil, about hopes that sprouted quickly only to die under life's harsh sun. Her husband's death had scorched so many dreams.

"Other seed fell among thorns, which grew up and choked the plants."

The Pharisees exchanged glances. Surely this simple agricultural tale had some deeper meaning. Was the teacher mocking their detailed interpretations of the Law? Were they the thorns in his metaphor? Judas Iscariot, standing with the other disciples on the shore, unconsciously touched the money bag at his waist. He had his own thorns—ambitions and frustrations that seemed to choke his joy in following this unconventional rabbi.

"Still other seed fell on good soil, where it produced a crop—a hundred, sixty, or thirty times what was sown."

A collective intake of breath swept the crowd. Such yields were the stuff of dreams, the kind of harvest that meant not just survival but abundance. Children would eat their fill, debts could be paid, and offerings could be made with joy rather than obligation.

Jesus paused, letting the image sink deep. Then, with a voice that carried both invitation and challenge: "Whoever has ears, let them hear."

The crowd stirred uneasily. That phrase—they'd heard it from prophets, from teachers who weren't content with surface understanding. It meant there was more here than agricultural advice. But what?

A young scribe, bolder than his companions, called out, "Teacher, what does this mean? Surely you speak of more than farming!"

Jesus's eyes found the questioner—earnest, eager, but also guarded. How much truth was the young man prepared to receive?

"The knowledge of the secrets of the kingdom of heaven has been given to you," Jesus said, addressing not just the scribe but all who genuinely sought understanding. "But to those who choose blindness, everything remains in parables."

One of the Jerusalem Pharisees, a man named Eleazar, stepped forward. His voice dripped with barely concealed disdain. "So you claim secret knowledge? You set yourself up as a mystery teacher, speaking in riddles to confuse the simple?"

"On the contrary," Jesus replied, his tone gentle but firm. "I speak in stories because they reveal truth to those who truly seek it, while concealing it from those who would use it as a weapon." He looked directly at Eleazar. "Tell me, teacher of the Law, when you expound on the commandments for hours in the synagogue, using words the common people can barely understand, are you illuminating or obscuring?"

Eleazar's face reddened, but before he could respond, a fisherman's wife called out, "Then help us understand, Master! We're simple people. What does the seed mean?"

Jesus smiled at her honest plea. "Come closer, all who wish to understand. Let me explain this first story, and then you'll begin to see the others more clearly."

The crowd pressed forward until some stood waist-deep in the water. Children found perches on their fathers' shoulders. Even some of the Pharisees inched closer, though they maintained expressions of scepticism.

"The farmer is anyone who speaks the word of God," Jesus began. "The seed is that word—living, potent, capable of transformation. But notice: the same seed falls on different types of ground. The seed doesn't change. The soil makes all the difference."

He pointed to the packed earth of the path running along the shore. "When anyone hears the message about the kingdom and does not understand it, the evil one comes and snatches away what was sown in their heart. This is the seed sown along the path. The ground is so hard, so travelled by the feet of tradition and preconception, that truth cannot penetrate. It sits on the surface until the birds—the forces that oppose God's kingdom—snatch it away."

Marcus, the Roman centurion, shifted uncomfortably. How many times had he heard Jewish teachings and dismissed them as foreign superstition? Was his heart that hardened path?

"The seed falling on rocky ground," Jesus continued, "refers to someone who hears the word and at once receives it with joy. But since they have no root, they last only a short time. When trouble or persecution comes because of the word, they quickly fall away."

Young Benjamin, who had left his father's fishing business to follow Jesus just a week ago, swallowed hard. His father's anger still rang in his ears. Would he be rocky ground when family pressure intensified?

"The seed falling among the thorns refers to someone who hears the word, but the worries of this life and the deceitfulness of wealth choke the word, making it unfruitful."

Joanna involuntarily glanced at her expensive robe. How many times had palace concerns crowded out spiritual contemplation? How often had she chosen comfort over conviction?

"But the seed falling on good soil refers to someone who hears the word and understands it. This is the one who produces a crop, yielding a hundred, sixty or thirty times what was sown."

"But Teacher," called out Thaddeus the vineyard keeper, "how do we become good soil? I was born on rocky ground—my father was hard, my grandfather harder still. Can the soil change its nature?"

Jesus's eyes lit with approval at the question. "You begin to understand, Thaddeus. The beauty of this kingdom is that rocky ground can be broken up, hard paths can be plowed, thorns can be uprooted. The farmer doesn't just scatter seed—he prepares the soil. And the wise farmer works with the Great Farmer, allowing his heart to be cultivated."

He stood in the boat, balancing easily despite its gentle rocking. "But come, let me tell you another story. The kingdom of heaven is like a man who sowed good seed in his field."

The crowd settled again, eager for more. Even the sceptical Pharisees leaned in, despite themselves.

"But while everyone was sleeping, his enemy came and sowed weeds among the wheat and went away. When the wheat sprouted and formed heads, then the weeds also appeared."

Farmers in the crowd groaned in recognition. They knew these weeds—darnel, probably, which looked exactly like wheat until the heads formed. By then, the roots were so intertwined that pulling the weeds would destroy the wheat.

"The owner's servants came to him and said, 'Sir, didn't you sow good seed in your field? Where then did the weeds come from?'

"'An enemy did this,' he replied.

"The servants asked him, 'Do you want us to go and pull them up?'

"'No,' he answered, 'because while you are pulling the weeds, you may uproot the wheat with them. Let both grow together until the harvest. At that time I will tell the harvesters: First collect the weeds and tie them in bundles to be burnt; then gather the wheat and bring it into my barn.'"

This story created more murmuring than the first. The Pharisees whispered furiously among themselves. Was Jesus suggesting that evil should be tolerated? That the unrighteous should be allowed to remain among the faithful?

Simon the Zealot, standing among the disciples, clenched his fists. He had joined Jesus hoping for revolution, for the violent overthrow of Roman oppression. This talk of letting weeds grow alongside wheat seemed like dangerous passivity.

But Mary of Magdala understood. She had been a weed once—demon-possessed, ostracised, and written off by religious society. Yet Jesus had seen great potential in her weedy existence. He had waited for the right moment to separate her from what bound her, without destroying her in the process.

"Teacher," called out Nathan, the synagogue ruler, his tone challenging, "are you saying we should not maintain purity among God's people? Should we not separate ourselves from sinners and Gentiles?"

Jesus's gaze was steady and compassionate but uncompromising. "Tell me, Nathan, can you always distinguish wheat from darnel in the early stages? Have you never mistaken one for the other? And even if you could, would your violent uprooting not damage the good plants growing nearby?"
He spread his arms wide, encompassing the entire diverse crowd. "The kingdom of heaven is patient. It knows that final judgement belongs to God alone. We are not called to be premature harvesters, but faithful growers. Tend your own roots. Bear your own fruit. The harvest will reveal what each plant truly is."
Before Nathan could respond, Jesus had already begun another parable. "The kingdom of heaven is like a mustard seed, which a man took and planted in his field."
Several people laughed. Mustard seed? The smallest of all seeds? How could the kingdom of heaven be compared to something so insignificant?
"Though it is the smallest of all seeds, yet when it grows, it is the largest of garden plants and becomes a tree, so that the birds come and perch in its branches."
Rebecca, holding her infant son, felt tears prick her eyes. She had felt so small since her husband's death, so insignificant in a world that had little use for widows. But if the kingdom of heaven could start as small as a mustard seed...
"The kingdom of heaven is like yeast that a woman took and mixed into about sixty pounds of flour until it worked all through the dough."

The women in the crowd exchanged knowing glances. They understood yeast—how a tiny amount could transform entire batches of dough, working invisibly but irresistibly. Was Jesus saying the kingdom worked the same way? Not through dramatic conquest but through quiet transformation?

Peter called from the boat's bow: "Master, the sun grows high. Should we return to shore so the people can seek shade?"

But Jesus was far from finished. The stories poured from him like water from a spring, each one revealing new facets of this kingdom he proclaimed.

"The kingdom of heaven is like treasure hidden in a field. When a man found it, he hid it again, and then in his joy went and sold all he had and bought that field."

Old Samuel the merchant stroked his beard thoughtfully. He had made such a purchase once—bought what seemed like worthless land because he'd discovered a vein of copper. But a kingdom worth everything one owned? What kind of treasure was that?

"Again, the kingdom of heaven is like a merchant looking for fine pearls. When he found one of great value, he went away and sold everything he had and bought it."

"But Teacher," interrupted Abigail, the pearl trader's daughter, "that's poor business! No single pearl is worth a merchant's entire inventory. He'd have nothing left to trade!"

Jesus smiled at her practical objection. "Exactly, Abigail. The kingdom of heaven overturns normal business practices. It demands everything because it gives everything. The merchant doesn't become poor—he becomes possessed of ultimate value. Would you rather have a hundred ordinary pearls or one beyond all price?"

The stories continued, each building on the last, creating a mosaic of meaning. Some in the crowd began to see patterns—the kingdom was hidden yet working, small yet powerful, costly yet invaluable. It challenged every assumption about how God worked in the world.

As the sun reached its zenith, Jesus told one more story that seemed to disturb even his disciples. "The kingdom of heaven is like a net that was let down into the lake and caught all kinds of fish. When it was full, the fishermen pulled it up on the shore. Then they sat down and collected the good fish in baskets but threw the bad away. This is how it will be at the end of the age. The angels will come and separate the wicked from the righteous and throw them into the blazing furnace, where there will be weeping and gnashing of teeth."

The image was stark and troubling. Peter and Andrew, who had sorted countless catches, understood the metaphor too well. Not every fish that entered the net was kept. There was judgement, separation, and finality.

"So," Jesus concluded, looking directly at the teachers of the Law who had been critiquing his every word, "every teacher of the law who has become a disciple in the kingdom of heaven is like the owner of a house who brings out of his storeroom new treasures as well as old."

It was an olive branch of sorts—acknowledging that the old treasures, the Law and the Prophets, still had value. But they must be combined with new treasures, new understanding, new wine in new wineskins.

The boat rocked gently as Jesus fell silent. The crowd stood in expectant quiet, processing the flood of images and ideas. Some faces showed enlightenment, others confusion, and still others resistance.

"Master," John called from the shore, "shall we bring the boat in?"

Jesus nodded, suddenly looking tired. Speaking in parables was exhausting work—each story had to be precisely crafted to reveal truth to seekers while protecting it from those who would misuse it. As Peter and Andrew poled the boat back to shore, Jesus noticed the disciples already organising the crowd for an orderly dispersal.

But before he could step onto dry land, the Pharisee Eleazar pushed forward.

"Teacher," he said, loudly enough for all to hear, "you speak of the kingdom of heaven as if you have special knowledge of it. But you're a carpenter's son from Nazareth. By what authority do you interpret God's kingdom?"

The crowd held its breath. This was the challenge they'd all been waiting for—credentials demanded, authority questioned.

Jesus stepped from the boat, his wet feet leaving prints in the sandy shore.

"Eleazar, you're a learnt man. Tell me, when David ate the consecrated bread, by what authority did he override the Law?"

"He was the Lord's anointed, fleeing for his life—"

"And was the Law diminished by his actions, or revealed more fully? Did God's mercy override God's holiness or demonstrate it?" Jesus stepped closer to the Pharisee. "You study the Scriptures diligently because you think that in them you have eternal life. These are the very Scriptures that testify about me, yet you refuse to come to me to have life."

"You claim the Scriptures speak of you?" Eleazar's voice rose in incredulity. "You make yourself the subject of holy writ?"

"I make myself nothing," Jesus replied. "But the Father makes me everything. The stories I've told today—they're not clever inventions. They're windows into reality. The kingdom of heaven is breaking into this world, whether you recognise it or not. The seed is being sown. The yeast is working. The net is being cast. And you, teacher of Israel, must decide what kind of soil you will be."

Before Eleazar could respond, a commotion arose from the back of the crowd. A man pushed forward, carrying his paralysed daughter. "Master," he cried, falling to his knees in the shallow water, "I've heard your stories. I believe the kingdom you speak of has power. My daughter—"

Jesus had already moved toward the child, compassion replacing confrontation in his features. As he laid hands on her, he spoke quietly: "The kingdom of heaven is also like this—a father's love that won't give up, meeting the power that makes all things new."

The girl's eyes fluttered open. Colour returned to her pallid cheeks. She sat up, looking around in wonder, then threw her arms around her father's neck. The crowd erupted in amazement.

"You see?" Jesus said, addressing everyone but looking at Eleazar. "The stories aren't just stories. They're announcements. The kingdom of heaven is here, working like seed, like yeast, like hidden treasure. Those with ears to hear, let them hear."

As the crowd began to disperse, many lingered, discussing the parables in small groups. The disciples moved among them, answering questions and offering clarifications. Jesus sat on a large stone near the water's edge, watching.

Mary Magdalene approached with a waterskin. "Master, you must be thirsty."

He accepted it gratefully, drinking deeply. "Thank you, Mary. Tell me, which story spoke most clearly to you?"

She considered carefully. "The weeds among the wheat, Lord. I was a weed once. Seven demons made me worse than darnel. But you saw what possibility was in me. You waited for the right time, then separated me from what I was not." Tears gathered in her eyes. "I understand patience now. I understand mercy."

"And that understanding will help you help others," Jesus said. "Each person here heard what they needed to hear. The farmer heard about soil. The merchant heard about pearls. The fisherman heard about nets. But they all heard about the kingdom."

Peter approached, still damp from managing the boat. "Master, I must confess—I don't understand all the stories. The yeast one especially. My wife uses yeast, but how is the kingdom like that?"

Jesus smiled at his disciple's honesty. "Peter, what happens when your wife forgets to add yeast to the dough?"

"We eat flatbread for a week, and she's frustrated with herself."

"And when she remembers?"

"The dough rises. The bread is light and satisfying. A little yeast changes everything." Peter's eyes widened with understanding. "Oh! The kingdom works quietly, invisibly, but transforms everything it touches!"

"Now you're beginning to see," Jesus affirmed. "Each parable is a door. Some will walk through immediately. Others will stand at the threshold for years before entering. But the doors remain open to all who knock."

Thomas joined them, his perpetual furrow of doubt deepened by the day's teaching. "Teacher, the story about the net troubles me. If the kingdom gathers all kinds of fish, but some are thrown away... how can we know we're the good fish?"

It was Judas who answered, surprising them all. "Maybe that's not for us to worry about," he said slowly, as if working out the thought as he spoke. "Maybe our job is to stay in the net, to trust the Fisherman's judgement rather than jumping back into the sea."

Jesus looked at Judas with an expression of profound sadness mixed with love. "Wisdom sometimes comes from unexpected sources. Yes, Judas. Trust the Fisherman. Stay in the net."

As afternoon shadows lengthened, the crowd finally dispersed completely. Some walked away puzzled, others enlightened, and still others resistant to truths that challenged their comfortable assumptions. The Pharisees from Jerusalem huddled together as they walked, planning their report to the Sanhedrin. The stories would be dissected, analysed for heresy, tested against tradition.

But in homes throughout Capernaum that night, ordinary people would repeat the parables to their families. Children would ask what mustard seeds had to do with God's kingdom. Wives would look at their yeast with new eyes. Farmers would think differently about sowing seed.

Jesus remained by the shore as his disciples cleaned up, mending nets that had been damaged by the day's unusual use. The Sea of Galilee lapped gently at the shore, its rhythm eternal and soothing.

"Lord," Andrew said, working beside his brother to repair a tear, "will you always teach in parables now?"

"When the message is too bright for eyes accustomed to darkness, we must filter it through story," Jesus replied. "Direct light blinds. Reflected light illuminates. The parables are mirrors in which people see truth at the angle they can bear."

"But some will never understand," James observed, frustration edging his voice. "Those Pharisees—they listened to every word looking for accusations, not truth."

"Even that serves the kingdom's purpose," Jesus said. "Their opposition forces believers to dig deeper, to move beyond surface understanding. Persecution produces perseverance. Opposition creates opportunity. The kingdom of heaven advances not despite resistance but through it."

As twilight approached, they made their way back to Peter's house. The courtyard was already filling with people who had heard about the day's teaching and wanted to learn more. Some brought sick relatives, hoping for healing. Others carried scrolls, wanting to compare the parables to ancient prophecies.

Jesus paused at the entrance, watching the gathering crowd. These were the good soil people—hungry for truth, ready to be transformed. They would take the seeds planted today and nurture them, sharing them with others, multiplying the harvest.

"Master," Matthew said, "shall I take notes? These parables—they should be preserved exactly as you spoke them."

"Write what you remember," Jesus instructed. "But know that the stories themselves are less important than what they produce. A seed preserved in a jar feeds no one. Only when planted, dying to what it was, does it fulfil its purpose."

Inside, Peter's wife had prepared a simple meal. As they reclined around the low table, the disciples continued processing the day's events. Each had heard the parables differently, understood different aspects, and been challenged in unique ways.

"The treasure in the field," Nathanael mused. "I keep thinking about that one. The man found it accidentally while doing ordinary work. Is that how most people find the kingdom? Not through intense searching but through stumbling upon it in daily life?"

"Yet the pearl merchant was actively searching," Philip countered. "He knew what he was looking for, even if he didn't know he'd find that one perfect pearl. Maybe the kingdom comes both ways—to seekers and to the surprised."

Jesus broke bread, blessed it, and passed it around. "You're both right. The kingdom meets people where they are. The religious scholar finds it through study. The simple fisherman finds it through relationship. The outcast finds it through acceptance. But all must value it above everything else. That's why both men sold all they had."

"I struggle with that," Judas admitted, fingering his money pouch. "Complete abandonment seems... impractical. How do we eat? How do we support the ministry?"

"The same God who provides seed for the sower provides bread for the eater," Jesus replied. "But note—I didn't say the men became destitute. They exchanged lesser wealth for greater. They invested everything in ultimate value. Poverty isn't the goal; priority is."

Late into the evening, people continued arriving. Jesus taught in the courtyard, expanding on the day's parables, answering questions, and healing those who came in faith. The kingdom of heaven was manifesting in a fisherman's house—small as a mustard seed, working like yeast, gathering all kinds of fish into its net.

Finally, as the moon rose over Galilee, Jesus withdrew to the roof for prayer. Below, his disciples continued discussing, debating, and discovering. The seeds were taking root. The soil was proving good.

Peter found him there an hour later. "Master, are you satisfied with today's teaching?"

Jesus looked out over Capernaum, where lamplight flickered in windows and the sound of families sharing evening meals drifted on the breeze. In how many homes are the parables being retold right now? How many children were falling asleep to stories of seeds and pearls and fishing nets?

"The sower has sown," he said simply. "Now we wait for the harvest."

"And tomorrow?"

"Tomorrow we sow again. The field is vast, Peter. The seed is plentiful. But the workers are few." He turned to his disciple. "Are you beginning to understand why I called you to fish for people instead of fish?"

Peter nodded slowly. "Fish die when caught. People live. The kingdom net doesn't destroy—it delivers."

"Now you're thinking in parables," Jesus said with a smile. "Careful, or you'll become a teacher yourself."

They stood in companionable silence, teacher and student, master and disciple. Below, Capernaum slept. But throughout the town, seeds were germinating in the soil of human hearts. Some would spring up quickly and fade. Others would struggle with thorns. But some—enough—would sink deep roots and produce abundant harvest.

The kingdom of heaven was like many things—seed and yeast, treasure and pearl, net and field. But most of all, it was like this: a teacher who cared enough to craft truth into stories, disciples willing to wrestle with meaning, and ordinary people whose lives would never be the same after encountering extraordinary love.

Tomorrow would bring new crowds, new challenges, and new opportunities to scatter seed. The religious leaders would intensify their opposition. The political powers would grow nervous. The cosmic conflict between light and darkness would escalate.

But tonight, the kingdom of heaven grew quietly in Capernaum, working like yeast through the whole batch of dough, transforming everything it touched with invisible but irresistible power. And Jesus, watching over the town like a shepherd over sheep, knew that his father's purposes would not fail.

The parables had been spoken. The seed had been sown. The kingdom of heaven was at hand for all who had ears to hear.

As Peter made his way back downstairs, Jesus remained on the roof, praying for each person who had heard the stories that day. He prayed for the hard-packed soil to be broken up, for the rocky ground to be deepened, for the thorns to be cleared away. He prayed for the good soil to remain receptive, to produce abundant fruit, and to multiply the kingdom's impact.

The Sea of Galilee reflected moonlight like scattered pearls across its surface. Somewhere out there, fishermen were casting nets, hoping for a good catch. They had no idea that the greatest fisherman of all had cast his net that very day, using stories as his mesh, drawing hearts toward heaven.

The kingdom of heaven was like a story that seemed simple on the surface but contained infinite depth. It was like a teacher who knew exactly what each listener needed to hear. It was like truth dressed in familiar clothes, walking among people who didn't recognise its royal identity.

Most of all, the kingdom of heaven was like love that refused to give up, that kept sowing seed despite poor soil and enemy interference, that believed in the harvest even when evidence seemed scarce. It was patient and persistent, gentle and powerful, hidden and revealed.

And in a world hungry for meaning, thirsty for truth, and desperate for hope, the kingdom's stories were finding eager ears and open hearts. The revolution had begun—not with swords and armies, but with carefully chosen words that would echo through centuries, transforming lives long after the speaker's voice fell silent.

The parables would outlive empires. The stories would survive persecutions. The truth wrapped in familiar metaphors would penetrate cultures and cross continents, always finding new soil in which to grow.

But that was tomorrow's harvest. Tonight, Jesus simply stood watch over the freshly sown field of Capernaum, praying for rain and sun in proper measure, trusting the seed's inherent power, and loving each precious soul who had ventured close enough to hear heaven's secrets told in earth's common tongue.

The kingdom of heaven had come near. And it looked like a teacher in a borrowed boat, telling stories that would change the world.

Chapter 14: Lord of Wind and Wave

The sun hung low over the Sea of Galilee, painting the water in shades of copper and gold. Peter stood at the water's edge, his practiced eye reading the subtle signs that only a lifetime on these waters could teach. The way the wind shifted. The particular quality of the light. The behaviour of the birds wheeling overhead.

"Storm coming," he muttered to Andrew, who was coiling rope nearby. His brother glanced at the clear sky sceptically. "Not a cloud to be seen."

"Since when do Galilee storms give warning?" Peter kicked at a piece of driftwood. "Mark me, brother. Before the night's through, we'll see weather."

They had spent the entire day here on the shore near Capernaum, part of a crowd so large it seemed half of Galilee had emptied itself to hear the Teacher. Jesus had taught from Peter's boat again, his voice carrying across the water to reach the thousands pressed along the beach. Parable after parable had flowed from him—seeds and soils, wheat and weeds, mustard seeds and hidden treasures.

Peter had tried to follow it all; he really had. But his mind kept drifting to practical matters. The crowd would need feeding soon. Where would all these people sleep? And why did the master insist on speaking in riddles when plain words would serve better?

"Peter!" James bar Zebedee called from where he and his brother John were preparing their boat. "The master's asking for you."

Peter made his way through the crowd, no easy task. People pressed in from every direction, reaching out to touch Jesus as he passed, calling out questions, and pleading for healing. The disciples had formed a protective circle around their teacher, but even so, the crush was overwhelming.

He found Jesus still sitting in the boat, though he'd pulled it slightly offshore to create some breathing room. The master looked exhausted. His voice was hoarse from speaking all day, his tunic soaked with sweat. Yet his eyes remained kind as he blessed a child someone held up to him.

"You wanted me, Rabbi?"

Jesus looked up at him with that penetrating gaze that still, after all these months, made Peter feel like his soul was being read like an open scroll. "Tell the others to prepare the boats. We're crossing to the other side."

Peter glanced at the crowd. "Now? Master, there must be five thousand people here, maybe more. They've come from as far as Tyre and Sidon to hear you. Shouldn't we—"

"Peter." Just his name, spoken quietly, but it stopped his protest mid-sentence. "We're crossing to the other side."

"Yes, Rabbi." Peter had learnt that tone. Discussion was finished. He turned to relay the orders, then paused. "Master, about the weather..."

But Jesus was already turning to address the crowd, raising his voice with effort. "The Kingdom of God has come near to you today. Go to your homes. Ponder what you've heard. Let those who have ears to hear, hear."

A murmur of disappointment rippled through the throng. They wanted more—more teaching, more healings, more of whatever it was that drew them to this Galilean carpenter like iron filings to a lodestone. But something in Jesus's manner brooked no argument. Slowly, reluctantly, they began to disperse.

Philip approached, ever the practical one. "Rabbi, should we arrange to meet them again tomorrow? I could send word to—"

"No plans," Jesus said wearily. "Tomorrow will worry about itself. Tonight, we sail."

The twelve moved with practiced efficiency now, preparing the boats. They had made this crossing many times—the Sea of Galilee was their highway, connecting the Jewish western shore with the largely Gentile eastern regions. Peter's boat would carry Jesus and several others. The Zebedee brothers' vessel would take the rest.

As they loaded supplies, Thomas pulled Peter aside. "Does he seem different to you today?"

Peter considered. There was something different about the Master this evening. A weight to him, as if the parables had cost him more than words. "He's tired. Who wouldn't be after speaking all day?"

"No, it's more than that." Thomas frowned, his natural scepticism showing. "Some of those stories today... did you understand them? The one about the wheat and the weeds?"

"He explained that one," Peter reminded him. "The field is the world; the good seed are the children of the kingdom..."

"Yes, but why not just say that plainly? Why wrap truth in riddles?"

Matthew, overhearing, joined them. "Isaiah prophesied it. 'Hearing they hear not, seeing they perceive not.' The parables reveal and conceal simultaneously."

"More riddles," Thomas muttered.

"Not riddles," Matthew insisted. "Invitations. Those hungry for truth will dig deeper. Those satisfied with surface understanding will walk away fed but not transformed."

Peter left them to their theological debate. He had a boat to prepare and a weather eye to keep. The sun was touching the horizon now, and that peculiar quality to the light had intensified. The air felt heavy, expectant. Even the usual evening breeze had stilled to nothing.

"Andrew," he called. "Double-check those sail lashings. And make sure we have the storm anchor aboard."

His brother nodded without question. When Peter's weather sense spoke, wise men listened.

Jesus was the last to board, helped by John and James. He moved slowly, each step deliberate, and Peter was struck again by how thoroughly the day had drained him. Teaching might not leave calluses like fishing, but it took its own toll.

"Where to, Master?" Peter asked as he took the tiller.

"The country of the Gadarenes," Jesus replied, settling himself in the stern. "Near the tombs."

Peter exchanged glances with Andrew. The tombs? Why would anyone want to go there? The eastern shore was Gentile territory, unclean by Jewish law. And the particular area Jesus mentioned... Peter had heard stories. They said a madman lived among those tombs, possessed by demons, so violent that chains couldn't hold him.

But orders were orders. Peter called out commands, and they pushed off from shore. The second boat followed, keeping pace. For a while, they rowed in the still air, making good progress. The last protesters on shore dwindled to specks, then vanished altogether.

"Why do they come, do you think?" Nathanael asked suddenly. He was one of the quieter disciples, given to deep thoughts. "All these people. What are they really seeking?"

"Healing," James suggested. "Free food, like when he multiplied the loaves."

"Entertainment," Judas added cynically. "How often does a prophet come to their villages? It breaks the monotony."

"Hope," said John quietly. "They come seeking hope."

Jesus, who had seemed to be dozing, opened his eyes. "And what do you seek?"

The question hung in the air like the calm before lightning. Each man examined his own heart, finding different answers. Peter knew what he sought—or thought he did. A kingdom. A restoration of Israel's glory. A place of honor beside the Messiah when he claimed David's throne. But lately, the Master's words had been painting a different picture. All this talk of suffering, of service, of losing life to find it.

"I seek to understand," Philip said finally. "To make sense of what I see and hear."

"I seek justice," Simon the Zealot declared. "For Rome to fall and Israel to rise."

"I seek truth," Thomas said, then added honestly, "though sometimes I'm not sure I'd recognise it if it struck me like lightning."

Jesus smiled at that, the exhaustion lifting from his features for a moment. "Keep seeking, Thomas. Those who seek, find. For those who knock, the door opens. Those who ask—"

He broke off, yawning hugely. "Forgive me. The spirit is willing, but the flesh..." He settled back against the cushion someone had placed in the stern. "Wake me when we reach the other side."

Within moments, his breathing deepened into sleep. The disciples continued rowing in companionable silence, each lost in his own thoughts. The last light faded from the sky, leaving them navigating by stars and long familiarity with these waters.

It was Matthew who first noticed the change. "The stars," he said, pointing. "They're going out."

Peter looked up and cursed under his breath. Clouds were racing in from the north—black, roiling masses that devoured the sky like a living thing. The temperature dropped ten degrees in as many seconds. The dead calm erupted into gusting wind that set the boat rocking.

"Storm sail!" Peter barked. "Andrew, help me with the mainsheet. James and John, get those oars in before we lose them. Everyone else, tie down anything loose."

They moved with the efficiency of experienced sailors, but Peter knew it wouldn't be enough. This wasn't one of the usual evening squalls that plagued the lake. This was a storm with teeth, the kind that left boats as splinters on the shore and men as food for fish.

The first wave hit them broadside, nearly capsizing them. Water poured over the gunwale, soaking everyone. In the other boat, Peter could hear similar shouts of alarm and see their sail being hastily reefed.

"Bail!" he shouted. "Nathanael, Philip, get those water jars emptied and start bailing. Thomas, help me with this tiller."

Another wave, larger than the first. The boat climbed it like a mountain, teetered at the crest, then plunged into the trough with a stomach-dropping fall. Judas lost his footing and would have gone overboard if Simon hadn't grabbed him.

And through it all, Jesus slept.

Peter couldn't fathom it. How could anyone sleep through this chaos? The wind howled like a living thing. Waves crashed over them in continuous assault. Lightning split the sky, revealing mountainous seas that made Peter's blood run cold. He had fished these waters since boyhood, but he had never seen a storm rise this fast or rage this fiercely.

"We're taking on too much water!" Andrew yelled. "The bailing's not keeping up!"

It was true. Despite their frantic efforts, the boat rode lower with each passing moment. The wind had shredded their sail, leaving them at the mercy of waves that seemed intent on their destruction. In the brief illumination of lightning, Peter saw the other boat faring no better.

"Master!" John was shaking Jesus's shoulder. "Master, wake up!"

Nothing. The teacher slept on, seemingly immune to the water pouring over him, the violent pitching of the boat, and the screams of wind and men.

A wave larger than all the rest rose before them, black as night and crowned with foam. Peter had a moment to think, *"This is how I die." Not in bed as an old man, but here on the sea I thought I knew.* Then it crashed down on them with the force of a collapsing building.

The boat disappeared beneath tonnes of water. Peter felt himself lifted, spun, and slammed back down. His hands cramped around the tiller, the only solid thing in a world gone liquid. He couldn't breathe, couldn't see, and couldn't tell which way was up.

Then, miraculously, they broke through. The boat bobbed up like a cork, water streaming from its sides. Half the disciples were sprawled in the bottom, coughing up water. The mast was cracked, hanging at a dangerous angle. They were still afloat, but barely.

"Teacher!" This time it was Peter himself shouting, abandoning the tiller to grab Jesus by the shoulders. "Lord, save us! We're perishing!"

Jesus opened his eyes slowly, as if waking from a pleasant dream. He looked around at the chaos—his disciples soaked and terrified, the boat filling with water, the storm raging like the end of the world—and his expression was… disappointed?

"Where is your faith?" he asked quietly.

Before anyone could answer, he stood. In a boat pitching like a wild horse, with waves towering over them and wind that could knock a man flat, he stood as steady as if on solid ground.

"Peace," he said to the storm. "Be still."

Peter would remember that moment for the rest of his life. The way Jesus spoke to the storm was like a master addressing an unruly servant. Not shouting over the wind, not dramatic gestures—just two words spoken with absolute authority.

And the storm obeyed.

The wind died instantly, not gradually diminishing but simply... stopping. Like a door slamming shut on chaos. The waves, robbed of their driving force, began to settle. Within moments, the sea was as smooth as glass, reflecting stars that had emerged from the fleeing clouds.

The silence was deafening. After the howling wind and crashing waves, this sudden calm felt unnatural, impossible. Water dripped from rigging. Men's harsh breathing was the loudest sound. In the distance, Peter could see the other boat, its occupants as motionless as statues, staring across the water at them.

Jesus sat back down, wringing water from his cloak. "Why are you so afraid?" he asked, and there was genuine puzzlement in his voice. "Do you still have no faith?"

Peter tried to answer, but his throat had closed up. His mind struggled to process what he had just witnessed. He had seen Jesus heal the sick, cast out demons, and multiply food. But this... this was different. This was nature itself bowing to his word. Wind and wave recognising their master.

"Who is this man?" Thomas whispered, voicing what they all were thinking. "Even the wind and sea obey him?"

It was Andrew who found his voice first, speaking the words of the psalm: "He stilled the storm to a whisper; the waves of the sea were hushed."

"You were testing us," Philip said accusingly. "You knew this storm was coming. That's why you insisted we cross tonight."

Jesus shook his head. "I test no one. But the Father allows tests, that faith might grow. A muscle unused grows weak. Faith unchallenged remains infantile."

"We could have died!" Judas protested.

"Could you?" Jesus fixed him with that penetrating gaze. "While I was in the boat?"

"You were asleep!" several voices said at once.

"My body slept. Do you think the Father sleeps? Do you think his care for you depends on my wakefulness?" He looked around at their faces, reading confusion, fear, and awe. "Oh, you of little faith. When will you understand? The same power that spoke the seas into existence sails with you. The voice that said, 'Let there be light,' shares your bread. Yet you fear wind and water?"

Peter found his voice at last. "Master, forgive us. We're just men. Fishermen. Tax collectors. Zealots. We see the impossible, and our minds rebel. How do we grow this faith you speak of?"

Jesus's expression softened. "By going through storms, Simon Peter. By discovering in your moment of desperation that I am there. By learning that sleeping or waking, I am who I am." He stood again, looking toward their destination. "But enough teaching for tonight. Row, my friends. The other shore waits, and work remains to be done."

They rowed in stunned silence. The sea remained preternaturally calm, their oars dipping into water smooth as oil. The other boat pulled alongside, its occupants staring at Jesus with expressions that mirrored their own shock.

"Did you see—" James Bar Alphaeus started.

"We saw," Peter cut him off. What else was there to say? They had witnessed something beyond human understanding. The very elements served this man they followed.

As they rowed, Peter's mind raced. He remembered the day Jesus had called him, standing on this very shore. "Follow me, and I will make you fishers of men." Peter had thought he understood. The Messiah needed followers, disciples, to help establish his kingdom. Peter knew fish and boats and nets—surely he could learn to catch men instead.

But this... who was this Jesus really? Peter had called him Messiah, Christ, and the Anointed One. But those were titles for a human king, a descendant of David who would restore Israel's fortunes. What human commanded storms? What son of man spoke to wind and wave as if they were servants awaiting orders?

"Peter." Jesus's voice broke into his thoughts. "What troubles you?"

"I thought I knew you," Peter admitted. "I thought I understood who you were and why I was following you. But tonight..." He gestured helplessly at the calm sea.

"And who do you say I am?" Jesus asked, and there was something urgent in the question, as if Peter's answer mattered deeply.

"I... I don't know anymore," Peter confessed. "The Christ, yes, but more than that. Something greater. Something that makes my mind reel and my knees weak."

"Good," Jesus said surprisingly. "The beginning of wisdom is admitting ignorance. You cannot be filled while convinced you're already full." He pointed ahead, where the eastern shore was becoming visible in the starlight. "Soon, Peter, you'll understand more. But first, you must see why we've crossed this sea, why the storm couldn't prevent our passage."

"The tombs," Peter remembered. "You said we were going to the tombs."

"A man waits there," Jesus said. "A man so tormented that hell itself seems to pour from his mouth. The religious leaders would write him off as unclean and unredeemable. Rome would execute him as a public menace. His own family has abandoned him to the dead." His voice grew fierce. "But I have come to seek and save the lost. No storm of nature or hell will prevent me from reaching even one tortured soul."

They were close to shore now, the boats grinding against the gravelly beach. As they pulled them up above the waterline, Peter could see the tombs in the distance—carved into the hillside, dark mouths gaping in the rock. Even from here, he could hear something that made his skin crawl. Howling. Like a wolf, but wrong somehow. Human and inhuman at once.

"Master," Simon the Zealot said nervously, "perhaps we should wait for daylight. The tombs at night—"

"Evil doesn't wait for convenient times," Jesus replied. "Neither shall we." He started up the path, and after a moment's hesitation, they followed.

The howling grew louder as they climbed. It echoed off the rocks, seeming to come from everywhere and nowhere. Other sounds joined it—the clank of chains, guttural cursing in multiple languages, and screams that spoke of torment beyond physical pain.

"How can one man make all those sounds?" Matthew whispered.

"Because," Jesus said grimly, "he is not one."

They crested a rise, and the tombs spread before them. Ancient carved facades, some collapsed, others gaping like mouths frozen in silent screams. The Romans had long ago given up burying their dead here—the place had an evil reputation that transcended cultural boundaries.

Movement in the shadows. Peter's hand went instinctively to the fishing knife at his belt, though what good it would do against whatever lurked here, he couldn't say.

Then the man emerged, and Peter's courage nearly failed him entirely. He was huge, muscles rippling under skin caked with filth and blood. Chains hung from his wrists and ankles, broken, the iron links snapped like thread. His hair was a wild tangle reaching to his waist. His eyes... Peter had seen madness before, but this was something beyond. Those eyes held torment that seemed to stretch back to the foundation of the world.

The man saw them and charged, moving with inhuman speed despite the dragging chains. The disciples scattered, all except Jesus, who stood calmly as if waiting for an old friend.

The demoniac skidded to a halt mere feet from Jesus, and something extraordinary happened. This man who terrorized the region, who broke chains like cobwebs, who had been declared untouchable by every authority—fell to his knees.

"What have you to do with me, Jesus, Son of the Most High God?" The voice that came from his throat was not one but many, a horrible chorus of different tones and accents. "I adjure you by God, do not torment me!"

Peter's mind reeled. The demons knew Jesus. Knew him by name, by title. Called him Son of the Most High God. The same recognition he'd seen in other possessed individuals, but multiplied, intensified.

"Come out of the man, you unclean spirit," Jesus commanded.

The man convulsed, multiple voices screaming from his throat. But he didn't collapse as others had when Jesus expelled demons. Instead, he writhed, fighting against the command.

"What is your name?" Jesus asked.

The man's face contorted through multiple expressions—rage, fear, cunning, and desperation. When he spoke, it was in that horrible multiple voice: "My name is Legion, for we are many."

Legion. Peter's blood ran cold. A Roman legion comprised thousands of soldiers. Were there truly thousands of demons in this poor wretch?

"We beg you," Legion continued, the voices shifting between pleading and threatening, "do not send us out of the country. Do not send us into the abyss."

Peter noticed movement on the hillside above the tombs. A large herd of pigs rooted among the rocks, watched by several swineherds who had frozen at the scene below. Pigs—unclean animals by Jewish law. Another reminder they were in Gentile territory.

"If you cast us out," Legion bargained desperately, "send us into the pigs. Let us enter them."

Jesus studied the writhing man for a long moment. Peter couldn't read his expression—sorrow? Anger? Calculation? Then he spoke a single word: "Go."

What happened next defied belief, even after everything Peter had witnessed. The man convulsed one final time, a shriek tearing from his throat that seemed to split the very air. Then a sound like rushing wind, though the night was still. The pigs on the hillside suddenly went mad.

They squealed in terror, eyes rolling white. As one, the entire herd—there must have been two thousand—turned and stampeded. Not scattered running, but a unified charge straight toward the cliff that overlooked the sea.

"No!" one of the swineherds shouted. "Stop them!"

But there was no stopping them. The pigs poured over the cliff like a waterfall of flesh, their squeals cut short by the impact below. Within moments, the entire herd was gone, drowned in the sea that Jesus had so recently calmed.

The silence that followed was absolute. The swineherds stared in shock, then at Jesus and his disciples, then at the man who had been Legion.

He sat quietly now, the chains having fallen away completely. The wild look was gone from his eyes, replaced by confusion and dawning awareness. He looked down at his naked, filthy body as if seeing it for the first time.

"Where... where am I?" His voice was hoarse but singular, human.

"You're free," Jesus said simply. He removed his own outer cloak and draped it around the man's shoulders. "What's your name?"

"Marcus," the man said wonderingly. "My name is Marcus. I had forgotten..." Tears began streaming down his face. "How long? How long was I...?"

"It doesn't matter," Jesus said gently. "You're yourself again. The past is past."

Peter watched in amazement as the other disciples slowly gathered around. The transformation was total. Where a moment ago had been a creature more beast than man now sat someone's son, someone's brother. Thin, scarred, traumatised, but human.

The swineherds had fled, running toward the nearby city. Peter knew they would spread the word. Soon, the whole region would know what had happened here.

"We should go," Judas said nervously. "Those pigs were valuable property. There will be consequences."

"Let them come," Jesus replied. He was helping Marcus to his feet, supporting him as muscles long abused remembered how to function. "The value of one human soul outweighs all the pigs in the world."

"But Master," Philip protested, "we're in Gentile territory. We have no authority here. If they demand compensation—"

"Then we'll address it when it arises," Jesus cut him off. "For now, this man needs food, clean water, and proper clothing. See to it."

They made camp there among the tombs, bizarre as it seemed. Marcus ate like a starving man, which he essentially was—who knew how long he'd survived on scraps and whatever the demons allowed him? Between bites, his story emerged.

He'd been a merchant, married with two children. The possession had started slowly—voices no one else could hear, fits of rage he couldn't control. His family tried to help and brought in priests and physicians. Nothing worked. The voices multiplied, and the violence grew worse. After he nearly killed his own son during an episode, they had him chained.

But the chains never held. The demons gave him unnatural strength and drove him from town into these tombs. His family held a funeral for him, considering him dead. Years passed in a haze of torment, multiple consciousnesses warring for control of his body, driving him to hurt himself and others.

"I was aware sometimes," he said quietly, staring into the fire they'd built. "Trapped inside while they used my body, they made me watch the horrible things they did. I prayed for death, but they wouldn't let me die. Said they had uses for me yet."

"Why so many?" Thomas asked. "I've seen possessed people before, but never a legion."

Marcus shuddered. "They said I was a gathering point. A stronghold. Through me, they could influence the whole region. Every act of violence, every bitter word, every small cruelty in the surrounding towns—they fed on it, grew stronger from it."

"And now they're gone," Matthew said, "drowned with the pigs."

"Not gone," Jesus corrected. "Spirits don't die with flesh. But their power here is broken. Their stronghold is freed." He looked at Marcus. "You understand you can never let them back in? The house has been swept clean—you must fill it with better things, or they'll return sevenfold."

"I understand," Marcus said firmly. "I want..." He paused, struggling for words. "I want to follow you. Wherever you go. You gave me back my life, my mind. Let me serve you."

Jesus smiled sadly. "Your heart is good, but that's not your path. Return to your home, to your family. Tell them what the Lord has done for you and how he had mercy on you. Your witness here will accomplish more than following me to places where my name is already known."

Before Marcus could respond, they heard voices approaching. Many voices and the clatter of weapons. The swineherds had been busy.

The crowd that crested the hill was substantial—city officials, merchants, curious citizens, and armed guards. They stopped short at the sight of the campfire, of Jesus sitting calmly with his disciples, and—they had to look twice—of the madman of the tombs, clothed and sane.

An official in Roman dress stepped forward. "You!" he pointed at Jesus. "Are you the one who destroyed our pigs?"

"I destroyed nothing," Jesus replied evenly. "I freed a man from torment. What happened to the pigs was a consequence, not an intention."

"Two thousand swine!" another man shouted. "Do you have any idea of the economic loss? Those pigs fed half the region and provided livelihood for dozens of families!"

"And this man?" Jesus gestured to Marcus. "What was his worth in your economy?"

"He was mad," the official said dismissively. "A public menace. We tolerated him in the tombs because at least there he only disturbed the dead."

"I see," Jesus said, his voice growing hard. "Pigs have value. Human beings are tolerated menaces. This is your justice?"

The crowd stirred uneasily. Many of them knew Marcus from before and remembered him as a successful merchant, a family man. Seeing him sitting there coherent was disturbing in ways they couldn't articulate.

"Who are you?" a woman called out. "What power do you have over demons?"

"I am who I am," Jesus replied. "The power is not mine but the Father's who sent me."

"Jewish sorcery," someone muttered. "We want no part of it."

The murmur grew, hostile now. Peter's hand went again to his knife. They were vastly outnumbered, in foreign territory, with no legal standing.

"Please," the Roman official said, and now his tone was less aggressive and more fearful. "We ask you to leave our region. Take your disciples and go. We want no trouble with whatever power you serve, but neither do we want that power among us."

Peter expected Jesus to argue, to proclaim his message as he did in Jewish towns. Instead, the master simply nodded. "As you wish. We'll leave with the dawn."

Relief washed over the official's face. "That's... that's good. Yes. And the man?" He gestured to Marcus.

"The man is your neighbour," Jesus said pointedly. "Treat him as such."

The crowd dispersed slowly, many casting wondering looks at Marcus, who bore their scrutiny with newfound dignity. When they were gone, Peter couldn't contain himself.

"Master, why? These people need your message as much as any. More, perhaps—they're Gentiles, without knowledge of the true God."

"You cannot force-feed bread to those who insist they're not hungry," Jesus replied. "They've seen the power of the Kingdom and found it too disturbing to their comfortable lives. Their pigs matter more than their people. So be it. Dust off your feet—others wait who will receive gladly what these reject."

They spent the night there, taking turns keeping watch, though no one really slept. The events of the evening—the storm, the deliverance of Legion, the rejection by the townspeople—swirled in their minds like eddies in a disturbed pool.

As dawn broke, they prepared to leave. Marcus stood apart, clearly torn between obedience to Jesus's command and desire to remain with his deliverer.

Jesus went to him, placing both hands on his shoulders. "Remember—you are free. No chain can hold you, and no voice can control you. You belong to yourself and to God. Use this freedom wisely."

"How can I ever repay you?" Marcus asked.

"By living," Jesus said simply. "By loving. By telling others that the Kingdom of God shows mercy even to those the world writes off as lost." He smiled. "And by raising your children to know that no darkness is so deep that light cannot penetrate it."

They embraced, teacher and freed man, and then Jesus led his disciples back to the boats. As they pushed off, Peter saw Marcus still standing on the shore, watching. Then he turned and began walking—not to the tombs, but toward the city, toward home, toward a life reclaimed.

"Where now, Master?" Peter asked as they rowed.

"Back to Capernaum," Jesus replied. "More crowds wait. More needs press. More hearts hunger." He looked at each of his disciples in turn. "But you twelve—you've seen something crucial tonight. You've seen that my authority extends over both natural and supernatural storms. Wind and wave, demon and disease—all must bow to the Father's will."

"We've seen," Peter agreed. "But Master, I'll be honest—it terrifies me as much as it amazes me. Who are you, truly?"

Jesus smiled that enigmatic smile that could mean anything or nothing. "Keep following, Simon Peter. Keep watching. The answer to that question is not given in words but in witness. Tonight you saw me calm a storm and free a legion. Before all is done, you'll see greater things than these."

"Greater than commanding nature itself?" Thomas asked sceptically.

"Much greater," Jesus assured him. "For any god can still storms and cast out demons. But only the true God can transform human hearts, turn hatred to love, and raise the dead to life—not just life of body but life eternal."

They rowed in contemplative silence after that, each man wrestling with what he'd witnessed. The Sea of Galilee stretched before them, calm now in the morning light, giving no sign of the violence it had displayed hours before. Like a servant who had thrown a tantrum and been rebuked, it now served them with docile compliance.

Peter found himself studying Jesus, who had moved to the bow and stood facing the wind. His clothes were still damp from the storm, his hair tangled from their night among the tombs. He looked thoroughly human—tired, weathered, in need of a good meal and better rest.

And yet.

And yet this same man had stood in a sinking boat and commanded creation itself. Had faced down a legion of demons and won without breaking a sweat. The disconnect between appearance and reality made Peter's head spin.

"Andrew," he said quietly to his brother. "What have we gotten ourselves into?"

Andrew smiled, the simple faith that had always characterised him shining through. "Something wonderful, brother. Something terrible and wonderful and beyond our understanding."

"Aren't you frightened?"

"Terrified," Andrew admitted cheerfully. "But where else would we go? Who else has words of eternal life? Who else shows us the very face of God?"

As if he'd heard—and perhaps he had—Jesus turned from the bow. His eyes met Peter's across the length of the boat, and in them Peter saw something that drove away fear. Love. Infinite, inexhaustible love. Not just for Peter, but for the whole broken world. For the crowds that pressed him past exhaustion. For the religious leaders who plotted against him. For Legion in his torment. For the townspeople who chose pigs over miracles.

This, Peter realised with stunning clarity, *is the power that calms storms and casts out demons. Not force, not violence, not domination. Love so pure and fierce it reorganises reality around itself.*

"Peter," Jesus called. "Take us home."

Home. Capernaum. Peter's house, where Jesus stayed, was where miracles had become almost commonplace. Where Peter's mother-in-law, healed of fever, now cooked for thirteen hungry men without complaint. Where crowds gathered before dawn hoping for a touch, a word, or a glimpse of the Kingdom breaking through.

"Yes, Master," Peter called back. "Taking us home."

But even as he steered toward familiar shores, Peter knew something fundamental had changed. After tonight, could anywhere truly be home? Once you'd seen the raw power of God unleashed, once you'd witnessed the cosmic battle between light and darkness played out in human lives, could you ever again be satisfied with ordinary existence?

The sun climbed higher, warming their faces and drying their clothes. Other fishing boats were putting out from Capernaum, their occupants waving greetings. *Normal life is resuming. The mundane world reasserting itself.*

But Peter had seen behind the veil. Had glimpsed forces and powers that undergirded reality. Had watched his teacher reveal himself as master of both natural and supernatural realms.

"Lord of wind and wave," he murmured, testing the title.

"What's that?" James asked.

"Nothing," Peter said. Then, louder: "Pull hard, boys! People are waiting. The Kingdom doesn't proclaim itself!"

They bent to their oars with renewed energy. Behind them, the eastern shore receded, taking with it the memory of tombs and demons. Ahead, Capernaum beckoned with its familiar skyline. Between—the sea, calm now, keeping its secrets.

But Peter knew better. Calm was temporary. Storms would come again—natural ones and spiritual ones. The battle they'd witnessed among the tombs was just one skirmish in a war that stretched from Eden to whatever end God had planned.

But they had Jesus in the boat. The lord of wind and wave, the master of demons, the proclaimer of the kingdom. And that, Peter was beginning to understand, made all the difference.

The harbour of Capernaum came into view, already busy with morning traffic. Peter could see a crowd gathering—word of their crossing must have spread. They would want to hear what had happened, why Jesus had insisted on crossing at night, what wonders had been performed on the other side.

"What do we tell them?" Nathanael wondered. "About the storm, the demons, the pigs?"

"The truth," Jesus said simply. "Those with ears to hear will understand. Others will add it to their collection of wonder stories, missing the deeper meaning."

"Which is?" Philip prompted.

Jesus smiled. "That the Kingdom of God cannot be stopped by any storm, natural or spiritual. That no soul is so lost that grace cannot find it. That what you think you know about power and authority is about to be turned upside down."

They were entering the harbour now, Peter skilfully navigating between other vessels. On the shore, he could see familiar faces—followers, sceptics, the curious, and the desperate. Another day's work beginning. But it's different now. Everything is different after last night.

As they pulled the boat onto the beach, Jesus placed a hand on Peter's shoulder. "Well done, fisherman. You got us through the storm."

"You got us through the storm," Peter corrected. "I just held the tiller."

"Sometimes," Jesus said with that mysterious smile, "holding the tiller while heaven rearranges the world is the greatest act of faith. Remember that when your time comes to steer the ship."

Before Peter could ask what he meant, Jesus was moving toward the crowd, arms open in greeting. The sick pressed forward. Questions flew. Children ran to embrace his legs. The relentless pace of ministry resumed.

But Peter lingered by the boat, his hand still on the worn wood of the tiller. *When your time comes to steer the ship.* What ship? What time?

"Peter!" someone called. "Tell us about the crossing! We heard there was a storm!"

He shook himself from reverie and waded into the crowd. There would be time later to ponder mysterious words and future responsibilities. For now, there was a story to tell. A story of storms and calm, of demons and deliverance, of a teacher who was so much more than he appeared.

"Gather round," Peter said, his fisherman's voice carrying over the noise. "Let me tell you what we witnessed when the Master decided to cross to the other side..."

The sun climbed toward noon, warming the shores of Galilee. In the distance, clouds gathered—there would be another storm by evening, Peter's weather sense told him. But that was hours away. For now, there was this moment, this crowd, and this story that needed telling.

And somewhere in the gathering, perhaps, another soul waited who needed to hear that storms could be calmed, that demons could be cast out, that the Kingdom of God was breaking into the world one miracle at a time.

Peter took a breath and began. "We had been teaching all day by the shore..."

Chapter 15: Legion Becomes Freedom

The storm had passed, leaving the Sea of Galilee eerily calm in the pre-dawn darkness. Jesus stood at the boat's prow, his robes still damp from spray, watching the eastern shore emerge from shadow. Behind him, his disciples worked in exhausted silence, bailing water and checking the nets they'd barely managed to secure during the tempest.

Peter's hands trembled as he coiled rope. Just hours ago, he'd watched his master stand and command the very elements to stillness. The wind had died mid-howl. Waves as tall as houses had collapsed into glassy calm. And Jesus had turned to them with something like disappointment in his eyes, asking why they had such little faith.

"Rabbi," Andrew ventured, breaking the silence, "where are we landing?"

Jesus didn't turn, his gaze fixed on the dark shoreline ahead. "Where we're needed."

James and John exchanged glances. The eastern shore meant Gentile territory—the Decapolis, where Greek culture flourished and Jewish law held little sway. Swine grazed these hills; temples to foreign gods crowned the cities. No self-respecting rabbi would set foot there without cause.

But then, Jesus had never been what they expected a rabbi to be.

The boat's hull scraped against pebbles, the sound sharp in the morning quiet. Thomas jumped out first, splashing through knee-deep water to pull them further ashore. The others followed, their movements mechanical, minds still processing the night's impossibilities.

"Should we make camp?" Matthew asked, ever practical. "The sun will rise soon."

Jesus stepped onto the shore, his sandals crunching on wet stones. "No camps. Not here."

Something in his tone made them all freeze. Peter's hand went instinctively to the knife at his belt—a fisherman's tool, not a weapon, but comforting nonetheless. The shore stretched empty in both directions, backed by limestone cliffs pocked with caves. Tombs, Peter realised with a chill. They'd landed at a burial ground.

A sound drifted from the cliff face—not quite human, not quite animal. A howl that raised the hair on their necks and set their teeth on edge. Several disciples stepped back toward the boat.

"Master," Judas said carefully, "perhaps we should find another place—"

"No." Jesus walked forward, each step deliberate. "He's been waiting long enough."

"Who?" Peter fell into step beside him, loyalty overcoming fear. "Who's been waiting?"

The howl came again, closer now, and with it the rattle of chains. Heavy chains, dragging across stone. Peter's question died in his throat as understanding dawned. They all knew the stories—the madman of Gadara, possessed by demons, living among the dead. Too violent for any prison to hold, too dangerous for any village to harbour.

"Stay back," Philip urged, catching Jesus's sleeve. "Master, the man is legendary. He's broken every chain they've put on him. Killed a merchant who ventured too close last summer. Even the Romans won't—"

Jesus gently removed Philip's hand. "Stay here if you wish. But I'm going to him."

The disciples stood frozen, torn between terror and devotion. It was young John who moved first, squaring his shoulders. "Where you go, Master, we follow."

One by one, they fell in behind Jesus, though Peter noticed how they unconsciously grouped together, hands near whatever might serve as weapons. Only Jesus walked as if strolling through a garden, his pace unhurried, his face serene.

The tombs loomed before them—ancient caves carved into limestone, their mouths dark as wounds. The stench hit them first: decay, human waste, and the copper tang of old blood. Then they saw the chains—broken lengths scattered across the ground, some still bearing manacles twisted by inhuman strength.

Movement in the largest cave mouth. A figure emerged, and several disciples gasped.

He had been a man once. That much was clear from the frame—tall, broad-shouldered, built for labour. But humanity had long fled those features. His hair hung in filthy mats to his waist. His beard was a wild tangle stained with things best not examined closely. Naked save for tattered remnants clinging to his waist, his skin bore the map of his torment—scars from chains, gashes from stones, and wounds in various stages of healing or infection.

But it was his eyes that struck horror into watching hearts. They rolled and darted without focus, sometimes showing only whites, sometimes blazing with unnatural light. When he opened his mouth, multiple voices poured out—screaming, laughing, and cursing in languages none of them recognised.

"Run!" Peter grabbed for Jesus, but his master had already stepped forward. The demoniac's chaotic movements suddenly focused. Every twitching muscle stilled. Those terrible eyes fixed on Jesus with laser intensity. Then, with a shriek that sent birds exploding from nearby trees, he charged.

The disciples scattered despite themselves. The man-thing moved with impossible speed, covering the rocky ground in bounds that defied human limitation. Stones flew from beneath his feet. Spittle flew from his mouth. The morning air filled with his wordless roar.

Twenty feet. Ten. Five.

Jesus never moved.

At the last instant, when collision seemed inevitable, the demoniac threw himself to the ground. Not in attack, but in prostration. His forehead pressed to the dirt at Jesus's feet, his whole body trembling like a leaf in a gale.

"What have you to do with me, Jesus, Son of the Most High God?" The voice that emerged wasn't human—too deep, too layered, as if a chorus spoke through one throat. "I beg you by God, do not torment me!"

The disciples stood frozen. He knew. This mad creature who lived among corpses, who broke chains like thread—he knew who Jesus was. Had known the instant he saw him.

Jesus looked down at the writhing form with infinite compassion. When he spoke, his voice carried that same authority that had stilled the storm. "Come out of the man, you unclean spirit."

The demoniac convulsed, his back arching impossibly. Foam tinged with blood frothed from his mouth. His fingers clawed furrows in the ground. But the spirits didn't flee. Instead, that horrible layered voice spoke again: "Please, Son of the Most High, I beg you—do not send us into the abyss! Not yet! The time hasn't come!"

"What is your name?" Jesus asked, though Peter suspected he already knew.

The man's head lifted, and for a moment, something almost human flickered in those tormented eyes. His mouth worked soundlessly, as if he himself tried to answer. Then the demons reasserted control, and that awful chorus returned:

"Legion. We are Legion, for we are many."

Peter's knees nearly buckled. A Roman legion contained six thousand soldiers. Six thousand demons in one man? How was he even alive?

"Many," the voices continued, each word a struggle. "So many. Sent to destroy him. Sent to make him a warning. Look what opposing the kingdom of darkness costs. Look what we do to those who might have stood for light."

"His name," Jesus said quietly. "Tell me his name."

The demoniac writhed, multiple voices arguing in languages both familiar and unknown. Finally, one voice emerged clearer than the rest—still inhuman, but tinged with mockery:

"Marcus. His name was Marcus. Marcus Aurelius Gavius. Citizen of Rome. Veteran of the Twelfth Legion. Seeker of truth. Protector of the weak." The voice became a sneer. "Look at your protector now."

Matthew stepped forward despite his fear, stylus and tablet already in hand. "A Roman? But why—"

"SILENCE!" The roar sent Matthew stumbling back. The demoniac—Marcus—half-rose, muscles bunching with inhuman tension. "You dare document this? You dare make a record of our work?"

"Peace." Jesus's single word acted like a leash, yanking the possessed man back to his knees. "Continue. Tell us all of it."

The demons resisted, Marcus's body contorting in ways that made joints pop audibly. But they couldn't disobey that command. The story poured out in fragments, different voices taking turns:

"Stationed in Caesarea... saw too much... questioned too much..."

"...the centurion who crucified innocents for sport..."

"...the tax collector who starved widows..."

"...the priest who sold temple sacrifices with false weights..."

"He documented it all. Fool! As if Roman justice cared about Jewish lives!"

"They came for him at night. Not soldiers. Servants of the god of this world."

"He fled here. Thought the tombs would hide him."

"We found him first."

"One by one, we entered. He fought—oh, how he fought!"

"Trained soldier. Iron will. It took hundreds of us to break him."

"But we did break him. Shattered his mind like pottery."

"Made him an example. This is what happens to those who stand against the darkness."

"This is what awaits any who truly follow the light."

The voices died away, leaving only the sound of Marcus's laboured breathing. The disciples stood in stunned silence, processing the horror of it. This wasn't random possession. This was targeted torture, spiritual warfare on a scale they'd never imagined.

Nathanael found his voice first. "Master, if they could do this to a Roman soldier, a trained warrior—"

"Fear not," Jesus said, not looking away from Marcus. "Greater is He who is in you than he who is in the world." He knelt, bringing himself to eye level with the tormented man. "Marcus. I know you can hear me. I've come to set you free."

The reaction was instant and violent. Marcus's body slammed backward as if pulled by invisible hands, his spine bending until his head nearly touched his heels. The screaming began—not one voice but thousands, a cacophony of rage and fear that made the disciples cover their ears.

"NO! He is ours! Bought with blood! Sealed with madness! You cannot—"

"I can." Jesus stood, and suddenly he seemed taller and broader, as if another presence superimposed itself over his human form. The morning light brightened around him, though the sun hadn't yet breached the horizon.

"By what authority do you claim him?"

"By right of conquest!" The demons shrieked. "By the law of sin and death! By the power of the prince of this world! He sought to fight darkness—darkness consumed him! The law stands!"

"I am the lawgiver," Jesus replied. "And I say: Enough."

The very air seemed to tremble. Peter felt it in his bones, a vibration that had nothing to do with sound. The demons felt it too. Marcus's body went rigid, every muscle locked in supernatural tension.

"Please!" The voices turned pleading. "Son of the Most High, have mercy! Do not send us to the abyss before the time! We know who you are! We know why you've come! But the hour hasn't arrived! The final judgement isn't yet!"

Jesus considered this, his expression unreadable. The disciples held their breath. Then his gaze swept the hillside, noting what they'd missed in their fear—a massive herd of swine rooting along the slopes, at least two thousand strong. Unclean animals by Jewish law, but valuable commodities in Gentile lands.

"If I cast you out," Jesus said slowly, "where would you go?"

Hope flickered in those inhuman voices. "The swine! Send us into the swine! Let us enter them instead!"

Peter started to protest—surely giving demons any foothold was dangerous. But Jesus had already made his decision.

"Go."

The word carried finality like a judge's gavel. What happened next burnt itself into the disciples' memories forever.

Marcus's body convulsed one final time, his mouth opening impossibly wide. What emerged wasn't breath or sound but shadow—visible darkness pouring from him like smoke from a burning building. The darkness writhed and twisted, forming shapes that hurt to perceive directly. Faces that weren't faces. Forms that violated the very concept of form.

The shadows streamed toward the hillside, a black river defying gravity. The swine felt them coming. The animals' contentment turned to panic in an instant. Squeals of terror split the morning as two thousand pigs suddenly went mad.

The herd moved as one, no longer animals but vessels of chaos. They turned not away from the cliff but toward it, running with the single-minded purpose of the destroyed. Their handlers screamed warnings and tried to turn them, but nothing could stop that headlong rush toward oblivion.

The thunder of four thousand hooves shook the ground. The disciples watched in horrified fascination as the leading edge of the herd reached the cliff's edge and didn't stop. Pigs poured over the precipice like a waterfall of flesh, their squeals dopplering as they fell. The splash as they hit the water below was audible even from a distance.

In moments, it was over. Two thousand swine drowned or were drowning, the Sea of Galilee frothing with their death throes. The swineherds stood frozen in shock, then as one turned and ran toward the city, their livelihoods destroyed, their minds reeling from the impossible.

But the disciples barely noticed the devastation. Their attention fixed on the figure still kneeling before Jesus.

Marcus—for it was truly Marcus now, not Legion—slowly raised his head. His eyes were clear. Haunted, exhausted, bearing the weight of years of torment, but human. Beautifully, wonderfully human.

"Master?" His voice came out as a croak, unused to forming words instead of screams. He looked down at his scarred, naked body as if seeing it for the first time in years. His hands rose to his face, fingers exploring features he'd forgotten he possessed.

"Peace, Marcus," Jesus said gently. "You're free."

"Free." Marcus tasted the word like foreign wine. Then the reality of it hit, and he began to weep. Not the wild tears of madness, but the clean grief of a man remembering how to feel. "I... I remember. All of it. Every moment. Everything they made me do. Every person I hurt. The merchant—I killed him. I couldn't stop myself. His family... oh God, his family..."

"That wasn't you," Peter found himself saying, moved by compassion despite his lingering fear. "The demons—"

"Used my hands." Marcus's voice broke. "My strength. I was aware, always aware, trapped inside while they..." He curled into himself, shame a visible weight.

Jesus knelt again, his hands gentle on Marcus's shoulders. "Look at me."

It took visible effort, but Marcus met his gaze.

"You are not defined by what was done to you," Jesus said. "Or by what they forced you to do. You are defined by who God says you are. And He calls you His son."

"After everything? After the blood, the blasphemy, the—"

"After everything." Jesus helped him to his feet, and the disciples saw what they'd missed in their terror. Beneath the scars and filth stood a man, perhaps forty years old, with the remains of Roman bearing in his posture. "Come. Let's get you cleaned and clothed."

Andrew and John already moved to the boat, retrieving spare tunics and cloaks. Philip found fresh water in their supplies. What followed was a humble resurrection—washing away years of degradation, clothing naked shame, and restoring human dignity to one who'd been reduced to less than an animal.

Marcus submitted to their ministrations with wondering gratitude, flinching occasionally as if expecting the voices to return. But they were gone, drowned with the swine, and in their absence, his true self slowly emerged.

"You're really a Roman soldier?" Thomas asked as they helped him dress.

"Was." Marcus's voice grew steadier with use. "Honourably discharged after twenty years. Settled in Caesarea to start a trading business. Import/export. I'd made connections throughout the Empire during my service." A shadow crossed his features. "That's how I started noticing the patterns."

"What patterns?" Matthew had his stylus ready again, unable to resist documenting.

Marcus glanced at Jesus, who nodded encouragement. "Shipments that didn't match manifests. Temple taxes that never reached the Temple. Roman justice for sale to the highest bidder. I'd fought for the Empire, bled for it. Thought Rome brought order to chaos. But the chaos was coming from within."

He sat heavily on a boulder, still weak from his ordeal. "I started keeping records. Names, dates, amounts. Thought if I gathered enough evidence, presented it to the right authorities..." He laughed bitterly. "Naive fool. The corruption went all the way up. The procurator, the high priest's family, even the legion commanders—all feeding from the same trough."

"So they silenced you," Judas said, understanding in his eyes.

"Tried to buy me first. When that failed, they tried to threaten me. When that failed..." Marcus gestured at himself. "They had other resources. I fled when I realised men in armour weren't my only enemies. Came here because the tombs were considered cursed ground, where even Roman patrols wouldn't venture. But the servants of darkness have no fear of death."

"How long?" Jesus asked quietly.

Marcus closed his eyes, calculating. "Three years. Maybe four. Time... blurred. There were seasons of greater torment, when they'd force me to travel, to be seen. To remind people what happened to those who challenged the powers that be. Then seasons here, among the dead, when they'd simply... feast on my suffering."

"Your family?" Mary Magdalene asked gently. She'd been hanging back, but compassion drew her forward.

"Dead before this began, thank God." His voice caught. "My wife died in childbirth along with our son. My daughter took fever the following winter. I thought I had nothing left to lose." He looked at his scarred hands. "I was wrong."

Silence fell over the group, each processing the horror and heroism of Marcus's story. Here was a man who'd tried to stand against systemic evil and paid a price beyond imagining. Yet Jesus had found him, freed him, and restored him.

"What now?" Marcus asked, looking at Jesus with eyes that held both gratitude and uncertainty. "I'm free, but... where does a man go after being Legion? Who would receive me? What life is possible after such darkness?"

Before Jesus could answer, shouts rose from the direction of the city. The swineherds had spread their tale, and already a crowd approached—merchants, officials, and curious citizens drawn by the incredible story.

"Master," James warned, "they don't look happy."

Indeed, the approaching crowd bristled with anger and fear. The loss of two thousand swine represented economic catastrophe for the entire region. Someone would have to pay.

"Should we return to the boat?" Andrew suggested, already calculating escape routes.

"No." Jesus stood, positioning himself between Marcus and the approaching mob. "They need to see."

"See what?"

"That the Kingdom of God values one human soul above all the swine in the world."

The crowd arrived like a breaking wave, their voices a babel of accusation and demand. Jesus stood calmly in their midst, letting their anger wash over him without response. But gradually, the shouting died as they noticed the figure sitting clothed and coherent among the disciples.

"Is that...?" A merchant pointed with a trembling hand. "It can't be. The madman?"

"Marcus Aurelius Gavius," the former demoniac said clearly. "Citizen of Rome. Merchant of Caesarea. Man of Gadara. And no longer Legion."

The crowd recoiled as if slapped. They'd seen this man—if man he could be called—raging naked among the tombs. They'd watched him break chains, heard his inhuman howls, and kept their children far from these cursed shores. Some bore scars from encounters with him during his possessed wanderings.

Yet here he sat, calm and clothed, speaking in measured tones. The impossibility of it struck them mute.

An official pushed through—a Roman administrator by his dress, responsible for maintaining order and collecting taxes. His face cycled through emotions: shock, calculation, and fear.

"What happened here?" He directed the question at Jesus, recognising authority. "The swineherds speak of demons and drowning pigs. Fables and madness. I need facts."

"Ask him." Jesus indicated Marcus. "He was there."

The administrator's eyes widened as he recognised the seated figure. "Impossible. You're dead. We recorded your death two years ago when you stopped appearing in the city."

"A kind of death," Marcus agreed. "But I live again, thanks to this teacher."

"Teacher?" The administrator's voice sharpened. "You're the Nazarene. The one performing miracles in Galilee." His eyes narrowed. "Judea has no authority here. This is the Decapolis. Free cities under Roman protection."

"I claim no earthly authority," Jesus replied. "Only the authority to free those who are bound."

"At the cost of two thousand swine!" A merchant pushed forward, face red with rage. "My entire investment, gone! Who will repay me?"

"Who repaid Marcus for his years of torment?" Jesus asked mildly.

"He was mad! Possessed! A danger to—"

"To those who profited from corruption?" Marcus stood slowly, Roman steel entering his voice despite his weakness. "I remember you, Quintus. You were one of them. Taking bribes to let spoilt grain pass inspection. How many sickened from bread made with your approved wheat?"

The merchant—Quintus—paled. "Lies. The ravings of a madman."

"I kept records," Marcus continued. "I hid them before I fled. Names, dates, transactions. The demons knew many things, but not that." He looked at the administrator. "Gaius Petronius, isn't it? You were new when I... left. But your predecessor, Lucius Varro—he was deep in the conspiracy. Taking a percentage of every illegal shipment that passed through the port."

The crowd stirred uneasily. Many recognised the names Marcus mentioned and saw how certain faces in the crowd went pale or angry.

"This is irrelevant!" Quintus snarled. "Whatever fantasies you harboured, they don't restore my swine!"

"Your swine purchased with blood money?" Marcus stepped forward, and though he stood in a borrowed tunic instead of armour, something of the soldier remained. "How appropriate that they rushed to destruction. As all things built on an evil foundation must eventually fall."

"Master," Peter murmured, "the mood is turning ugly."

Indeed, the crowd seemed balanced on a knife's edge. Some looked at Marcus with wonder and growing hope—if such a man could be restored, what other miracles were possible? But others, particularly those with wealth and position, saw only threat. The supernatural destruction of the swine was disturbing enough. A restored Marcus who remembered their crimes was worse.

"You should leave," the administrator said finally, addressing Jesus. "Take your disciples and return to Galilee. We want no prophets here, no workers of wonders. We have an order. We have prosperity."

"Built on the suffering of the innocent," Marcus said quietly.

"The world is built on suffering!" The administrator's mask of civility cracked. "The strong rule, the weak serve. Rome conquered through strength, not miracles. We've achieved peace through power, not... whatever this is."

"Peace?" Jesus looked around the crowd, meeting eyes that quickly looked away. "Is it peace when a man seeking justice is tormented by demons for years while you prosper from the very corruption he tried to expose? Is it peace when evil spirits are more welcome in your region than the Spirit of God?"

"We don't want your god!" someone shouted from the back. "We have our own gods, and they serve us well!"

"Do they?" Jesus asked. "Then why did your gods not free Marcus? Why did they allow Legion to make their home among your tombs, terrorising your children, mocking your powerlessness? Where were your gods when evil walked naked among you?"

Silence answered him. Even the waves seemed to quiet, waiting.

"Please," another voice said—softer, broken. A woman pushed through the crowd, elderly but straight-backed. She approached Marcus with tears streaming. "My son. The merchant you... you killed. Do you remember?"

Marcus's face crumbled. He dropped to his knees before her. "Every moment. His face haunts me. I fought against the demons and tried to warn him to run, but my voice was not my own. My hands..." He held them out, seeing blood that had long since washed away. "I'm sorry. So sorry. It means nothing, changes nothing, but—"

The woman studied him for a long moment. Then, to everyone's shock, she reached out and took those scarred hands in her weathered ones.

"I see," she whispered. "It wasn't you. You were a prisoner too." She looked at Jesus. "Rabbi, is he truly free? Will the demons return?"

"He is free indeed," Jesus assured her. "What God has cleansed, no power can defile again."

The woman nodded slowly, then did something that drew gasps from the crowd. She helped Marcus to his feet, this mother lifting the man who'd killed her son.

"Then I forgive you," she said simply. "My Joseph is beyond pain now. But you—you've suffered enough for crimes that weren't truly yours. Be at peace."

Marcus broke down completely then, sobbing like a child while the old woman held him. The crowd watched in stunned silence as Grace accomplished what violence never could—true healing, true restoration.

But the moment couldn't last. The administrator, recovering his composure, raised his voice again. "Touching as this is, it doesn't address the economic devastation. Someone must pay for the lost swine. If not this teacher, then..." His eyes fixed on Marcus. "Then the madman himself. Seize him!"

"No!" Several voices cried out, but Roman efficiency was already in motion. Guards pushed through the crowd, hands on sword hilts.

Jesus stepped between them and Marcus. "You would arrest a man for the crime of being healed?"

"For the destruction of property," the administrator corrected. "The law is clear."

"Your law," Jesus said quietly, "or God's?"

"In the Decapolis, Roman law is God's law."

The blasphemy hung in the air like a challenge. Peter's hand found his knife again, and he saw other disciples tense for violence. But Jesus raised a hand, and they stilled.

"Then we will leave," he said simply. "As you wish. But know this—today salvation came to this shore, and you begged it to depart. Today the Kingdom of God touched your land, and you chose the kingdoms of this world. The time will come when you remember this moment and weep for what you've lost."

He turned to Marcus. "Come with us."

"Master, I..." Marcus looked around at the crowd, at the city beyond, and at the tombs he'd called home. "I want to follow you. Let me be your disciple. I'll serve you unto death—a better death than I've known."

Jesus smiled but shook his head. "Not yet. Return to your home, to Caesarea. Tell them what great things the Lord has done for you and how He had mercy on you."

"But they'll kill me! The same powers that sent the demons—"

"Cannot touch what God protects." Jesus gripped his shoulders. "You have a testimony they need to hear. You've seen both the depths of darkness and the heights of God's delivering power. Who better to speak truth to those enslaved by lesser demons—greed, pride, and the lust for power?"

"What of my records? The evidence I gathered?"

"Retrieve them. Use them. But not for revenge—for redemption. Some who profited from evil might yet turn to good if shown the way."

Marcus nodded slowly, understanding dawning. "You're sending me back as a witness."

"The first of many in these lands. The Decapolis will not always reject the Kingdom. Seeds planted today will bear fruit in season."

"Teacher!" The administrator's patience had ended. "Leave now, or face arrest yourself!"

Jesus looked at him with something between pity and sorrow. "We go. But Marcus stays—a free citizen of Rome, guilty of no crime save being oppressed by forces you pretend don't exist. Touch him at your peril."

Something in Jesus's tone made the guards step back despite themselves. The administrator's face flushed, but he too hesitated. There was authority here beyond his understanding, power that made Roman might seem suddenly fragile.

"Master," Marcus said urgently, "will I see you again?"

"In this life or the next," Jesus promised. "But you'll hear of me. As I travel and teach, as the Kingdom grows, you'll hear. And when you do, remember this day. Remember that no darkness is so deep that light cannot pierce it. No chain is so strong that truth cannot break it."

He turned to his disciples. "Come. Our work here is finished."

They walked through the crowd that parted like water, no one quite willing to impede their passage. Behind them, Marcus stood straight and tall, no longer Legion but himself, testimonial proof that transformation was possible.

As they reached the boat, Peter couldn't help looking back. The crowd had turned on itself, some arguing for Marcus's arrest, others defending him. The old woman who'd forgiven him stood at his side like a guardian. Already, the seeds of division were visible—those who'd witnessed grace warring with those who feared change.

"Master," Peter said as they pushed off, "was it worth it? One man freed, but a whole city rejecting you?"

Jesus settled into the boat, his eyes still on the shore where Marcus stood watching them go. "Peter, if you had a hundred sheep and one went lost, would you not leave the ninety-nine to find it?"

"Of course, but—"

"There are no 'buts' in the mathematics of heaven. One soul restored outweighs all the swine in the world. Marcus will speak truth in places we cannot go, witnessing powers we won't directly confront. Through him, many will be freed from subtler demons."

"And the swine?" Judas asked, ever practical. "The economic loss was real. Families will suffer because of what we did today."

"What the demons did," Jesus corrected. "I merely gave them what they asked for—a habitation they couldn't sustain. The destruction revealed their true nature. As for the economic loss..." He sighed. "Yes, some will suffer. But they suffered already under a system that created men like Marcus's tormentors. Sometimes a false peace must be shattered for true peace to come."

They sailed in contemplative silence, each processing what they'd witnessed. The eastern shore fell away behind them, but its lessons remained. They'd seen the ultimate end of spiritual warfare—a man so thoroughly possessed that he'd become a living horror. Yet even such a one could be redeemed.

"I've been thinking," Matthew said eventually, "about the name. Legion. Six thousand demons in one man. If such forces of darkness exist, they marshal themselves against individuals who threaten their kingdoms..."

He didn't finish, but they all understood. If the enemy could do that to one Roman soldier who'd challenged corruption, what might they do to the One who challenged the very foundation of their power?

Jesus read their thoughts. "Fear not. What you saw today was victory, not defeat. Yes, darkness has power in this age. Yes, it can possess, torment, and destroy. But you also saw its limits. At my word, at just my word, six thousand demons fled like smoke before wind."

"Into pigs," Thomas noted with dry humour. "Somehow fitting."

That broke the tension, and they found themselves laughing—perhaps inappropriate given the morning's gravity, but necessary. Human hearts could only hold so much cosmic weight before requiring release.

"Will Marcus be safe?" John asked when the laughter died. "You sent him back to his enemies with only a promise of protection."

"Safer than he was among the tombs," Jesus replied. "The Father protects those who bear witness to His works. Marcus has a purpose now, a mission. That itself is a kind of armour against the darkness."

"And us?" Andrew gestured at the disciples. "We follow you daily. Does that make us targets for... Legion-level attention?"

Jesus was quiet for a moment, and when he spoke, his words carried weight. "I send you out as sheep among wolves. Yes, you'll face opposition—human and otherwise. But remember what you saw today. The strongest demons flee at the mention of my name. You carry that name, that authority. Use it wisely, but without fear."

The familiar western shore of Galilee came into view, and with it, a return to their usual ministry. But they were changed by what they'd witnessed. The cosmic battle between light and darkness was no longer theoretical. They'd seen its casualties and its victories.

As they pulled the boat ashore near Capernaum, Peter found himself looking back one more time toward the eastern shore, now invisible in the morning haze. Somewhere over there, Marcus was beginning his new life—testifying to power that could shatter the strongest chains, mercy that could restore the most shattered minds.

"Come," Jesus said, already moving toward the crowds gathering on their beach. "Others need freedom too. Different chains, subtler demons, but the same healing power."

They followed, as they always did. But now they understood better what they followed—not just a teacher or even a prophet, but one with authority over the very forces of darkness. Legion had named him truly: Son of the Most High God.

The morning sun climbed higher, burning away the last of the mist. A new day in Galilee, full of familiar challenges. But for twelve disciples who'd witnessed the transformation of Legion into Marcus, no day would ever be quite ordinary again.

Behind them, the Sea of Galilee lapped peacefully at the shore, holding its secrets. Somewhere beneath its waves lay two thousand drowned swine, testimony to the price of hosting darkness. And somewhere on its eastern shore walked a man made new, living proof that no one was beyond redemption's reach.

The Kingdom of God advanced one freed soul at a time, and today, despite rejection and economic loss, despite fear and misunderstanding, it had claimed another victory. Marcus was free. In the arithmetic of heaven, that was enough.

But in the boat, pushing through the shallows toward shore, the disciples couldn't shake the memory of those rolling, tormented eyes clearing into sanity, of that inhuman voice softening into grateful humanity. They'd witnessed resurrection of a different kind—a man brought back not from physical death but from something worse.

"Master," Peter said quietly as they secured the boat, "what you did today..."

"What the Father did through me," Jesus corrected gently. "Remember that, Peter. The power isn't mine alone. It flows from the Father, through me, and someday, through you."

"Through us?" Peter's voice cracked slightly. "Facing down legions of demons?"

"If necessary. But more often facing down the everyday demons—pride, greed, hatred, and fear. The spirits that possess without fanfare, that bind without chains. Those are the battles you'll fight most often."

They walked up the beach toward Capernaum, where everyday ministry awaited. But Peter noticed how each disciple walked a little taller and stood a little straighter. They'd seen the worst the enemy could do and watched their master defeat it with a word.

Whatever lay ahead—and Jesus's hints suggested struggles beyond their imagination—they would face it knowing that light was stronger than darkness, that love could shatter hatred, and that even Legion must bow before the Son of the Most High.

The ordinary world of fishing boats and tax booths, of sick children and worried parents, welcomed them back. But they brought with them the extraordinary truth of what they'd witnessed on the eastern shore. In hushed conversations and amazed whispers, the story would spread: the madman of Gadara was mad no more. Legion had become Marcus. The possessed had become a witness.

And somewhere in Caesarea, a Roman citizen was preparing to tell his own story, to show his scars and speak of healing, and to challenge the powers that had thought him destroyed. The ripples from one divine encounter would spread far beyond the Decapolis, touching lives the disciples would never know.

The Kingdom advanced, one freed soul at a time.

It was enough. It was everything.

Chapter 16: Desperate Faith, Timid Touch

The morning sun painted Capernaum's harbour in shades of gold and amber as Jesus and his disciples stepped from the boat onto the western shore of the Sea of Galilee. The crossing from the Gentile territory of the Gadarenes had been peaceful—a stark contrast to their storm-tossed journey eastward days before. Peter secured the mooring rope with practiced efficiency, his weathered hands working automatically while his eyes scanned the gathering crowd.

"They're already here," Andrew murmured, nodding toward the cluster of people hurrying down from the town. "Word travels fast."

Jesus stood at the water's edge, his feet still wet from wading ashore, watching the approaching crowd with that particular mixture of compassion and weariness his disciples had come to recognise. The past days in Gentile territory had been intense—the violent confrontation with Legion, the man possessed by a thousand demons, had drained them all. Yet here, on Jewish soil, the needs pressed in again like waves against the shore.

"Master," James said quietly, "perhaps we should find a place to rest first. You've barely slept since—"

But Jesus was already moving forward, arms open to embrace the first of the townspeople reaching them. An elderly woman grasped his hands, tears streaming down her weathered face.

"Rabbi, you've returned! My grandson—the fever broke just as you said it would before you left. He lives!" She pressed his hands to her lips. "He lives because of you!"

More pressed in—fishermen abandoning their nets, merchants leaving their stalls, mothers carrying infants, fathers supporting limping children. The disciples formed a protective circle around Jesus, trying to create space for him to move, but the crowd swelled like a living thing, each person desperate for a moment of attention, a word of hope, or a touch of healing.

Through the chaos, Peter noticed a disturbance in the crowd's flow. People were stepping aside, some bowing, others whispering urgently. A path opened, and through it strode a man whose very bearing commanded respect. His robes were of the finest linen, the blue and white prayer shawl draped over his shoulders was shot through with threads of gold, and his phylacteries were crafted of supple leather, the tiny scrolls within written by the most skilled scribes.

"Jairus," someone whispered, and the name rippled through the crowd like wind through grain.

Peter tensed. Jairus was the ruler of Capernaum's synagogue—the very synagogue where Jesus had taught with such authority, where he had cast out demons, and where the religious establishment had first begun to view him with suspicion. What did the synagogue ruler want? Had he come to challenge Jesus publicly? To demand he cease his teaching?

But as Jairus drew closer, Peter saw something in the man's face that shocked him. Gone was the dignified composure of a religious leader. His eyes were wild with desperation, his carefully groomed beard dishevelled as if he'd been tearing at it. His expensive robes were dusty and wrinkled.

The crowd fell silent as Jairus approached Jesus. For a moment, the two men regarded each other—the established religious authority and the radical teacher who had turned everything upside down. Then, in a movement that sent gasps through the crowd, Jairus fell to his knees in the dirt.

"Master," he said, and his voice broke on the word. "My daughter—my only daughter—she's dying."

The proud synagogue ruler prostrated himself completely, his forehead touching the ground at Jesus's feet. "Please," he whispered, and the word held all the desperation of a father watching his child slip away. "She's only twelve years old. The physicians can do nothing. She's... she's almost gone. Please, if you would just come and lay your hands on her, she would live. I know she would live."

The crowd held its collective breath. Everyone knew the tension between Jesus and the religious authorities. Just weeks ago, Pharisees from Jerusalem had accused him of casting out demons by Beelzebub. They had questioned his authority, challenged his interpretation of the Law, and whispered about blasphemy. And Jairus, as synagogue ruler, had been caught in the middle—privately moved by Jesus's teaching but publicly bound by his position.

Now all of that fell away. He was not a ruler or a religious authority. He was simply a father, broken and desperate, begging for his daughter's life.

Jesus reached down and gently lifted Jairus to his feet. "Tell me about her," he said softly.

Jairus's composure crumbled entirely. "Her name is Talitha. She loves to dance—always dancing, spinning in the courtyard until she's dizzy. She sings while she helps her mother with the bread. She..." His voice caught. "Three days ago, she complained of pain in her belly. By evening, the fever had taken her. We've tried everything—poultices, prayers, offerings at the Temple. The physicians bled her, but it only made her weaker. This morning, she didn't recognise me. She called for her grandmother—my mother, who died two years ago. Please, Master. I'll do anything. Take my position, my wealth, my life—just save my daughter."

"Take me to her," Jesus said simply.

Relief flooded Jairus's face. He turned and began pushing through the crowd, Jesus following close behind. The disciples scrambled to keep up, trying to maintain some order as the entire crowd surged after them. Everyone wanted to see what would happen when Jesus entered the synagogue ruler's house. Would he heal the child? Would the religious authorities try to stop him?

The narrow streets of Capernaum became a river of humanity. People pressed in from every side, reaching out to touch Jesus's robe, calling out their own needs and petitions. The disciples formed a moving barrier, but it was like trying to hold back the tide.

"Give the Master room!" Peter shouted, using his fisherman's strength to clear a path. "Let him through!"

But the crowd only pressed closer. In the midst of the chaos, a figure moved through the shadows between buildings, keeping pace with the procession but maintaining distance. She was wrapped in layers of cloth despite the morning warmth, her face hidden beneath a deep hood. Her movements were furtive and desperate, like a starving animal approaching a guarded feast.

Her name was Miriam, though few in Capernaum would remember it now. Twelve years ago, she had been the wife of a prosperous merchant, mother to three young sons, and respected in the community. Then the bleeding had begun.

At first, it was just an inconvenience—the normal flow of a woman's body refusing to cease at its appointed time. She had consulted the midwives and tried their remedies. But days became weeks, and weeks became months. According to the Law of Moses, she was unclean as long as the blood flowed. Everything she touched became unclean. Anyone who touched her became unclean.

Her husband had been patient at first. He built her a separate room and arranged for servants to bring her meals without contact. But as months became years, patience turned to frustration, then to disgust. The physicians demanded increasing fees for treatments that didn't work—burning cauterisations, foul-smelling potions, and endless dietary restrictions. Their life savings evaporated like morning dew.

When the money ran out, so did her husband's commitment. The letter of divorce was delivered by a servant who wouldn't meet her eyes. Her sons were taken to live with their paternal grandparents. She was forbidden to see them—what mother would willingly make her children unclean?

Twelve years. Twelve years of isolation, poverty, and shame. Twelve years of feeling her life drain away with the blood that wouldn't stop flowing. She had sold everything—her jewellery, her robes, even her hair to wig-makers. Now she survived on scraps and the occasional charity of those who remembered her from better days.

She had spent everything on physicians. One had made her drink a potion of ground pearls mixed with wine—three months' worth of earnings gone in a single gulp that did nothing but make her vomit. Another had prescribed sitting in increasingly hot baths until she fainted from the heat. A travelling Greek physician had suggested the problem was in her mind and prescribed meditation and philosophy. A Jewish healer had blamed secret sin and demanded she confess transgressions she hadn't committed.

Nothing worked. The bleeding continued, and with it, her exile from human touch, from worship, and from life itself.

But then she had heard about Jesus.

The stories seemed impossible at first. A teacher who healed with a touch, who cast out demons with a word, who even raised the dead. She had dismissed them as wishful thinking—she knew better than most how desperate people could deceive themselves with false hope.

But the stories persisted. Her neighbour's cousin swore she had seen a paralysed man walk. A fisherman at the market claimed his brother's leprosy had vanished at Jesus's command. Even the synagogue buzzed with whispers about the Nazarene who taught with unprecedented authority.

For the first time in years, Miriam felt something stir in her chest. Not quite hope—she had learnt the danger of hope—but a possibility. A what-if that wouldn't leave her alone.

She had tried to approach Jesus before, but always the crowds were too thick, her shame too great. How could she, an unclean woman, push through all those people? Her very presence would defile them. And if she spoke to Jesus directly and admitted her condition publicly, the humiliation would be unbearable. The crowd might stone her for bringing her uncleanness among them.

But today, watching from her hiding place as Jesus agreed to follow Jairus, she felt desperation override shame. The teacher was known for his compassion for outcasts—tax collectors, prostitutes, and lepers. Maybe, just maybe, he would have mercy on her too.

A thought formed in her mind, born of desperation and a peculiar kind of faith. She didn't need to speak to him, didn't need to make her shame public. If the stories were true, if he really carried the power of God, then wouldn't even his garments hold that power? Just a touch—the briefest contact with the edge of his robe—surely that would be enough.

It was a dangerous plan. If caught, she could be dragged before the synagogue authorities for defiling the crowd. But what did she have to lose? She was already as good as dead, a ghost haunting the edges of life.

As the crowd moved through the streets toward Jairus's house, Miriam slipped from her hiding place and merged with the flow of people. Her heart hammered against her ribs. When was the last time she had been in such close contact with others? The smell of unwashed bodies, the heat of the press, the casual touches as people jostled for position—it was overwhelming after years of isolation.

She pulled her hood lower and pushed forward. Through gaps in the crowd, she could see Jesus's back, see the blue and white of his prayer shawl, and the tassels swaying with his movement. According to the Law, those tassels—the tzitzit—were reminders of God's commandments. Each thread, each knot, held significance. If she could just touch one of those tassels...

Closer. She wormed between two large men arguing about whether Jesus was Elijah returned. Neither noticed the small figure slipping past. Closer still. A mother with a crying infant blocked her path. Miriam waited, trembling with urgency, until the woman shifted to comfort her child.

There. Just ahead. Jesus had paused as Jairus spoke urgently with someone—perhaps a servant from his house. The crowd pressed in from behind, pushing Miriam forward. This was her chance.

She dropped to her knees, ostensibly knocked down by the crowd's movement. On her knees, she could reach through the forest of legs, past the disciples who formed a protective barrier. Her hand shook as she extended it, twelve years of isolation screaming warnings in her mind. What if it didn't work? What if her uncleanness was too great even for his power? What if—

Her fingers brushed the tassel of his prayer shawl.

The effect was instantaneous and devastating. Power flowed into her—not harsh or violent, but warm and overwhelming, like stepping from a cave into full sunlight. She felt it race through her body, touching places that had been broken for so long she'd forgotten they could be whole. The constant drain, the weakness that had become her daily companion, the flow that had defined her existence for twelve years—gone. Simply gone.

She knelt there in the dust, surrounded by oblivious crowds, and felt her body obey her for the first time in over a decade. The weakness was gone. The pain was gone. She was... whole.

Tears poured down her face as she pressed her hands to her stomach, feeling the stillness there, the blessed absence of flow. Healed. The word rang in her mind like a bell. Healed. Whole. Clean.

She had to get away. Had to find somewhere private to process this miracle. She began to rise, to slip back through the crowd—

"Who touched me?"

Jesus's voice cut through the chaos like a sword. He had stopped walking and was turning in a slow circle, his eyes scanning the crowd. The disciples looked at him in confusion.

"Master," Peter said, gesturing at the press of bodies around them, "everyone is touching you. The whole crowd is pressing in."

But Jesus shook his head. "No. Someone touched me. I felt power go out from me."

Miriam's heart, so recently filled with joy, now pounded with terror. He knew. Somehow, he knew. She tried to shrink back, to disappear into the crowd, but her legs wouldn't obey. The same power that had healed her now held her in place.

The crowd began to murmur, people looking at each other with suspicion and curiosity. Who had touched the teacher? Why was he making such an issue of it?

Jairus shifted anxiously. "Master, please, my daughter—"

Jesus raised a hand gently, his eyes still searching the crowd. "Who touched my clothes?"

The disciples exchanged bewildered looks. "Master," James ventured, "you see the crowd pressing against you, and yet you ask, 'Who touched me?'"

But Jesus continued to look around, and Miriam knew with terrible certainty that he would not move until she revealed herself. The power that had healed her drew her forward even as her mind screamed retreat. On trembling legs, she pushed through the crowd until she stood before him.

The moment the crowd saw her clearly—the layers of clothing, the hood pulled low, the way she held herself apart—understanding dawned. Whispers rippled outward.

"She's unclean!"

"How dare she!"

"We've all been defiled!"

Miriam fell at Jesus's feet, her whole body shaking. The words poured out of her in a rush, twelve years of pain and shame compressed into a single confession.

"It was me, Master. I touched you. I've been bleeding for twelve years. Twelve years! I've spent everything on physicians who only made it worse. I lost my husband, my children, and my place in the community. I haven't felt a human touch in so long I'd forgotten what it was like. I heard about you, about your power, and I thought—I thought if I could just touch your robe, just the edge of it, maybe... And I did, and the bleeding stopped. I know it stopped. For the first time in twelve years, I'm whole. I'm sorry. I'm so sorry. I know I've made you unclean, made all these people unclean. I just... I couldn't bear it anymore. I just wanted to be well."

She waited for the condemnation, for the stones that surely would come. She had publicly admitted to defiling a rabbi and to moving through a crowd while unclean. The Law was clear about such things.

But no stones came. Instead, she felt a hand on her head—the first deliberate human touch she had experienced in twelve years. She looked up through her tears to find Jesus kneeling before her, his eyes filled not with anger but with compassion so deep it took her breath away.

"Daughter," he said, and the word was like water in the desert. When was the last time anyone had called her daughter? "Your faith has healed you. Go in peace and be freed from your suffering."

Daughter. Not "woman." Not "unclean one." Daughter.

The crowd stood in stunned silence. According to the Law, Jesus should now be unclean from touching her. He should be pronouncing the ritual requirements for purification. Instead, he was blessing her, affirming her healing, and calling her daughter.

"I felt it," Miriam whispered, wonder filling her voice. "The moment I touched your robe, I felt the healing flow through me. Like sunrise after endless night."

Jesus helped her to her feet, his hands steady and unashamed. "Your faith drew that power," he said, loud enough for all to hear. "Not the robe, not magic, but faith. For twelve years, you suffered. For twelve years, you persevered. Your faith, even when hope seemed dead, brought you to this moment."

He turned to address the crowd, many of whom were still muttering about defilement and propriety. "This woman, this daughter of Abraham, has been bound by suffering for twelve years. Twelve years—the same age as the child we go to heal. Is not her freedom a cause for rejoicing? Is not her faith an example to all?"

The parallel struck the crowd—twelve years of death-in-life for the woman, twelve years of life now threatened by death for Jairus's daughter. The anger began to dissipate, replaced by something like awe.

But even as Jesus spoke, a disturbance rippled through the crowd from the direction of Jairus's house. People parted to let through a small group of men, their faces grave, their clothes showing signs of hasty travel. Miriam recognised them as servants from the synagogue ruler's household.

They pushed past her without a glance—she might be healed, but habits of seeing her as invisible died hard—and approached their master. The lead servant, an elderly man named Samuel who had served Jairus's family for decades, couldn't meet his master's eyes.

"Sir," he said quietly, but in the sudden hush his words carried clearly. "Your daughter is dead. There's no need to trouble the teacher any longer."

The words hit Jairus like a physical blow. He staggered, his face draining of colour. "Dead?" The word came out as barely a whisper. "No. No, she can't be. I left her this morning. She was breathing. She knew I was going to find the teacher. She can't be..."

Samuel nodded miserably. "She passed just moments ago, sir. Your wife is with her. The mourners have already been summoned."

Jairus's legs gave out. He would have fallen if Jesus hadn't caught him, supporting the synagogue ruler as sobs tore from his chest. "Too late," he gasped. "I was too late. I should have come sooner. I should have ignored the council's warnings about you. My pride, my position—I let them matter more than my daughter's life, and now..."

"Jairus." Jesus's voice was firm but gentle. "Don't be afraid. Only believe."

Jairus looked up at him through his tears. "Believe? She's dead. You heal the sick, but dead? She's gone. My little girl is gone."

Jesus gripped his shoulders. "Did you not just witness this woman's faith rewarded after twelve years? Your daughter has lived twelve years. Do you think the God who numbers every hair on her head has forgotten her? Only believe."

Something in Jesus's eyes—a certainty that defied logic, a compassion that acknowledged the pain while promising something beyond it—made Jairus nod slowly. What else could he do? His daughter was dead. Following Jesus couldn't make things worse.

Jesus turned to the crowd. "No one follows from here except Peter, James, and John." His tone brooked no argument. The crowd muttered but began to disperse, sensing that what came next was too holy, too intimate for public spectacle.

Miriam caught Jesus's eye as she prepared to leave. "Thank you," she mouthed, pressing her hand to her heart. He smiled at her—a smile that said her story was far from over, that healing was just the beginning of what faith could bring.

As the crowd dispersed, she stood there for a moment, marvelling at the feeling of strength in her limbs, the absence of the constant drain that had defined her existence. Twelve years of death, and now life. She understood why Jesus had made her healing public—not to shame her but to testify. Her healing was not stolen in secret but given in love, acknowledged before the community that had excluded her.

She pulled back her hood, letting the sun touch her face. Tomorrow, she would go to the priests and perform the rituals that would officially declare her clean. She would find her sons, now young men, and see if reconciliation was possible. She would reclaim her name, her place, and her life.

But for now, she simply stood in the street and breathed deeply, tasting freedom with every breath.

The journey to Jairus's house took on a different quality without the pressing crowd. The four of them—Jesus and his three closest disciples—walked in silence through streets that grew progressively wealthier. Jairus's position afforded him a large house near the centre of town, close to the synagogue he administered.

As they approached, the sound of mourning reached them—the professional wailing of hired mourners, the discordant notes of flutes played in grief, and the rhythmic sound of hands striking chests in lamentation. The speed with which the mourning ritual had begun spoke to both Jairus's prominence and the Jewish community's practiced response to death.

"They've already started," Peter muttered. "The mourners, the flute players—it's official. The girl is dead."

Jairus flinched at the words but kept walking, his hand gripping Jesus's arm as if it were the only thing keeping him upright.

The house came into view—a two-story structure built around a central courtyard, its walls gleaming white in the sun. But the usual dignity of the home was shattered by the chaos of grief. Mourners filled the courtyard, their professional wails rising and falling in practiced cadence. Musicians played their funeral dirges. Neighbours pressed in, bringing food, offering condolences, and participating in the communal ritual of grief.

Jesus stopped at the entrance to the courtyard, surveying the scene. "Why all this commotion and wailing?" he asked, his voice cutting through the noise. "The child is not dead but asleep."

The mourning stopped abruptly, replaced by shocked silence. Then someone laughed—a harsh, mocking sound.

"Asleep?" It was one of the professional mourners, a woman whose job it was to lead the community in expressing grief. "I've been mourning the dead for thirty years, teacher. I know the difference between sleep and death. The girl is dead. I helped prepare the body myself."

Others joined in the derisive laughter. Who was this teacher to deny the reality of death? They had seen the girl's still form, felt the cooling of her skin, and witnessed the departure of breath. Death was death, final and irreversible. To call it sleep was to mock their grief and their intelligence.

Jesus's expression didn't change. He turned to Jairus. "Clear them out. All of them."

Jairus hesitated. These were neighbours, colleagues, and people whose respect he needed to maintain his position. But then he thought of his daughter lying still in the upper room, and position meant nothing.

"Everyone out," he commanded, his voice regaining some of its authority. "The teacher requires privacy."

The crowd protested, but Jairus was still the synagogue ruler. Reluctantly, muttering about disrespect and false prophets, they filed out. The professional mourners were the last to go, glaring at Jesus as they left, their livelihoods interrupted by his strange pronouncement.

Finally, only Jairus, his wife, Jesus, and the three disciples remained. Jairus's wife, Rebecca, stood at the top of the stairs leading to the upper room. Her face was ravaged by grief, her expensive robes torn in mourning, and ashes were in her hair. When she saw her husband with Jesus, a flicker of hope crossed her features before reality reasserted itself.

"She's gone, Jairus," she said, her voice hollow. "Our baby is gone. I was holding her hand when... when she just stopped. No final words, no goodbye. Just... stopped."

Jairus climbed the stairs and embraced his wife. They clung to each other, united in the devastating democracy of parental grief. Jesus followed, his disciples close behind.

The upper room was dim, windows covered according to mourning custom. On a low bed in the centre lay a figure so still it seemed carved from marble. Talitha, twelve years old, on the cusp between childhood and womanhood. Her face, which Jairus had described as always animated with laughter or song, was now composed in the terrible peace of death. Her dark hair had been carefully arranged, her best Sabbath dress smoothed over her still form. Peter, James, and John hung back near the doorway, uncertain. They had seen Jesus heal the sick, cast out demons, and calm storms. But death? Death was the final enemy, the one boundary even prophets couldn't cross. Elijah and Elisha had raised the dead, yes, but they were towering figures of ancient times. Could their teacher, this carpenter from Nazareth, truly command death itself?

Jesus approached the bed slowly, his eyes never leaving the girl's face. He sat on the edge of the bed, as natural as a parent checking on a sleeping child. Rebecca made a small sound of protest—to touch the dead was to become unclean—but Jairus held her back.

"Her name," Jesus said softly. "Tell me about her name."

"Talitha," Jairus whispered. "It means 'little lamb.' When she was born, she was so small, and she made these little bleating sounds when she cried. My mother said she sounded like a lamb, and the name stuck."

Jesus nodded, then took the girl's hand in his. It was small, cold, and lifeless. He held it gently, as if it were made of spun glass.

"She loved to hold hands," Rebecca said, the words tumbling out. "Even as she got older, she would still slip her hand into mine when we walked to market. She said it made her feel safe. These past days, when the fever was so high, holding her hand was all I could do. I held it until... until there was nothing left to hold onto."

Jesus looked at the grieving parents with infinite compassion. "What you held onto was not lost," he said. "Love doesn't end with breath. Faith doesn't stop at death's door. Watch and see the glory of God."

He turned back to the girl, still holding her hand, and spoke two words in Aramaic, the common tongue of their daily life: "Talitha koum."

Little lamb, arise.

The words were spoken quietly, conversationally, the way a parent might wake a child for morning prayers. No grand gestures, no invocation of divine names, no elaborate ritual. Just two simple words dropping into the silence like stones into still water.

For a moment, nothing happened. Peter found himself holding his breath, waiting. Then—

The girl's eyelids fluttered.

Rebecca gasped, her hand flying to her mouth. Jairus gripped the doorframe to keep from falling.

Talitha's eyes opened fully, blinking in confusion at the dim light. She turned her head, saw Jesus holding her hand, and smiled—a child's instinctive trust in a kind face.

"I'm thirsty," she said, her voice hoarse but unmistakably alive.

Then, as if waking from an afternoon nap, she sat up, looked around at the room full of stunned adults, and asked, "Why is everyone crying? And why are the windows covered? It's still daytime, isn't it?"

Rebecca let out a sound that was part sob, part laugh, and part prayer and flew to her daughter. She gathered Talitha in her arms, touching her face, her hair, and her hands, unable to believe the warm, living reality of her child.

"You were..." Jairus started, then stopped, overcome. "We thought... the sickness..."

"I had strange dreams," Talitha said, settling into her mother's embrace but looking at Jesus with curious eyes. "I dreamed I was walking in a garden, the most beautiful garden. There was a man there who said I needed to go back, that it wasn't time yet. Was that you?"

Jesus smiled. "Perhaps. Dreams can be mysterious things." He stood, addressing the parents. "Give her something to eat. She's been through an ordeal, and her body needs nourishment."

"Something to eat," Rebecca repeated, laughing through her tears. "Of course. Such a normal thing. Something to eat." She seemed almost hysterical with joy, clutching her living, breathing daughter.

"And tell no one what happened here," Jesus added, though his expression suggested he knew how impossible that command would be. How does one hide a resurrection? How does one explain a funeral becoming a feast?

Jairus found his voice. "Master, I... there are no words. My daughter was dead. I know death; I've presided over enough funerals. She was gone, and you... you just called her back. Like she was in the next room. How?"

"Faith," Jesus said simply. "You believed, even when belief seemed foolish. Your faith, like that woman's in the street, opened a door for God's power to flow through. Death is not the final word, Jairus. It never has been. It's just a sleep from which the Father can awaken His children."

He moved toward the door, motioning for his disciples to follow. They seemed frozen, staring at Talitha, who was now complaining about being hungry and asking why everyone was making such a fuss.

"Peter, James, and John," Jesus called. "Come. Our work here is done."

They followed him down the stairs and out of the house in a daze. Behind them, they could hear the beginning of commotion—Rebecca calling for food, Jairus's voice raised in joy, and Talitha asking questions about what had happened while she "slept."

Outside, a few neighbours lingered, curious about why the mourning had stopped. When they saw Jesus emerge, they pressed forward with questions, but he simply smiled and continued walking. Let Jairus decide what to tell them. Let the story spread as it would. The truth had a way of making itself known.

As they walked back toward Peter's house, the three disciples kept exchanging glances, trying to process what they had witnessed. Finally, Peter couldn't contain himself any longer.

"Master," he burst out, "she was dead. Actually dead. I've seen death and pulled drowned men from the sea. She wasn't breathing, her skin was cold, and you just... you just told her to get up. And she did!"

Jesus looked at his impetuous disciple with affection. "Does this surprise you, Peter? Have I not told you that the Son of Man has authority over all things? Disease, demons, nature itself—why should death be different?"

"But death is... death is final," James said, struggling to articulate thoughts that had never been challenged before. "It's the one thing that happens to everyone, the end of every story."

"Is it?" Jesus asked. "Or is it merely a chapter break? You've read the scriptures. What did God say to Moses at the burning bush? 'I am the God of Abraham, the God of Isaac, and the God of Jacob.' Not 'I was,' but 'I am.' To God, they live still. Death is real, yes, but it's not ultimate. Love is ultimate. Life is ultimate. God is ultimate."

John, the youngest of the three, had been silent since leaving the house. Now he spoke quietly. "The woman in the street—twelve years of living death. The girl—twelve years of life ended by death. Both healed, both restored. It's like... like you were showing us something about time, about how God sees differently than we do."

Jesus stopped walking and looked at John with pleased surprise. "You see clearly, John. Yes, twelve years. The woman's suffering began when the girl was born. Their stories intersected today for a reason. One had faith despite years of disappointment. The other had parents whose faith bridged the gap when she could not believe for herself. Both were daughters in need of restoration."

They resumed walking, passing through the market where normal life continued—merchants hawking wares, children playing, life in all its mundane glory. None of these people knew that death had been reversed just streets away, that the fundamental order they took for granted had been challenged and overcome.

"What do we do with this knowledge?" Peter asked. "How do we tell people that you can raise the dead? They already struggle to believe the healings."

"You don't tell them," Jesus said. "Not yet. Let them see the other signs first; let faith grow gradually. The time will come when death itself will be defeated publicly, finally, in a way that changes everything. But that time is not yet. For now, it's enough that you three have seen. You will need this memory in days to come."

He spoke the last words with a weight that made them shiver despite the warm afternoon. There was prophecy in his tone, a looking forward to events they couldn't yet imagine.

They arrived at Peter's house to find a crowd already gathered, word having spread about the healing of the woman with the issue of blood. People wanted to hear more, to understand how faith could draw power from a mere touch. Some had brought sick relatives, hoping for similar miracles.

Jesus sighed—the sigh of a man who knew his work was never done, that human need was as endless as the sea. But then he smiled, that transformative smile that reminded them why they had left everything to follow him.

"Bring them," he said to Peter. "All of them. While it is day, we must do the works of Him who sent me. Night is coming when no one can work."

As the afternoon wore on, Jesus taught and healed in Peter's courtyard. The disciples helped organise the crowd, their minds still reeling from what they had witnessed. Occasionally, they would catch each other's eyes, sharing silent amazement. They had seen the dead raised. They had watched their teacher speak life into death as easily as speaking words into air.

Meanwhile, across town, the story was already spreading despite Jesus's command for silence. How could Jairus and Rebecca explain their daughter's presence at the evening meal? How could they account for the dismissed mourners and the cancelled funeral? Neighbours who had seen Talitha's body carried to the upper room now saw her playing in the courtyard, helping her mother prepare bread, very much alive.

Miriam, the healed woman, had gone to the mikvah, the ritual bath, to formally mark her transition from unclean to clean. As she immersed herself in the living water, she thought about her twelve years of isolation ending just as a twelve-year-old girl's life was restored. There was poetry in it, divine symmetry that spoke of a God who noticed, who counted, who cared about individual stories.

She emerged from the water reborn in more ways than one. Tomorrow, she would begin the process of rebuilding her life. She would seek out her sons, find work, and rejoin the community of faith. But tonight, she simply wanted to sit in the synagogue—the place she had been barred from for over a decade—and offer prayers of thanksgiving.

As she entered the synagogue for evening prayers, she saw Jairus at the front, preparing to lead the service. Their eyes met across the room. He nodded to her, a nod that acknowledged their shared experience of miraculous intervention. Both had been desperate. Both had risked everything on faith in the teacher from Nazareth. Both had received back their lives.

The service began, ancient prayers rising like incense. When they reached the Shema—"Hear, O Israel, the Lord our God, the Lord is One"—Miriam's voice joined the congregation for the first time in twelve years. The words felt new in her mouth, charged with fresh meaning. The God who was One had shown His power through one man, bringing wholeness where there had been division, life where there had been death.

In his house, Jairus held his daughter's hand during the prayers, still marvelling at its warmth. Talitha sang the responses with her usual enthusiasm, as if she hadn't spent the afternoon in the realm of the dead. When the service ended, she tugged on his robes.

"Abba," she said, using the intimate form of father, "the man who woke me up—will we see him again?"

"I hope so, little lamb," Jairus said, scooping her into his arms despite her protests that she was too old for such treatment. "I very much hope so."

As night fell over Capernaum, the town buzzed with whispered conversations. In Peter's house, Jesus finally dismissed the crowds and retreated to the roof for prayer. His three witnesses joined him, still processing the day's events.

"You saw death reversed today," Jesus told them as they settled under the stars. "But you also saw something more. You saw faith transcend social boundaries—a desperate woman and a synagogue ruler, both brought low, both lifted up. You saw how the kingdom of God inverts expectations. The unclean made clean, the dead made alive, the last made first."

"But why, Master?" James asked. "Why these particular miracles? Why today?"

Jesus was quiet for a long moment, looking up at the stars—the same stars that had announced his birth to eastern sages, that had guided Israel through the wilderness, and that spoke silently of the God who numbers them all.

"Because the kingdom of heaven is at hand," he finally said. "Because people need to know that God has not abandoned them to sickness and death. Because faith, even faith as small as a mustard seed, can move mountains—or raise the dead. Because my Father is glorified when His children are restored to wholeness."

He turned to look at each of them in turn. "But also because you needed to see it. Dark days are coming when you will question everything, when death will seem to have the final word. Remember this day. Remember that I stood in a room with death and commanded it to flee. Remember that power flows from me to all who reach out in faith. Remember that no condition—not twelve years of bleeding, not death itself—is beyond the reach of God's healing touch."

Peter started to speak, probably to make some bold declaration about never doubting, but Jesus held up a hand. "Don't make promises about future faith, Peter. Just treasure what you've seen. Hide it in your heart. You'll need these memories when the storm comes."

They sat in silence after that, each lost in thought. Below them, Capernaum settled into sleep. In one house, a woman who had bled for twelve years slept peacefully, her body finally at rest. In another, a twelve-year-old girl dreamed ordinary dreams, her parents checking on her repeatedly, still barely believing she breathed.

And in houses throughout the town, people pondered what they had seen and heard. A teacher who welcomed the unclean, who raised the dead, and who spoke of God's kingdom as if it were breaking into the world at that very moment. Some believed. Some doubted. Some stored the stories away, waiting to see what would come next.

But for those who had experienced it—Miriam with her healed body, Jairus with his restored daughter, and three disciples with their expanded understanding—the kingdom of God was no longer a distant hope but a present reality. They had touched it, seen it, been transformed by it.

The teacher from Nazareth had come to their shore bringing more than words. He brought power over the fundamental forces that bound humanity—disease, isolation, and even death itself. And he wielded that power not as a tyrant or a showman, but as a servant, responding to faith wherever he found it, whether in a synagogue ruler's desperate plea or an unclean woman's secret touch.

As the stars wheeled overhead, marking time's passage, the witnesses to the day's miracles carried their stories into sleep. But the stories themselves remained awake, spreading from house to house, heart to heart, faith kindling faith, and hope breeding hope.

Tomorrow would bring new crowds, new needs, and new opportunities for the kingdom to break through. But today had been enough. Today, desperation had met divinity, and divinity had proven stronger than disease and death.

Today, in a small town by a lake in Galilee, heaven had touched earth, and those who witnessed it would never be the same.

The last sound Peter heard before sleep took him was Jesus's voice, still praying on the roof, still interceding for the broken world he had come to heal. And in that sound was the promise that what they had seen today was only the beginning.

The kingdom of heaven was indeed at hand. And it looked like a bleeding woman made whole and a dead girl eating dinner with her parents, both touched by the same hand, both raised by the same voice, both proof that in God's economy, nothing—not twelve years of suffering, not death itself—was wasted or beyond redemption.

Chapter 17: Sent Out Two by Two

The morning mist still clung to the Sea of Galilee when Jesus gathered the Twelve on the hillside above Capernaum. Peter noticed it first—that particular intensity in the master's eyes that meant something significant was about to happen. He'd seen it before the choosing of the Twelve, before the raising of Jairus's daughter, in those moments when heaven seemed to press close to earth.

"Sit," Jesus said simply, and they arranged themselves in a semicircle around him, the lake spreading like hammered silver below them. The familiar fishing boats looked like toys from this height, and Peter felt a pang of something—not quite homesickness, but an awareness of how far he'd travelled from the simple life of nets and scales.

Andrew settled beside him, close enough that their shoulders touched. The brothers had learnt to draw comfort from each other's presence in this strange new life they'd chosen. Or had it chosen them? Peter could never quite decide.

"The harvest is plentiful," Jesus began without preamble, his voice carrying that authority that still made Peter's spine straighten after all these months. "But the labourers are few."

Matthew, ever the scribe, had already produced his writing materials from somewhere in his robe. The former tax collector had adapted to discipleship with surprising grace, though Peter noticed he still sat slightly apart, as if unsure of his welcome even now.

"Master," John spoke up from his position at Jesus's right hand—the young disciple had an uncanny ability to position himself close to their teacher. "Are you sending us out?"

Jesus smiled, but it was tinged with something Peter couldn't quite name. Sorrow? Concern? "The time has come for you to go without me. Two by two, into every town and village of Galilee."

A ripple of unease passed through the group. They'd grown accustomed to following in Jesus's wake, watching him work wonders, and learning from his teachings. The thought of going out on their own felt like being asked to walk on water. Again.

"But Teacher," Philip protested, his practical nature asserting itself, "we're not ready. We don't have your authority, your power—"

"Don't you?" Jesus's question hung in the morning air. "What have I been showing you these many months? Have you learnt nothing of faith?"

Thomas, earning his reputation for blunt questions, asked what they were all thinking: "What if we fail? What if the demons don't listen to us? What if the sick remain sick?"

Jesus stood, and they all scrambled to their feet with him. He moved among them, placing a hand on Thomas's shoulder, meeting each of their eyes in turn. "I'm giving you authority over unclean spirits, to cast them out, and to heal every disease and every affliction."

The words should have been reassuring, but Peter felt the weight of them like a millstone. Authority was one thing when Jesus was there to catch them if they fell. But alone? Well, not alone—two by two, he'd said. Peter glanced at Andrew, seeing his own apprehension mirrored in his brother's face.

"Come," Jesus said, leading them further up the hillside to a level area where they could all stand comfortably. "There are things you must understand before you go."

What followed was unlike any teaching they'd received before. Jesus spoke not in parables but in direct, practical instructions that Matthew's stylus could barely keep pace with.

"Go nowhere among the Gentiles," Jesus began, and Peter saw Matthew's hand pause. The former tax collector had worked with Romans for years; this restriction clearly surprised him. "Enter no town of the Samaritans. Go rather to the lost sheep of the house of Israel."

James, the son of Zebedee, raised his hand like a schoolboy. "Only to Jews, Master?"

"For now," Jesus replied, and there was something in that "for now" that suggested larger plans, wider horizons. "Your message is simple: 'The kingdom of heaven is at hand.' Heal the sick, raise the dead, cleanse lepers, cast out demons."

"Raise the dead?" Thaddaeus's voice cracked on the words. The quiet disciple rarely spoke, but when he did, it was usually to voice what others were too afraid to say.

Jesus turned to him with infinite patience. "Did I stutter, Thaddaeus? You've seen me do it. The power isn't in you—it flows through you from the Father. You are merely the vessels."

"Empty vessels," Peter muttered, earning a sharp look from Jesus that somehow also contained affection.

"Exactly, Simon Peter. Empty vessels that God can fill. The moment you think the power is yours, you'll lose it."

Judas Iscariot, their treasurer, had been mentally calculating something. "Master, about provisions. How much silver should each pair take? The common purse has enough for—"

"You receive without paying; give without pay," Jesus interrupted. "Acquire no gold or silver or copper for your belts, no bag for your journey, no two tunics or sandals or staff."

Peter heard several sharp intakes of breath. No money? No extra clothes? No provisions at all? It was one thing to travel light when following Jesus, who somehow always ensured they had what they needed. But to go out completely dependent on strangers' hospitality?

"Teacher," Judas pressed, his face showing the strain of trying to reconcile this command with his careful bookkeeping, "surely some small provision—"

"The labourer deserves his food," Jesus said firmly. "Whatever town or village you enter, find out who is worthy in it and stay there until you depart. As you enter the house, greet it. If the house is worthy, let your peace come upon it, but if it is not worthy, let your peace return to you."

Simon the Zealot, who had spent years fighting Romans with more conventional weapons, looked troubled. "And if they reject us entirely? If they refuse to hear?"

Jesus's face grew stern. "If anyone will not receive you or listen to your words, shake off the dust from your feet when you leave that house or town." He paused, letting the weight of this settle. "Truly, I say to you, it will be more bearable on the day of judgement for the land of Sodom and Gomorrah than for that town."

The comparison to those famously destroyed cities sent a chill through the group. Peter had always thought of their message as good news, but here was its shadow side—the terrible responsibility of those who heard and rejected. "I am sending you out as sheep in the midst of wolves," Jesus continued, his voice taking on an urgent quality. "So be wise as serpents and innocent as doves."

"That seems contradictory," Nathanael observed. The man Jesus had praised for having no guile struggled with the concept of strategic wisdom.

"The serpent knows when to strike and when to retreat," Jesus explained. "It doesn't seek conflict but doesn't shrink from it when necessary. Yet your wisdom must be coupled with purity of motive. Be clever in avoiding unnecessary persecution, but never compromise the message."

He began to pace, and they unconsciously moved to maintain their semicircle around him. "Beware of men, for they will deliver you over to courts and flog you in their synagogues. You will be dragged before governors and kings for my sake, to bear witness before them and the Gentiles."

Peter felt his blood run cold. Flogging? Governors? They were fishermen and tax collectors, not revolutionaries. Well, except for Simon, but even he had laid down his dagger to follow Jesus.

"Master," Andrew's quiet voice somehow carried over the group's murmuring, "you speak of persecution as if it's certain."

"Isn't it?" Jesus turned to face them all, his expression a mixture of love and sorrow. "A disciple is not above his teacher, nor a servant above his master. If they have called the master of the house Beelzebul, how much more will they malign those of his household?"

They'd all heard the accusations from Jerusalem's religious elite—that Jesus cast out demons by the prince of demons. The blasphemy of it still made Peter's fists clench.

"But when they deliver you over," Jesus continued, "do not be anxious about how you are to speak or what you are to say, for what you are to say will be given to you in that hour. For it is not you who speak, but the Spirit of your Father speaking through you."

Matthew looked up from his frantic writing. "The Spirit will give us words?"

"Have I not always provided what you needed?" Jesus asked. "Why would words be different from bread or fish?"

It was a fair point, Peter had to admit. How many times had they seen Jesus provide? The wedding wine, the multiplied loaves, the nets breaking with fish. Provision was woven into the very fabric of following him.

But Jesus wasn't finished with the hard truths. "Brother will deliver brother over to death, and the father his child, and children will rise against parents and have them put to death."

The silence that followed was profound. James and John exchanged glances—the sons of thunder who had once wanted to call down fire on an inhospitable village were perhaps beginning to understand the real cost of the kingdom.

"You will be hated by all for my name's sake," Jesus said softly. "But the one who endures to the end will be saved. When they persecute you in one town, flee to the next, for truly, I say to you, you will not have gone through all the towns of Israel before the Son of Man comes."

That last phrase sparked a dozen questions, but Jesus held up his hand for silence. "Do not fear those who kill the body but cannot kill the soul. Rather fear him who can destroy both soul and body in hell."

Bartholomew, ever the philosopher among them, mused aloud, "So physical death is not the worst outcome?"

"Are not two sparrows sold for a penny?" Jesus replied, seeming to change subjects. "And not one of them will fall to the ground apart from your Father. But even the hairs of your head are all numbered. Fear not, therefore; you are of more value than many sparrows."

Peter unconsciously touched his own thinning hair, wondering at a God who kept such minute inventory. If the Father noticed every sparrow's fall, surely he would watch over his sent ones.

"Everyone who acknowledges me before men," Jesus continued, his voice gaining strength, "I also will acknowledge before my Father who is in heaven. But whoever denies me before men, I also will deny before my Father who is in heaven."

The weight of this pressed down on them like a physical thing. Peter remembered his own moment of walking on water, the split second when faith gave way to fear and he began to sink. What if that happened when facing a synagogue court? What if his courage failed when it mattered most? As if reading his thoughts—and perhaps he was—Jesus looked directly at him. "Do not think that I have come to bring peace to the earth. I have not come to bring peace, but a sword."

Even Simon the Zealot looked shocked at this. They'd all assumed the Messiah would bring peace and would unite Israel against her enemies. But this talk of division, of families torn apart...

"I have come to set a man against his father," Jesus elaborated, "and a daughter against her mother, and a daughter-in-law against her mother-in-law. And a person's enemies will be those of his own household."

Peter thought of his wife back in Capernaum, how she'd struggled to understand his decision to follow this rabbi. She supported him now, but what if persecution came? What if she had to choose between her husband and her safety?

"Whoever loves father or mother more than me is not worthy of me," Jesus said, each word falling like a hammer blow. "Whoever loves son or daughter more than me is not worthy of me. And whoever does not take his cross and follow me is not worthy of me."

Take his cross. They all knew what that meant. They'd seen the condemned carrying their crossbeams through the streets and seen the forests of crosses Rome planted as warnings. Was Jesus really comparing discipleship to that ultimate shame and agony?

"Whoever finds his life will lose it," Jesus continued, his voice now tender despite the hard words, "and whoever loses his life for my sake will find it."

John, young and passionate, suddenly burst out, "I'm not afraid to die for you, Master!"

Jesus turned to him with such love that it made Peter's throat tight. "I know, beloved. But dying is sometimes easier than living for me. Can you face the daily deaths—to pride, to comfort, to your own will?"

John's confident expression faltered, and he nodded slowly, perhaps beginning to understand.

"Now," Jesus said, his tone shifting to something more practical, "let me tell you about receiving and rewards." He gestured for them to sit again, and they gratefully sank back to the grass, emotionally exhausted from the intensity of his warnings.

"Whoever receives you receives me," he began, "and whoever receives me receives him who sent me. The one who receives a prophet because he is a prophet will receive a prophet's reward, and the one who receives a righteous person because he is a righteous person will receive a righteous person's reward."

"So those who welcome us are actually welcoming you?" Philip asked, working through the logic.

"And through me, the Father," Jesus confirmed. "Even a cup of cold water given to one of these little ones because he is a disciple—truly, I say to you, he will by no means lose his reward."

The sun had climbed higher during their teaching, and the morning mist had burnt away, leaving the lake sparkling beneath them. Jesus stood again, and they could sense the formal teaching was ending.

"Now, let me assign your partnerships," he said, and Peter felt his pulse quicken. Who would he be paired with? Surely Andrew, his brother. They'd worked together since childhood.

But Jesus's choices surprised them, as usual. "Peter, you'll go with John."

Peter blinked. John? The young mystic who spoke in poetry half the time? How were they supposed to work together?

"Andrew, you'll partner with Bartholomew."

Andrew nodded calmly, as he did most things. Bartholomew looked pleased—the philosopher and the practical fisherman might balance each other well.

"James and Matthew."

Now that was interesting. The son of thunder paired with the former tax collector. James had probably wanted to break Matthew's fingers a year ago. Now they'd be preaching together.

"Philip and Thomas."

The practical organiser and the sceptic. Peter could see the wisdom in it—Philip would push forward while Thomas would ask the hard questions.

"Thaddaeus and Simon."

The quiet one and the former Zealot. Another unexpected pairing.

"That leaves..." Judas looked around, realizing he was paired with James the son of Alphaeus by elimination. The treasurer and the contemplative. Not a natural match, but then, what did they know of Jesus's reasons?

436

"You'll leave tomorrow at dawn," Jesus instructed. "Tonight, pray. Fast if you feel led. Prepare your hearts more than your bags—remember, you take nothing but the clothes on your backs."

"Where should we go, Master?" Peter asked, already trying to plan despite the prohibition on provisions.

"The Spirit will guide you," Jesus replied. "Start with the villages nearest Capernaum and work outward. Some of you will go north toward Chorazin, others south toward Magdala, and some inland toward Cana. Don't plan too carefully—be ready to change direction as the Spirit leads."

He began to move among them again, placing hands on heads, speaking quiet words of encouragement to each pair. When he reached Peter and John, he smiled at Peter's still-obvious discomfort with the pairing.

"Iron sharpens iron, Simon," he said quietly. "John's passion needs your practicality. Your impulsiveness needs his reflection. Together, you'll be more than the sum of your parts."

To John, he said, "Learn from Peter's boldness. He may sink sometimes, but at least he gets out of the boat."

As the sun reached its zenith, Jesus dismissed them to prepare. But Peter lingered, as did several others, reluctant to leave their master's presence when they knew they'd be without it for... how long?

"Master," Peter finally asked, "when will we return to you?"

Jesus gazed out over the lake, then back at his anxious disciples. "When the towns have heard the message. When you've learnt what you need to learn. When the Father's purposes are accomplished."

It wasn't the specific answer Peter wanted, but he was learning that Jesus rarely gave those.

The walk back to Capernaum was subdued. Each man was lost in his own thoughts, processing the morning's intense teaching. Peter found himself walking beside Matthew, who was still scribbling notes as he walked—a feat that impressed the fisherman.

"Did you get it all down?" Peter asked.

Matthew looked up, his face troubled. "The words, yes. But the weight of them? How do you capture that in ink?"

"You don't," Peter said simply. "You carry it in your bones."

That evening, Capernaum's usual bustle seemed muted to Peter's eyes. Or perhaps it was just his own apprehension colouring everything. He found himself at his own home, something that happened less and less these days. His wife, Deborah, greeted him with a mixture of joy and concern. "You look troubled, husband. More than usual, I mean."

He told her about the morning, about the commission to go out preaching and healing. Her face went through a series of expressions—pride, fear, resignation, and finally a sort of determined support.

"How long will you be gone?"

"I don't know. Until the work is done," he said.

She busied herself preparing a simple meal, her movements sharp with suppressed emotion. "And you go with John? Not Andrew?"

"The Master's choice. He says we'll balance each other."

"Or drive each other mad," she muttered, then immediately looked contrite. "I'm sorry. I know this is important. I just..."

"You just wish your husband was a normal fisherman who came home every night smelling of fish instead of miracles?"

That earned him a small smile. "The fish smell was pretty bad, actually." She grew serious again. "Will it be dangerous?"

Peter thought of Jesus's warnings about persecution, about families divided, and about taking up crosses. "Probably," he admitted.

She was quiet for a long moment, then moved to an old chest in the corner. From it, she pulled out a worn prayer shawl. "This was my father's. He wore it every Sabbath until he died. Take it with you."

"But Jesus said no extra clothing—"

"It's not extra. It's armour. Spiritual armour." She pressed it into his hands. "If you're going to preach in synagogues, you'll need it."

That night, Peter couldn't sleep. He stood on his roof, looking out over the lake that had been his world for so long. Somewhere out there in the darkness, boats were fishing, men were working nets, and life was proceeding in its ancient rhythms. Tomorrow, he would step out of that rhythm into something unprecedented.

"Can't sleep either?"

Peter turned to find John climbing up onto the roof. The younger man's face was pale in the moonlight, making him look even younger than his years.

"Thinking about tomorrow," Peter admitted.

"I've been praying," John said, settling beside him. "Asking for courage. The Master's words today..."

"We're terrifying," Peter finished. "Let's be honest about it."

John smiled slightly. "I was going to say challenging, but yes, terrifying works too." He was quiet for a moment. "Why do you think he paired us together?"
Peter considered this. "You heard him—iron sharpening iron. Though I'm not sure which of us is supposed to be the iron."
"Both, I think. That's the point." John pulled his knees up to his chest, looking suddenly very young. "I've never preached without him there. What if I open my mouth and nothing comes out?"
"Then I'll jump in with both feet and probably say something stupid, and you'll have to fix it," Peter said, surprised to find himself comforting the usually confident young disciple. "Between the two of us, we'll manage."
"You really think the Spirit will give us words?"
Peter thought about all the times he'd seen Jesus do the impossible, all the moments when divine power had broken through into their ordinary world. "I think if we're stupid enough to go out with no money, no food, and no plan except 'the kingdom of heaven is at hand,' then yes, the Spirit had better show up."
John laughed, a sound that carried across the sleeping town. "When you put it that way, it does sound fairly insane."
"Following him usually does. Remember when he told me to walk on water?"
"You did it, though. For a few steps."
"Until I didn't." Peter's voice grew thoughtful. "But he caught me. Even when my faith failed, he caught me. I'm hoping that's still true tomorrow."
They sat in companionable silence for a while, each lost in his own thoughts. Finally, John stood to go. "We should try to rest. Dawn comes early."

"John," Peter called as the younger man started down. "We'll take care of each other out there, right? Whatever comes?"

John's smile was radiant even in the darkness. "Whatever comes, brother."

After John left, Peter remained on the roof a while longer. He thought about the eleven other men somewhere in Capernaum, probably experiencing their own dark night of the soul. Ordinary men called to extraordinary things. Tax collectors and zealots, fishermen and philosophers, all sent out to proclaim a kingdom they barely understood themselves.

But maybe that was the point. Maybe their very ordinariness was what qualified them. They knew what it was to struggle, to doubt, to fail. When they spoke of grace, it wouldn't be theoretical.

The eastern sky was just beginning to lighten when Peter finally climbed down from the roof. Deborah was already awake, packing food into a bag despite Jesus's prohibition.

"For tonight," she said firmly. "After that, you trust God. But for tonight, you eat your wife's bread."

He didn't argue. There were battles worth fighting and battles worth losing gracefully.

Andrew arrived as Peter was finishing his preparations. The brothers embraced, a lifetime of shared experience in that simple gesture.

"Strange to be going different directions," Andrew said.

"We've been going different directions since we started following him," Peter replied. "This is just more literal."

"Bartholomew thinks we should head toward Chorazin first. Says he has a cousin there who might give us a hearing."

"John wants to start with the fishing villages along the northern shore. Says fishermen understand about casting nets and hoping for catches."

Andrew smiled. "Sounds like you're both thinking strategically. The Master would be proud."

"The Master would tell us to stop thinking and start trusting," Peter corrected, but he was smiling too.

They walked together to the agreed meeting place—the same hillside where they'd received their commission the day before. The other disciples were already gathering, most looking as sleep-deprived as Peter felt. Jesus was there, sitting on a large stone, watching the sunrise paint the sky in shades of rose and gold.

He didn't speak at first, just let them assemble, find their partners, and work through their nervous energy. Thomas was peppering Philip with logistical questions. James and Matthew were clearly still figuring out how to relate to each other. Judas was trying to secretly slip coins to various disciples, while Simon the Zealot kept checking for the dagger he no longer carried.

Finally, Jesus stood. The simple motion brought immediate silence.

"The fields are white for harvest," he said, his voice carrying despite its quietness. "You are my first fruits, the beginning of the gathering. Go with my authority, my blessing, and my love."

He moved among them one more time, embracing each man, whispering final words of encouragement. When he reached Peter, he gripped his shoulders firmly.

"Remember, Simon Peter—when you speak, I speak through you. When you heal, I heal through you. You go in my name, not your own strength."

"What if I forget that?" Peter asked honestly.

"Then John will remind you," Jesus said with a slight smile. "And when he gets too mystical, you'll ground him. I didn't pair you randomly, Simon. Trust me."

"I do," Peter said, and found he meant it, despite all his fears.

Jesus stepped back, raised his hands in blessing, and spoke words that seemed to resonate in the very air around them: "Go therefore in the name of the Father, the Son, and the Holy Spirit. Proclaim the kingdom. Heal the sick. Cast out demons. Show them what God's reign looks like when it breaks into the world. And remember—I am with you always, even to the end of the age."

With that, he turned and walked away, not looking back. The message was clear—they were on their own now. Or rather, they were on their own, which was infinitely better and infinitely more terrifying.

The six pairs looked at each other, none wanting to be the first to leave.

Finally, Peter shouldered his nearly empty pack and looked at John. "North shore fishing villages?"

John nodded, shouldering his own pack. "We may as well start with what we know."

"Brothers," Peter called to the others, "we'll meet back here in... how long did the Master say?"

"He didn't," Thomas replied. "As usual."

"Then we'll know when we know," Peter decided. "God go with you all."

"And with you," came the chorus of replies.

The pairs began to disperse in different directions. Peter and John headed north along the lake shore, the familiar path taking on new significance. They were no longer just disciples following their master. They were apostles—sent ones, carrying his authority and message into the world.

The first village they came to was tiny—maybe a dozen families who made their living fishing the northern shallows. Peter knew some of them by reputation and had sold fish to them in better-provisioned towns. But knowing them as fellow fishermen was different from approaching them as... what? Prophets? Preachers? Wonder-workers?

"How do we start?" John asked as they paused at the village entrance.

Peter thought about it. "The same way we'd start anything, I suppose. We find someone willing to talk, and we talk."

An elderly man sat mending nets in the shade of an ancient sycamore. Peter recognised the careful, methodical movements of someone who'd been doing this task for decades. He approached with the easy gait of one fisherman to another.

"Peace be with you, Father," he said in the traditional greeting.

The old man looked up, squinting. "And with you. You're Simon bar Jonah, aren't you? From Capernaum?"

"I am. Or was. These days I go by Peter."

"Rock, eh?" The old man chuckled. "Bit presumptuous for a fisherman. You always were one for the grand gestures. I remember when you and your brother bought that second boat. Everyone said you were overreaching."

"Maybe I was," Peter admitted, settling down beside him. John hung back, letting Peter take the lead with someone from his world. "These days I'm fishing for something different."

"Ah." The old man's fingers never stopped their work. "You're with that teacher. The one who's been stirring things up."

"Jesus of Nazareth. Yes."

"My granddaughter was in Capernaum last month. Saw him heal a paralytic. Lowered through a roof, she said. Sounded like nonsense to me."

"I was there," Peter said simply. "It wasn't nonsense."

The old man's hands stilled for the first time. "You saw it?"

"I helped clear the debris afterward. The man walked out carrying his own mat.

"Hm." The fingers resumed their work, but Peter could see thoughts working behind those weathered features. "And now you're here because...?"

"Because the kingdom of heaven is at hand," John spoke for the first time, his young voice carrying surprising authority. "Because God is moving in Israel again, like in the days of the prophets."

The old man studied John with sharp eyes. "Another fisherman?"

"Of sorts," John replied with a small smile. "Also from Capernaum."

"The kingdom of heaven," the old man repeated slowly. "My grandfather used to talk about waiting for God's kingdom. Died waiting. My father too. Now I'm old, and Rome's boot is still on our necks. What makes your teacher different from all the others who've promised deliverance?"

Peter leaned forward. "He doesn't promise to overthrow Rome. He promises to overthrow everything—the way we think, the way we live, and the way we understand God himself."

"That's a large claim from a fisherman."

"It is," Peter agreed. "Would you like to hear more? Maybe gather others who might be interested?"

The old man considered this for a long moment. Then he carefully set aside his nets and stood with the careful movements of age. "My daughter's house has the largest courtyard. I suppose we could gather there after the evening meal. But I make no promises about reception."

"We ask for none," John said. "Only open ears."

As the old man shuffled off to spread word, Peter and John found themselves alone again.

"That went better than I expected," John admitted.

"Wait until tonight before you celebrate," Peter warned. "Curiosity is one thing. Response is another."

They spent the afternoon walking through the village, observing, praying, and occasionally engaging in small talk with villagers. Several people recognised Peter, which helped break down initial suspicion. By evening, word had spread that the fisherman-turned-disciple and his young companion had something to say about the controversial teacher from Nazareth.

The courtyard was fuller than Peter had expected. Maybe thirty people, ranging from children to elderly, had gathered. Oil lamps cast flickering shadows as the sun set over the lake. Peter felt his mouth go dry. Speaking to crowds when Jesus was there was one thing. This was entirely different.

"Tell us about the teacher," someone called out. "Is it true he makes blind men see?"

Peter looked at John, who nodded encouragingly. Taking a deep breath, Peter stepped into the centre of the courtyard.

"I was fishing," he began, falling back on what he knew. "My brother Andrew and I had just finished a terrible night. Empty nets, empty boats, empty hopes. Then this teacher asked to use my boat as a platform to teach from. When he finished, he told me to put out into deep water and let down my nets."

He had their attention now. Fishermen understood about empty nets and daytime fishing's futility.

"I almost laughed at him," Peter continued. "What did a carpenter know about fishing? But something in his voice... I did it. And the catch nearly sank two boats."

Murmurs rippled through the crowd. Exaggeration was common in fishing stories, but Peter's reputation was for plain dealing.

"But that wasn't the real miracle," Peter said, warming to his theme. "The real miracle was what he said next: 'Follow me, and I will make you fishers of men.' And I did. Left everything—boats, nets, livelihood—to follow a wandering teacher with no home and no salary."

"Why?" The question came from a young woman holding a baby.

Peter considered his answer carefully. "Because in his presence, I knew I was standing before more than a man. Because his words carried authority I'd never heard from any rabbi. Because..." He paused, then spoke the truth that still amazed him. "Because he saw who I could become, not just who I was."

"Tell them about the kingdom," John prompted softly.

Peter nodded. "He sent us here to tell you that God's kingdom is breaking into the world. Not with armies or politics, but with transformed hearts and healed bodies and freed spirits."

"Can you prove it?" This from a sceptical-looking man near the back. "Words are easy. If you carry his authority, show us."

Peter felt panic rise in his throat. This was the moment he'd dreaded. But before he could respond, a commotion arose near the entrance. A woman pushed through, half-carrying, half-dragging a boy of perhaps ten years.

"Please," she gasped, "my son. The fever came three days ago. The healer in the next village said there's nothing more to do. I heard you were here, that you follow the miracle worker. Please..."

The boy was clearly desperately ill. His skin burnt with fever, his eyes rolled back, and his breathing was shallow and rapid. The crowd instinctively stepped back, fearing contagion.

Peter froze. This was exactly what Jesus had commissioned them to do, but faced with the reality of a dying child, all his doubts crashed over him like a wave. What if nothing happened? What if the boy died right here in front of everyone?

Then John was beside him, young John who'd been leaning on Jesus's breast at their last meal together. "Remember what he said," John whispered. "It's not our power. We're just vessels."

Peter nodded, forcing his feet to move toward the sick child. He knelt beside the mother, acutely aware of every eye upon him. The boy's skin was furnace-hot under his touch.

"What's his name?" he asked the mother.

"David. Like the king." Her voice broke. "He's all I have left. His father died last winter."

Peter looked at the boy—David, not just "the sick child," but David, someone's everything. He thought of Jesus, how he always saw the person, not just the problem.

"David," he said firmly, placing both hands on the burning head. "In the name of Jesus the Messiah, be healed. Let the fever leave you and strength return."

For a moment, nothing happened. Peter could feel the crowd's scepticism growing and could sense John praying fervently beside him. Then, like a wave receding, he felt the heat begin to drain from beneath his hands. The boy's laboured breathing eased. Colour returned to his cheeks.

David's eyes fluttered open, focused, clear. "Mama?" he said in a perfectly normal voice. "I'm hungry."

The courtyard erupted. The mother clutched her son, weeping and laughing simultaneously. People pressed forward to touch the boy, to confirm the miracle. Others pulled back in fear or awe.

Peter stood on shaking legs, overwhelmed by what had just happened. He'd spoken, and heaven had answered. The authority Jesus had given them was real.

"The kingdom of heaven," he said, having to raise his voice over the commotion, "looks like this. It looks like fever fleeing and death retreating. It looks like hope returning to hopeless situations. This is what Jesus of Nazareth brings—not just words about God, but the very presence and power of God."

"How?" someone shouted. "How is this possible?"

"I don't fully understand it myself," Peter admitted with characteristic honesty. "But I know who he is. He's the one Israel has been waiting for. The one Moses and the prophets spoke about. And he's calling all of us to turn from our old ways and embrace God's new thing."

What followed was a flood of questions, requests, and discussions that lasted well into the night. More sick were brought—a woman with a withered hand, a man with clouded eyes, and a child who hadn't spoken since birth. Not all were healed; Peter learnt quickly that the Spirit moved according to divine wisdom, not human demand. But enough were touched that by midnight, the entire village was in uproar.

The old fisherman who'd first welcomed them pulled Peter aside as the crowd finally began to disperse. "I've lived seventy years by this lake," he said quietly. "I've seen would-be messiahs come and go, seen movements rise and fall. But this..." He gestured at David, now running around the courtyard with other children, fully restored. "This is different."

"Will you believe, then?" John asked gently. "Will you enter the kingdom?"

The old man smiled, years seeming to fall from his weathered face. "Son, I entered it the moment that boy opened his eyes. The question now is what to do about it."

Peter and John exchanged glances. They hadn't really thought beyond the proclamation and healing. What came next?

"Gather those who believe," Peter said, trusting instinct and what he'd observed from Jesus. "Pray together. Care for one another. Share what you have with those in need. Live as if God's kingdom is already here—because it is."

"And you? Will you stay and teach us more?"

"We have other villages to visit," John replied. "But perhaps we'll return. Or others will come. The Master has many disciples."

They were offered the best lodging in the village that night, but sleep eluded Peter. He lay on the simple pallet, staring at the ceiling, replaying the evening's events. The feel of fever leaving at his command. The authority flowed through him like water through a channel. The faces transformed by hope.

"Can't sleep?" John whispered from his own pallet.

"My mind won't stop spinning. Did that really happen?"

"It did. I saw it. More importantly, they saw it. The kingdom became visible tonight."

Peter rolled onto his side to face his young partner. "I was terrified. When that mother brought her son forward, all I could think was, 'What if it doesn't work?'"

"But you acted anyway. That's faith, Peter. Not the absence of doubt, but action in spite of it."

"When did you become so wise?"

John's smile was visible even in the darkness. "I've been listening to the Master. Really listening. You should try it sometime instead of always jumping in with questions."

Peter chuckled despite himself. "And there's the sharpening iron the master mentioned."

They left the village at dawn, pockets empty as commanded but hearts full. The old fisherman and several others saw them off, pressing bread and dried fish into their hands despite their protests.

"The labourer deserves his food," the old man quoted back at them with a grin. "You laboured well last night. Take it with our blessing."

The pattern repeated itself in the next village and the next. Sometimes the reception was warm, sometimes hostile. In one town, the synagogue ruler refused them entrance and warned others against listening to "followers of the blasphemer." They shook the dust from their feet as instructed and moved on, though it pained Peter to leave any place unreached.

In another village, the entire population seemed to turn out for healing. Peter and John prayed until their voices were hoarse and laid hands until their arms ached. Many were healed; some were not. The mystery of divine selection troubled Peter until John pointed out that Jesus himself hadn't healed every sick person in Israel.

"The healings are signs," John explained during one of their walks between villages. "Pointing to something greater. If everyone were healed all the time, it would become expected and mundane. The kingdom breaks in through surprises, disruptions of the normal order."

"You really have been listening to him," Peter marvelled.

Days blended into weeks. They developed a rhythm—arrive in a village, find someone willing to host them, gather people for teaching, demonstrate the kingdom's power as the Spirit led, establish the beginnings of believing communities, and move on. Peter's initial fears gave way to growing confidence, though he never lost the sense of utter dependence on power beyond himself.

The persecution Jesus had warned about manifested in various ways. In one town, they were dragged before the local council and accused of disturbing the peace. Peter found, to his amazement, that words flowed from his mouth—scriptures he didn't remember memorising, arguments he couldn't have constructed on his own. They were released with warnings, but not before several council members privately expressed interest in hearing more.

John proved an able partner, his mystical insights balancing Peter's practical approach. When Peter wanted to push too hard, John counselled patience. When John got lost in theological reflection, Peter reminded him that people needed bread as well as wisdom. They learnt to read each other's moods and to support each other's weaknesses.

One evening, perhaps three weeks into their mission, they sat by a small fire outside a village where they'd been poorly received. Only a handful had listened, and those fearfully. The synagogue leaders had made it clear that anyone associating with them risked expulsion.

"Do you think the others are having better success?" Peter asked, poking at the fire with a stick.

"Does it matter?" John replied. "We're not in competition. Each seed planted is precious, whether it's one or a hundred."

"I know. I just..." Peter struggled to articulate his frustration. "I want everyone to see what we've seen. To know him like we know him."

"Not everyone is ready. Remember the parable of the sower? Some soil isn't prepared for the seed yet."

They were silent for a while, listening to the night sounds of rural Galilee. Then John spoke again, his voice thoughtful.

"I've been thinking about what the Master said—about not going to the Gentiles or Samaritans. Just to the lost sheep of Israel."

"What about it?"

"It seems... limited. If this really is God's kingdom breaking in, shouldn't it be for everyone?"

Peter considered this. "Maybe it's about timing. Israel first, then the nations? Like light spreading from a single lamp?"

"Maybe." John pulled his cloak tighter against the evening chill. "Or maybe we're not ready yet. Maybe we need to understand it fully ourselves before we can translate it for those outside the covenant."

"Always thinking deep thoughts," Peter said with affection. "Sometimes I'm glad the Master just tells me to cast nets or walk on water. Clear instructions, even if they're impossible."

"But that's just it," John said eagerly. "The impossible becomes possible in his presence. We've seen it. We've done it! These past weeks, how many impossibilities have we witnessed?"

Peter thought back—fevers fled, demons cast out, blind eyes opened, deaf ears unstopped, and communities transformed. "Too many to count," he admitted. "It's becoming almost normal, which probably should worry me."

"Or encourage you. The kingdom is becoming natural to us. We're learning to live in it, not just visit it."

A rustling in the bushes made them both tense, but it was only a village boy, perhaps eight years old, approaching nervously.

"Sirs?" he said in a small voice. "My grandmother sent me. She couldn't come herself—her legs don't work right. But she wanted to know... is it true what you said about God loving even the broken ones?"

Peter's heart melted. "What's your name, son?"

"Eli."

"Well, Eli, not only does God love the broken ones, sometimes he uses us to fix them. Would you like us to come see your grandmother?"

The boy's face lit up. "Would you? The elders said we shouldn't talk to you, but Grandmother said, "Any god who cares about people like her is worth the risk.""

They followed Eli through darkened streets to a tiny house on the village's edge. Inside, by the light of a single lamp, an elderly woman sat twisted by what looked like years of joint disease.

"So," she said without preamble, "you're the troublemakers. You don't look like much."

"We're not much," Peter agreed, kneeling beside her. "But we serve someone who is everything."

"Tell me about him," she commanded. "Not the miracles—I've heard about those. Tell me about the man."

So they did. John spoke of Jesus's compassion, how he wept over Jerusalem. Peter told of his patience with thick-headed disciples. They painted a picture of someone utterly holy yet utterly approachable, someone who touched lepers and ate with tax collectors, who blessed children and challenged religious authorities.

"He sounds like someone I'd like to meet," the woman said when they finished. "Too bad these old bones won't make the journey to find him."

"You don't need to," John said gently. "He's already here, in us, through his Spirit. May we pray for you?"

She nodded, and they placed their hands on her gnarled fingers. This time, Peter felt no anxiety, only compassion for this woman who'd lived with pain for so long. The prayer came naturally, words of blessing and healing flowing like water.

The cracking sounds were audible as joints realigned, as decades of damage reversed. The woman gasped, not in pain but in wonder, as she slowly straightened fingers that had been clawed for years.

"Oh," she breathed, flexing her newly mobile hands. "Oh my."

"Stand up, grandmother," John encouraged gently.

She did, slowly at first, then with growing confidence as legs that had barely supported her now bore her weight easily. Eli watched with wide eyes as his grandmother took her first pain-free steps in decades.

"This," she said firmly, "changes everything. Eli, run and fetch your parents. Then the neighbours. Elders or no elders, people need to hear about this."

What started as a rejected mission became a midnight revival. People crept from their houses, drawn by Eli's excited proclamations. The healed grandmother became an evangelist, her transformed body a sermon more powerful than any words.

By dawn, half the village had gathered, including some shamefaced elders who'd been among the most vocal opponents. Peter, exhausted but exhilarated, found himself thinking that this was exactly what Jesus had intended—not just proclamation but demonstration, not just words but power.

"The kingdom of heaven is like yeast," he found himself saying to the crowd, remembering one of Jesus's parables. "It starts small, hidden, but it works through everything it touches until all is transformed. That's what's happening here. That's what's happening throughout Galilee. God is on the move."

They stayed an extra day in that village, teaching, praying, and organising the new believers. The grandmother became their chief advocate, her testimony carrying weight that no outsider's words could match.

As they finally prepared to leave, she pulled them aside. "I'm old enough to speak plainly," she said. "This kingdom you preach—it's going to cost, isn't it? The powerful don't give up power easily."

"The Master warned us," Peter acknowledged. "Division, persecution, maybe worse."

"But still worth it?"

"Worth everything," John said with quiet conviction. "To see God's will done on earth as in heaven? Worth any price."

She nodded, satisfied. "Then we'll pay it. We've been paying the wrong prices for the wrong things for too long. At least this suffering will mean something."

They left that village different from how they'd entered it—not just because of the healings, but because they'd seen how rejection could turn to reception, how one transformed life could catalyse a community's transformation.

The weeks rolled on. Villages blurred together, yet each remained distinct—the fishing community where entire boats' crews decided to follow Jesus's way, the agricultural town where they were run out for "disrupting the harvest," and the mixed Jewish-Gentile settlement where they had to carefully navigate ethnic tensions while maintaining Jesus's command to focus on Israel.

Peter learnt to read crowds, to sense when to push forward with bold proclamation and when to retreat into parables and questions. John developed a gift for discerning spirits, knowing instinctively which suffering came from physical ailment and which from spiritual oppression.

They also learnt the cost of constant ministry. There were nights when they collapsed exhausted, unable to eat the offered food. Days when the weight of others' suffering felt crushing. Times when they missed Jesus so acutely it was like a physical ache.

"Do you think he knew it would be this hard?" Peter asked one evening as they nursed blistered feet by a stream.

"He told us we'd be sheep among wolves," John reminded him. "I don't think he's ever lied to us about the cost."

"No, but experiencing it is different from hearing about it." Peter winced as he examined a particularly nasty blister. "I used to think following him was the hard choice. Now I realise it was the easy one. He did most of the heavy lifting. This—carrying it ourselves—this is harder."

"Not ourselves," John corrected gently. "His Spirit through us. When you start thinking it's your power, that's when you'll really struggle."

Peter nodded, accepting the rebuke. It was a lesson he had to learn repeatedly—the difference between being a channel and being the source.

One day, perhaps six weeks into their mission, they crested a hill to find a familiar sight—the other disciples, or at least some of them. Andrew and Bartholomew were approaching from the opposite direction, looking as travel-worn as Peter felt.

The reunion was joyful, with brothers embracing and stories immediately beginning to flow. They made camp together that night, sharing provisions and experiences.

"You won't believe what happened in Chorazin," Andrew began, his usually calm demeanour animated with excitement. "The entire synagogue leadership repented. They're reorganising their whole community around Jesus's teachings."

"Any persecution?" Peter asked.

"Some. Bartholomew got hauled before the local authorities for 'disturbing the peace.' You should have heard him—he quoted the entire scroll of Isaiah from memory, proving Jesus's legitimacy from Scripture. They let us go, and two of them followed us afterward to hear more."

Bartholomew smiled modestly. "The Spirit gave me recall I didn't know I had. Though I think my years of study helped prepare the vessel."

They talked late into the night, sharing victories and defeats, lessons learnt, and questions raised. It emerged that all the pairs had experienced similar patterns—initial rejection often giving way to acceptance, healings serving as door-openers for deeper teaching, and small communities of believers forming in village after village.

"It's like a net," Andrew observed at one point. "Each village connected to others through family and trade. The message spreads along existing relationships."

"The Master knew," Peter said with growing certainty. "He knew exactly what would happen when he sent us out. We're not just preaching—we're planting. By the time we return to him, all of Galilee will have heard."

"But will they respond?" Bartholomew asked, ever the thinker. "Hearing is one thing. Changing your life is another."

"That's not our responsibility," John said firmly. "We plant and water. God gives the growth."

They parted the next morning, agreeing to meet again if their paths crossed but not forcing it. There was too much work to do, too many villages yet unreached.

The final weeks of their mission took Peter and John into regions they'd never visited, hill country where Jewish communities clung to ancient ways and viewed outsiders with deep suspicion. Here, their message met the strongest resistance yet.

In one synagogue, Peter was literally thrown out mid-sentence when he proclaimed Jesus as Messiah. The bruises lasted for days, but worse was the sense of failure. John had to remind him repeatedly of Jesus's words about shaking off dust and moving on.

Yet even in the resistant areas, there were breakthrough moments. A shepherd boy healed of lameness became their guide through the hill country, his testimony opening doors that would have remained closed to strangers. A widow whose only son was raised from a death-like fever became a fierce advocate, shaming village elders into at least giving the disciples a hearing.

Peter noticed changes in himself as the weeks progressed. The impulsive fisherman who'd tried to walk on water was still there, but tempered now by experience. He learnt when boldness served and when it hindered. He discovered depths of compassion he hadn't known he possessed, finding himself weeping with mourners and rejoicing with the healed.

John changed too, his mystical bent finding practical expression in the gift of knowing exactly what each person needed to hear. The "son of thunder" became a son of consolation, his words bringing comfort to the afflicted and affliction to the comfortable.

Their final stop before returning to Capernaum was a village perched high above the lake, offering a panoramic view of the region they'd spent months traversing. As they sat teaching in the small synagogue, Peter found himself overwhelmed by the journey's magnitude.

Down there, scattered across the landscape like seeds, were dozens of villages where they'd proclaimed the kingdom. In each one, people whose lives had been transformed. Communities are beginning to reorganise around Jesus's teachings. A network of faith spreading like roots through the soil of Galilee.

"What are you thinking?" the synagogue ruler asked, noticing Peter's distant gaze.

"I'm thinking about fishing," Peter replied, earning puzzled looks. "My master said he'd make us fishers of men. I used to think that meant catching them one at a time. But it's not that at all. It's about casting a net so wide it encompasses everything, drawing all of it toward the kingdom."

That night, their last in the field, Peter couldn't sleep again. But this time, it wasn't anxiety keeping him awake—it was anticipation. Tomorrow, they'd see Jesus again. They'd report what they'd seen and done. They'd hear what the other pairs had experienced.

Most of all, they'd be back in the presence of the one who'd sent them. After months of representing him, of speaking in his name, of channelling his power, they'd be with him again. The thought made Peter's heart race like a youth in love.

"Ready to go home?" John asked from his pallet.

"Home," Peter repeated, tasting the word. "Is that what Capernaum is now?"

"Home is where he is," John said simply. "Everything else is just geography."

They set out at dawn, walking with energy that belied their months of travel. As they descended toward the lake, they encountered other pairs also heading back—James and Matthew from the east, and Philip and Thomas from the south. The reunion was moving, with disciples embracing like long-lost family.

"Look at us," James laughed, surveying their ragged band. "We look like beggars, not apostles."

"Maybe that's the point," Matthew suggested. "We went out with nothing and returned with nothing—except the kingdom breaking out all over Galilee."

They entered Capernaum together, a dozen tired, dusty men whose appearance gave no hint of the spiritual revolution they'd been part of. But Peter noticed people recognising them, pointing, and whispering. Word of their missions had preceded them.

Jesus was waiting at Peter's house, sitting in the courtyard as if he'd known exactly when they'd arrive. Which, Peter realised, he probably had. The sight of him—calm, powerful, radiating that indefinable presence—made Peter's throat tight with emotion.

"Master," he began, then found he couldn't continue. How did you summarise months of miracles, struggles, and revelations?

Jesus rose and embraced each of them in turn, his eyes speaking volumes. When he'd greeted them all, he stepped back and smiled—that radiant expression that made all their hardships worthwhile.

"Come," he said simply. "Tell me everything."

They talked for hours, stories tumbling over each other, twelve voices trying to capture the magnitude of what they'd experienced. Jesus listened with perfect attention, asking occasional questions, drawing out details they might have overlooked.

When they finally ran out of words, exhausted by their own testimonies, Jesus leaned back with satisfaction. "The seventy-two I will send out next will go because of your faithfulness. You've proven that ordinary men can carry extraordinary authority when they go in my name."

"Will we go out again?" Peter asked, surprised to find he hoped the answer was yes despite the hardships.

"You'll go to the ends of the earth eventually," Jesus said, his eyes holding depths Peter couldn't fathom. "But for now, rest. Reflect on what you've learnt. Let it sink deep into your bones. You'll need these lessons for what's coming."

What's coming? The phrase hung in the air like a promise or a warning. Peter didn't ask for clarification. He'd learnt that Jesus revealed things in his own time.

That evening, they gathered for a meal—the Twelve, Jesus, and some of the women who supported their ministry. It felt like a feast after months of accepting whatever was offered. Peter found himself sitting between John and Andrew, perfectly content.

"So," Deborah asked, having heard his initial reports, "was it worth it? The blisters, the rejection, the uncertainty?"

Peter thought of the grandmother dancing on legs that had been crippled for decades. The fever left young David at his command. The villages transformed by hope. The kingdom seeds planted throughout Galilee.

"Worth it?" He smiled at his patient wife. "It was just the beginning. The harvest he spoke of—we've seen it starting. And somehow, I don't think we'll ever be the same."

John raised his cup. "To the kingdom," he said simply.

"To the kingdom," they echoed, twelve voices united in purpose.

Outside, Galilee went about its evening routines, unaware that everything had changed. In villages throughout the region, new believers gathered to pray and break bread. Healed bodies bore witness to divine power. Communities began to reorganise around radical teachings about love and forgiveness.

The nets had been cast. The fishing had begun. And Peter, the impulsive fisherman who'd left everything to follow a carpenter from Nazareth, knew with bone-deep certainty that this was what he'd been born for.

As the meal continued around him, he caught Jesus's eye. The Master smiled and nodded slightly, acknowledging what Peter couldn't put into words. They'd passed the test. Proven faithful in smaller things. Now, perhaps, they were ready for whatever came next.

The thought should have terrified him. Instead, Peter felt only anticipation. If going out in pairs could transform Galilee, what might happen when the full force of the kingdom was unleashed?

He would find out soon enough. But tonight, surrounded by brothers in faith and the presence of the one who'd called them, Peter was content to simply be. Tomorrow would bring its own challenges and glories.

The kingdom of heaven was at hand. They'd proclaimed it throughout Galilee. Now, they would watch it grow, participate in its expansion, and pay whatever price its establishment required.

Peter the fisherman had become Peter the fisher of men. The transformation was complete. Or perhaps, he thought as he watched Jesus laughing at something Matthew had said, it was just beginning.

Either way, he was ready. They all were. Sent out two by two, they'd discovered that ordinary men could do extraordinary things when empowered by heaven. It was a lesson that would echo through the centuries, inspiring countless others to go and do likewise.

But that was for tomorrow and all the tomorrows to come. Tonight, they were home. Together. Victorious. And grateful beyond words for the privilege of being part of something infinitely larger than themselves.

The kingdom of heaven was at hand. And they were its heralds, its witnesses, its living proof that God had not forgotten his people. It was enough. More than enough.

Chapter 18: The Voice Silenced

The fortress of Machaerus squatted on its mountaintop like a vulture waiting for something to die. Built by Herod the Great as a bulwark against his enemies, it now served his son Antipas as both palace and prison, luxury and cruelty existing side by side within its black basalt walls.

In the depths below the palace, where no silk cushions softened the stone and no perfume masked the stench of human misery, John the Baptist sat in darkness. Six months he'd been here. Six months since he'd dared to speak truth to power, to name the sin that everyone else pretended not to see.

"It is not lawful for you to have your brother's wife."

Those eight words had cost him everything. Eight words spoken in the wilderness, carried on the wind to Herod's ears, and now here he sat, the voice that had shaken Israel reduced to whispers in the dark.

But even whispers could be dangerous. Even in chains, John remained a threat to those who built their kingdoms on lies.

Above him, three stories up where windows caught the morning light, Herodias stood before a mirror of polished silver, painting her face for war. Today was Antipas's birthday, and the elite of Galilee and Perea would gather to grovel before their puppet king. Today, she would finally silence the voice that haunted her marriage bed.

"Mother?"

Salome appeared in the doorway, sixteen years old and beautiful in the way that weapons are beautiful—sharp, gleaming, and designed to cut. Herodias had shaped her carefully, this daughter who was both her greatest creation and her most useful tool.

"Come," Herodias said, not turning from the mirror. "Let me look at you."

Salome approached, her movements already carrying the studied grace of a dancer. She wore the costume Herodias had commissioned—silk so fine it seemed made of spiderwebs and jewels that caught the light with every breath. Modest enough to avoid immediate scandal, revealing enough to destroy a man's reason.

"You remember what we discussed?" Herodias asked, adjusting a fold of fabric.

"I dance. When Herod offers me a reward, I ask for guidance. You provide it."

"And if he hesitates?"

"I remind him of his oath. In front of his guests. A king who breaks his word is no king at all."

Herodias smiled, the expression sharp as a blade. "My clever girl. Today, we remove the last stone in our path."

Salome's eyes—so like her mother's—flickered with something that might have been conscience. "The prophet? But he's already imprisoned. What harm can he do?"

"You're young," Herodias said, finally turning to face her daughter. "You don't understand how ideas work. That man down there, rotting in his cell—he's more dangerous than an army. Every day he lives, people whisper. They say God speaks through him. They say our marriage is cursed. They wait for his prophecies to come true."

She gripped Salome's shoulders, nails digging in just enough to hurt. "Dead men tell no prophecies. Dead men become footnotes, not martyrs. Do you understand?"

Salome nodded, though something in her eyes suggested she understood more than her mother realised. "I'll dance well, Mother. He won't be able to refuse me."

"No," Herodias agreed. "He won't."

In the banquet hall, preparations were reaching their peak. Slaves scurried between tables, laying out golden plates and cups encrusted with gems. The wine had been brought from Rome itself, the food was prepared by cooks borrowed from the Emperor's own kitchens. No expense had been spared. Herod Antipas might rule only a fragment of his father's kingdom, but tonight he would pretend to greatness.

The man himself stood on a balcony overlooking the Dead Sea, that body of water so thick with salt that nothing could live in it. Fitting, he thought, for a man whose life had become equally barren of anything real or growing.

"My lord?"

He turned to find Chuza, his steward, waiting with the diplomatic expression that meant bad news.

"What is it?"

"The prisoner, my lord. He's been asking to see you."

Antipas's jaw tightened. "The answer remains no."

"He says it concerns a dream. A warning."

"He's had six months to deliver warnings. I'm not interested in the ravings of madmen."

But that wasn't true, and they both knew it. John haunted Antipas like a guilty conscience. How many times had he almost released him? How many nights had he woken from dreams where the prophet's eyes burnt with holy fire, where his voice thundered judgement like the old prophets of Israel?

"Shall I tell him—"

"Tell him nothing. Let him rot."

Chuza bowed and withdrew, but not before Antipas caught the flash of something in his eyes. Disgust? Pity? Even his own servants judged him now. That was what came of showing weakness, of letting them see him wrestle with conscience.

His father would have killed John immediately. No hesitation, no midnight wrestling with guilt. Herod the Great had murdered his own sons without losing sleep. But Antipas was not his father and had never been his father, and that was both his salvation and his doom.

"Brooding again?"

Herodias glided onto the balcony, beautiful and poisonous as nightshade. She'd been Philip's wife first—his brother Philip, safe in his distant tetrarchy, probably grateful to be rid of her. Antipas had met her on a visit to Rome and fallen like a stone into dark water. His first wife, the Nabatean princess, had fled back to her father the moment she heard. Another enemy made, another bridge burnt for the sake of this woman who wore his weakness like jewellery.

"Thinking," he said.

"About the prophet?" She moved behind him, hands sliding over his shoulders. "Today that ends. After tonight, no one will remember his name."

"You're very confident."

"I have reason to be." Her breath was warm against his ear. "I've prepared a special entertainment for your birthday. Something your guests will never forget."

He turned to look at her, seeing the triumph already gleaming in her eyes. "What have you done?"

"Given you what you want but are too weak to take yourself." She kissed him, tasting of wine and scheming. "Trust me. By dawn, your kingdom will be cleaner."

She left him there, staring at the dead water, wondering how his life had become a Greek tragedy performed for an audience of vultures. Inside, he could hear the first guests arriving, their laughter already too loud, too desperate. Everyone was trying to forget they were dancing on the edge of a blade, that Rome's patience was finite, and that they were all one rebellion away from annihilation.

In his cell, John heard the music beginning and knew his time was short. He'd felt it in the air all day, the way animals sense earthquakes before they strike. Death was coming, dressed in silk and moving to the rhythm of drums.

He didn't fear it. Six months in darkness had burnt away everything but the essential. He was the voice crying in the wilderness, and he had cried. He was the messenger preparing the way, and the way was prepared. His work was finished. Only the dying remained.

But there were things that troubled him. Questions that gnawed at him in the dark hours. Had he been wrong about Jesus? His cousin from Nazareth had baptised thousands, performed miracles, and spoken with authority that made religious leaders tremble. But was he the one? The Messiah who would restore Israel, establish justice, and bring down the proud from their thrones?

The Jesus he'd known hadn't seemed like a conquering king. Too gentle, too willing to eat with tax collectors and sinners. Where was the fire? Where was the judgement John had promised would come?

"Lord," he prayed, pressing his forehead against the cold stone. "If I die tonight, let me die knowing I pointed to the right man. Let me die without doubts."

No voice from heaven answered. No light pierced the darkness. But somewhere deep in his bones, deeper than thought or reason, he felt a settling. A peace that had nothing to do with circumstances. Yes. Yes, Jesus was the one. Different than John had imagined, working in ways that defied expectation, but the one nonetheless.

John smiled in the darkness. Let them come. He was ready.

The banquet hall filled as the sun set, casting long shadows through windows designed to frame views of the fortress's power. The guests were a careful mixture—Jewish nobility who'd made their peace with Rome, Greek merchants who controlled the trade routes, and Roman officials who ensured the taxes flowed steadily to Caesar. All of them were bound together by compromise and the mutual understanding that principles were luxuries none of them could afford.

Antipas received them from his throne, Herodias beside him like a beautiful poison. He knew what they thought of him. Weak, compared to his father. A puppet whose strings showed. But tonight, surrounded by wealth and sycophants, he could pretend otherwise.

The feast began with wine—always wine first, to soften edges and blur judgement. Then came the food, dish after dish designed to overwhelm. Roasted peacock stuffed with dates and almonds. Fish from the Sea of Galilee prepared seven different ways. Fruits soaked in honey and wine until they seemed more drug than food.

"Magnificent!" declared Marcus Quintus, the Roman procurator's representative. He was already on his third cup, face flushed with wine and political calculation. "Your father himself couldn't have done better."

It was a lie, and everyone knew it. Herod the Great's banquets had been legendary, excess elevated to art. This was mere imitation, a child playing with his father's crown. But Antipas smiled and accepted the flattery, because what else could he do?

"You honour us with your presence," he replied. "Rome's friendship is worth more than gold."

"Speaking of gold," said Matthias the merchant, leaning forward with the eager expression of a man who smelt profit, "I hear the tax revenues from Galilee have exceeded expectations this quarter."

"The people prosper under just rule," Antipas said carefully. It was dangerous territory. Tax collection was the eternal balance—take too little and Rome grew suspicious, take too much and rebellion fermented like wine. John's arrest had sparked riots in some territories. Nothing major, quickly suppressed, but enough to remind him how thin the ice beneath his feet really was.

"And yet you keep the Baptist alive," observed Nathan ben Azariah, one of the few Pharisees who'd accepted the invitation. "Some might call that... merciful."

The word hung in the air like an accusation. Mercy was a weakness in this company. Mercy was what lesser men showed when they lacked the stomach for necessary cruelty.

"The prophet is contained," Herodias interjected smoothly. "His words reach no one. He's less than a memory now."

"Memories can be dangerous," Nathan murmured into his wine cup. "Especially memories of holy men wrongly imprisoned."

Antipas felt heat rise in his face. "Are you questioning my judgement?"

"Never, my lord. I merely observe that the people have... attachments to such figures. They remember Elijah. They remember Jeremiah. Prophets in prison become symbols."

"Dead prophets become martyrs," Marcus added helpfully, already too drunk for diplomacy. "Better to let him rot quietly, I say. Unless he attempts escape or incites rebellion..."

The conversation was veering toward dangerous ground. Antipas raised his cup. "Tonight is for celebration, not politics. To friendship between nations!"

The toast was echoed with varying degrees of enthusiasm. The moment passed, but Antipas caught the satisfied gleam in Herodias's eyes. She was counting on conversations like this, he realised. Planting seeds that would flower into inevitability.

The evening wore on, wine flowing like water, inhibitions dissolving with each cup. A troupe of acrobats performed, twisting their bodies into impossible shapes. Musicians played, the drums growing louder as the night deepened. Dancers whirled, their movements becoming less artistic and more provocative as the audience's tastes coarsened.

Then, at some signal Antipas missed, the regular entertainers withdrew. The drums fell silent. In the sudden hush, every head turned toward the main entrance.

Salome entered like a vision from fever dreams.

She moved as if the air itself were water, flowing rather than walking. Her costume caught the lamplight and threw it back multiplied, creating the illusion that she was clothed in living flame. But it was her face that held them—young enough to evoke protection, beautiful enough to destroy wisdom, with eyes that promised everything and nothing.

Even before the music began, Antipas knew he was lost.

The dance started slowly, almost modestly. A lifted arm here, a turned ankle there. But with each movement, she claimed more of the room, more of the air, and more of the rational thought from every man present. This was not the crude writhing of common dancers. This was art elevated to a weapon, beauty deployed with surgical precision.

Antipas tried to look away and found he couldn't. His cup sat forgotten in his hand. Around him, he was dimly aware that every other man was equally transfixed. Even Marcus, who usually preferred boys, stared with slack-jawed fascination.

The tempo increased. Salome spun, her hair whipping around her like dark silk. The jewels on her costume created patterns in the air, hypnotic and mesmerising. She danced as if telling a story—innocence transforming into knowledge, knowledge into power, and power into something darker still.

Herodias watched from her throne with the satisfaction of a general whose battle plan unfolds perfectly. Every rehearsal, every carefully choreographed moment was having its intended effect. She saw the hunger in Antipas's eyes, the way his hands gripped the throne's arms until his knuckles went white. Perfect.

The music reached a crescendo. Salome spun faster and faster until she seemed less human than an elemental force. Then, at the perfect moment, she collapsed at Antipas's feet, prostrate but somehow still in control, her hair spread across the floor like spilt ink.

The silence that followed was deafening. No one breathed. No one moved. The very air seemed to wait.

"Rise," Antipas managed, his voice hoarse. "That was... extraordinary."

Salome looked up at him through her lashes, and in that moment she was both child and woman, innocent and knowing, everything a man might want and everything he should fear.

"I dance for your glory, my lord," she said, her voice carrying despite its softness. "To honour your birthday."

"And you have honoured it beyond measure." He was sweating despite the evening coolness. "Name your reward. Anything. I swear before all these witnesses—whatever you ask, up to half my kingdom, it's yours."

The words hung in the air like a sword waiting to fall. Around the room, men who'd made and broken a thousand deals recognised the trap closing, but wine and beauty had made them slow, made them forget that in palaces, every gift had teeth.

Salome rose with careful grace, as if the offer were unexpected. "You're too generous, my lord. I... I don't know what to ask. May I seek counsel?"

"Of course."

She glided to her mother, and every eye followed. They bent their heads together, the picture of filial devotion. But Matthias, sitting closest, would later swear he heard Herodias hiss like a serpent speaking to Eve.

When Salome returned, something had changed in her face. The innocence was still there, but sharpened now, like a blade wrapped in silk.

"I have decided," she announced.

"Speak, and it's yours."

"I want the head of John the Baptist."

If the silence before had been deafening, this was the silence of tombs. Antipas felt the blood drain from his face. Around him, cups stopped halfway to lips, and smiles froze into rictus masks.

"Surely," he began, then had to clear his throat. "Surely you jest. A beautiful girl like you—jewels would be better. Gold. Estates…"

"I want his head," Salome repeated, her voice carrying that same soft clarity. "On a platter. Now."

Nathan the Pharisee made a sound—protest or prayer, impossible to tell. Marcus giggled, a high, drunk sound that cut off when he saw no one else was laughing.

"Be reasonable," Antipas tried again. "The prophet is a holy man. The people revere him. To kill him without trial—"

"You swore an oath." Herodias's voice cut through his objections like a sword through parchment. "Before all these witnesses. Before God Himself. Will you be known as an oath-breaker? Will men say Herod Antipas's word means nothing?"

She was on her feet now, every inch the outraged queen. "My daughter honoured you with her art. You promised her anything. Will you make her a liar before this company? Will you shame us all with your cowardice?"

The word hit like a slap. Cowardice. His father's ghost seemed to laugh from the shadows. "Weak," it whispered. Always weak. Can't even keep a simple promise.

"My lord," Marcus slurred, trying to be helpful, "it's just one fanatic. There are a dozen more in the wilderness. Who'll miss him?"

"God will miss him," Nathan said quietly. "The people will miss him. History will remember this moment."

"History remembers winners," Herodias snapped. "It forgets the rest."

Antipas looked around the room, seeing his future in their faces. If he refused, word would spread that his oaths meant nothing. That he could be manipulated by prisoners, controlled by fear of the mob. Weak. The word would follow him like a shadow.

But if he agreed...

"Please," Salome said, and there was something terrible in the sweetness of her voice. "You promised."

The trap was perfect. Inescapable. He'd walked into it with his eyes open, led by wine and lust and the need to seem powerful. Just like his marriage. Just like every compromise that had brought him to this moment.

"Very well," he heard himself say. The words seemed to come from very far away. "Guards!"

Two soldiers stepped forward, faces carefully neutral. They'd served in palaces too long to show surprise at any depravity.

"Go to the lower cells. The prisoner called John the Baptist..." His voice failed. He swallowed and tried again. "Execute him. Bring his head. Quickly."

"On a platter," Salome added helpfully. "Don't forget the platter."

The guards saluted and left. The room remained frozen, everyone processing what they'd just witnessed. A man had danced himself to death, and they'd all watched it happen.

"Music!" Herodias commanded. "Wine! This is a celebration!"

The spell broke, sort of. Musicians began playing, but the melodies were uncertain and faltering. Servants poured wine with shaking hands. Conversations resumed in whispers, everyone pretending they hadn't just witnessed judicial murder served as entertainment.

Antipas drank deeply, trying to drown the voice in his head that sounded like prophecy: "It is not lawful for you to have your brother's wife."

In the depths of Machaerus, John heard the footsteps long before they reached his cell. Not the shuffling gait of the usual guards bringing water and mouldy bread. These were measured, purposeful—the walk of men on deadly business.

He rose from his knees, prayer still warm on his lips. So. The time had come. He thought there might be fear but found only a strange lightness, as if chains he hadn't known he carried were already falling away.

The door opened. Two soldiers entered, and John could read his fate in their carefully blank expressions. Behind them, incongruously, a slave carried a silver platter.

"By order of Herod Antipas," the senior guard began, then stopped. What was the point of formal pronouncements? They all knew why they were here.

"I forgive you," John said quietly. "And I forgive him."

The guard's mask slipped for just a moment, showing the man beneath—tired, disgusted, trapped in his own chains of duty and survival.

"Make it easy on yourself, prophet. Don't fight."

"I've never fought. I've only spoken truth."

"Truth." The younger guard spat. "Look where truth got you."

John smiled, and something in that smile made both soldiers step back.

"Truth got me exactly where I need to be. I decrease so another can increase. The friend of the bridegroom rejoices when he hears the bridegroom's voice. My joy is complete."

"Mad," the younger guard muttered. "They're all mad."

"On your knees," the senior guard said, not unkindly. "Close your eyes. It'll be quick."

John knelt on the stone floor where he'd spent so many hours in prayer. But he didn't close his eyes. Instead, he looked up at the small window where a single star was visible.

"Lord," he said clearly, "into Your hands I commit my spirit. Let my blood water the seeds of Your kingdom. Let my silence speak louder than my voice ever could."

The sword was already moving. John had one last moment of perfect clarity—seeing not this dungeon but the Jordan River, watching his cousin emerge from the water while heaven split open and a dove descended. The voice that had spoken then echoed now in his heart: "This is my beloved Son, in whom I am well pleased."

Yes, John thought. Yes, I chose correctly. The Lamb of God who takes away the sins of the world. I saw him. I pointed to him. My work is—

The blade fell. Silence descended on the cell, broken only by the sound of blood dripping onto stone. The younger guard turned away, retching. The older one remained professional, lifting the severed head with practiced efficiency and placing it on the platter.

"God have mercy," the slave whispered, his hands shaking so badly the platter rattled.

"There is no God in Herod's palace," the senior guard said. But his voice lacked conviction, and he was careful not to look at the prophet's face, where the eyes remained open, seeming to see into worlds beyond this one.

They climbed back toward the light and music, a macabre procession carrying death to a birthday feast. With each step, the sounds of celebration grew louder, more jarring. How could they be laughing? How could they not feel the weight of what had just happened?

The throne room doors swung open. The music stuttered to a stop. Every head turned to see the guards enter, the slave between them carrying his terrible burden.

The head of John the Baptist lay on the silver platter, blood still dripping from the severed neck. His hair, which had never been cut in accordance with his Nazirite vow, spread around him like a dark halo. His eyes were open, fixed on some distant point, and his lips were slightly parted as if he'd been interrupted mid-sermon.

A woman screamed. Someone's wine cup shattered on the floor. Nathan the Pharisee began reciting prayers for the dead, his voice rising and falling in ancient rhythms.

Salome stepped forward, no hesitation in her movements. She took the platter from the trembling slave as if it weighed nothing, as if she carried such burdens every day. Then she turned and walked to her mother, presenting it like a gift.

"As you wished, Mother."

Herodias gazed down at the face of the man who'd tormented her, who'd dared to name her sin before all Israel. She'd expected to feel triumph. Instead, there was only a hollow sensation, as if she'd won a battle that turned out to be meaningless.

"Take it away," she said, her voice less steady than she'd intended. "Throw it to the dogs."

"No." The word came from Antipas, who looked like he'd aged a decade in the last few minutes. "His disciples will want the body. For burial. Give it to them."

"You show mercy to the dead that you denied the living?" Herodias's voice could have etched glass.

"I show decency," he replied, not looking at her. "If any remains in this place."

The party was effectively over. Guests made excuses and fled, suddenly remembering urgent business elsewhere. Marcus had to be carried out, finally succumbing to wine and horror. Nathan left without another word, but his eyes promised that this story would be told in every synagogue in Galilee.

Soon only the royal household remained, surrounded by the debris of celebration. Food congealed on golden plates. Wine pooled on the floor like blood. The head still sat on its platter, a centrepiece for a feast no one could stomach.

"You did well," Herodias told Salome, who hadn't moved since delivering her prize. "You've secured our future."

"Have I?" Salome's voice was very young suddenly. "I've never seen a dead man before. He doesn't look dangerous. He looks... sad."

"The dead always look sad. It means nothing."

"His disciples," Salome continued as if her mother hadn't spoken. "They say he baptised thousands. That he prepared the way for someone greater. What if—"

"Enough." Herodias gripped her daughter's arm. "What's done is done. Tomorrow, no one will remember his name. That's how the world works. The strong survive, the weak perish, and prophets die when they inconvenience kings."

But even as she spoke, Herodias felt a chill that had nothing to do with the night air. Something had shifted with John's death, some cosmic balance disturbed. The silence that followed his execution wasn't the silence of victory but of a gathering storm.

Antipas sat alone on his throne long after everyone else had gone. The platter remained before him, John's dead eyes seeming to watch with terrible patience. He tried to look away and couldn't. Those eyes had seen heaven open. What did they see now?

"Chuza," he called, and his steward appeared from the shadows where servants learn to wait. "Send word to John's disciples. Tell them they can claim the body."

"Yes, my lord."

"And Chuza? What was it he wanted to tell me? The dream he mentioned?"

Chuza hesitated. "He said... he said he dreamed of a fox trying to catch a lamb. But every time the fox pounced, the lamb became a lion. He said you would understand."

Antipas closed his eyes. A fox—that's what his enemies called him. Herod the Fox, too clever for his own good. And the lamb... he thought of the rumours from Nazareth, of the teacher who spoke with authority, who John had claimed was the Messiah.

"My lord? Shall I send a reply?"

"He's beyond replies now." Antipas opened his eyes to find John still watching. "We all are."

The disciples came at dawn, moving through the fortress gates like men in a dream. Andrew and Philip, James and Bartholomew—men who'd left everything to follow a voice in the wilderness, now come to collect that voice's remains.

The guards, shame-faced and silent, led them to where the body had been laid. Someone—a servant with more compassion than sense—had tried to clean him, washing away the blood and closing the terrible wound. But there was no disguising what had been done.

Andrew wept openly as they wrapped John in burial cloths. Philip's hands shook as he helped lift the body. They'd prepared for this possibility and had known since the arrest that it might end this way. But knowing and experiencing were different things.

"Where will you take him?" one guard asked quietly.

"To his own people," James replied. "He'll be buried with his fathers."

They carried him out as the sun rose over the Dead Sea, painting the water the colour of blood. Behind them, Machaerus squatted on its mountain, already trying to forget what had happened within its walls.

But forgetting would prove impossible. By noon, the story was spreading through the marketplace. By evening, it had reached every village in Galilee. The voice crying in the wilderness had been silenced, but its echo grew louder with each telling.

In Capernaum, Jesus stood very still as Andrew and Philip told him the news. His face showed no surprise—had he known? Had some divine telegraph warned him?— but his grief was real and sharp as nails.

"How?" was all he asked.

"Herod's birthday feast. The girl danced. Herodias demanded his head as payment." Andrew's voice broke. "We buried him this morning."

Jesus nodded slowly. "Come away with me to a quiet place. We need to mourn. We need to pray. And then..." He looked toward Jerusalem, toward a future that had just become more certain and more terrible. "Then we continue what he started."

"Master," Philip ventured, "the people are saying Herod fears you now. That he thinks you might be John returned from the dead. Perhaps we should—"

"Fear makes men do terrible things," Jesus interrupted gently. "We don't run from frightened foxes. We continue toward Jerusalem, knowing the path leads through suffering to glory."

He turned to gather the other disciples to begin the retreat that would let them process this loss. But Andrew caught his words and filed them away. Through suffering to glory. Was that what John had found in his final moments? Was that the secret written in his dead eyes?

Back in Machaerus, Antipas couldn't eat, couldn't sleep, and couldn't escape the memory of that severed head. He ordered the banquet hall sealed, claimed he was renovating, but really he couldn't bear to enter the space where he'd been trapped by his own words.

Herodias watched him deteriorate with disgust and calculation. She'd removed one threat to their power, but her husband was becoming another. Weak men were dangerous in their own way, prone to sudden attacks of conscience or equally sudden cruelties.

"You need to assert yourself," she told him one morning, finding him staring at the spot where John had been executed. "Show strength. The people are restless."

"The people mourn him," Antipas replied. "They light candles. They are fast. They whisper that God's judgement is coming."

"Then give them something else to whisper about. A new building project. A military campaign. Anything but this... wallowing."

He turned to her, and she saw something in his eyes that made her step back. "Do you ever wonder if he was right? If our marriage really is cursed?"

"Don't be ridiculous."

"My first wife's father prepares for war because of our insult. Rome watches for any sign of weakness. Now I've killed a prophet." He laughed, the sound sharp and brittle. "My father killed babies and slept soundly. I kill one holy man and can't close my eyes without seeing his face."

"Your father was strong—"

"My father was a monster!" The words exploded from him. "He killed his own sons! He murdered anyone who threatened him! And I swore I'd be different, better. Instead, I'm just a pale echo, committing smaller murders for pettier reasons."

Herodias straightened her spine. "You did what was necessary. What I made possible because you lacked the courage to do it yourself. Don't blame me for your weakness."

"No," he agreed quietly. "I blame myself. For everything."

She left him there, already calculating alternatives. If Antipas fell, she'd need another patron, another path to power. Survivors always did.

Alone again, Antipas returned to his vigil. Somewhere in the distance, he could hear singing—John's disciples or sympathisers, keeping watch, maintaining memory. The voice in the wilderness had been silenced, but its echo refused to die.

"I'm sorry," he whispered to the bloodstained stones. "I'm so sorry."

But the dead keep their own counsel, and forgiveness, if it existed, would have to come from the living. Antipas doubted he'd live long enough to find it.

The festival of Tabernacles came and went. Then Passover approached, bringing with it crowds and tension and memories of other deaths. Reports reached Machaerus of Jesus's growing ministry, of thousands fed with a few loaves, of storms calmed and demons cast out.

"He's John returned," Antipas said with certainty that bordered on madness. "John has come back to haunt me."

"John is dead," Herodias reminded him, patience worn thin by months of his obsession. "This is another charlatan, nothing more."

"You didn't see his eyes. You didn't see what I saw in that cell, on that platter. He knew something. Saw something. And now..."

"Now you're seeing ghosts and jumping at shadows. Very kingly."

Their marriage, built on passion and ambition, crumbled like walls undermined by truth. They still shared a bed but not warmth. Still ruled together but not united. The blood between them had dried but was never washed clean.

Salome, meanwhile, had retreated into silence. The girl who'd danced with such calculated sensuality now spent hours in prayer, as if trying to wash the memory from her movements. Herodias found her one day by the fortress walls, staring toward the wilderness.

"What are you looking for?"

"I dream about him," Salome said quietly. "The prophet. He speaks to me in dreams."

"The dead don't speak."

"These do." She turned to her mother, and Herodias was shocked to see tears. "He forgives me. Every night, he forgives me. And every night, I wake knowing I don't deserve it."

"You did what was necessary."

"I did what you told me to do." The accusation hung between them like a blade. "I was your weapon, aimed at your enemy. But weapons can turn in the hand, Mother. Be careful how you use them."

She walked away, leaving Herodias alone with the uncomfortable realisation that in winning her battle, she might have lost her daughter.

Years passed. The teacher from Nazareth continued his work, gathering disciples, challenging authorities, and performing signs that made even hardened sceptics wonder. Antipas tried twice to meet him, driven by guilt and curiosity and the mad hope that seeing him would either confirm or deny his fears about John's return.

Both times, Jesus evaded him. "Tell that fox," he said once, the message carried back by trembling servants, "that I cast out demons and perform healings today and tomorrow, and on the third day I will complete my work."

A fox. So the prophet—this prophet—knew him too. Knew his nature, his small cunning, his scavenging existence. The fox who'd caught the voice in the wilderness but found it turned to poison in his mouth.

Then came another Passover, another feast turned to horror. Pilate, faced with an impossible choice, sent a prisoner to Antipas—Jesus of Nazareth, worker of miracles, threat to stability. Here was Antipas's chance to meet the man who haunted him, to look into eyes that might or might not be John's reborn.

But when Jesus stood before him, silent and dignified despite chains and mockery, Antipas saw only his own condemnation reflected back. This wasn't John—the features were different, the bearing more regal than wild. But the same fire burnt behind those eyes, the same truth that refused to bend before power.

"Perform a miracle," Antipas commanded, hearing the desperation in his own voice. "Show me a sign. Speak!"

Silence. Jesus wouldn't even dignify him with refusal. He simply stood, patient as stone, letting his presence say everything that needed saying.

"He's yours," Antipas told Pilate's soldiers eventually, dressing Jesus in a mock-royal robe to hide his own relief. "I find no fault requiring death."

But he knew, even as he washed his hands of another prophet's blood, that he was lying. The fault was everywhere—in the system that crushed truth-tellers, in the powerful who chose comfort over conscience, and in his own heart that had learnt to justify murder for the sake of a dance.

He would never see Jesus again. Within hours, Roman nails would accomplish what Herodian swords had begun. Another voice silenced, another prophet's blood crying from the ground.

But Antipas would live with the knowledge that he could have prevented both deaths. Could have chosen differently at a dozen crucial moments. Instead, he'd danced to Herodias's tune as surely as his court had danced to Salome's, and the music had led them all to damnation.

In the end, when Antipas's own fall came—defeated in battle, exiled by Rome, stripped of everything he'd killed to keep—he thought of John's eyes on that platter. Patient. Knowing. Waiting for justice that comes as slow but certain as sunrise.

The voice in the wilderness had been silenced. But silence, Antipas learnt too late, could speak louder than any cry. In every quiet moment for the rest of his life, he heard it—the absence where truth should have been, the hollow where a prophet's voice once rang.

He died in exile, far from the fortress where he'd traded his soul for a dance. But distance made no difference. Some chains are forged from choices, not iron. Some cells are built from memory, not stone.

And in the histories written afterward, in the stories told by survivors and witnesses, a curious thing happened. Herod Antipas, who'd ruled for decades, who'd built cities and commanded armies, was remembered for essentially one thing—as the weak man who killed John the Baptist for the sake of a promise he should never have made.

The powerful disappeared into footnotes. The prophet lived forever.

The voice, even silenced, still cried in the wilderness. And somewhere, always, there were those who stopped to listen, who heard in that silence a call to prepare the way, to make straight the paths, to announce the coming of a kingdom that no earthly power could contain or kill.

John had decreased so another could increase. His death had watered seeds that would grow into a movement that would outlive empires. The fox had caught his prey, only to discover he'd swallowed something that would devour him from within.

In the end, the last word belonged not to kings or dancers or silver platters, but to the truth John had proclaimed with his living and his dying: "Behold the Lamb of God, who takes away the sin of the world."

The lamb the fox could never catch. The lamb who became a lion. The lamb whose kingdom would have no end.

The voice was silenced. But the Word it had proclaimed echoed into eternity, and no power in heaven or earth could call it back.

Printed in Dunstable, United Kingdom